A TOAST TO TRAVEL

... but it's not always lovely

Fraser Beath McEwing

Published in Australia by Sid Harta Books & Print Pty Ltd,
ABN: 34632585293
23 Stirling Crescent, Glen Waverley, Victoria 3150 Australia
Telephone: +61 3 9560 9920, Facsimile: +61 3 9545 1742
E-mail: author@sidharta.com.au

First published in Australia 2022
This edition published 2022
Copyright © Fraser Beath McEwing 2022

Cover design, typesetting: WorkingType
(www.workingtype.com.au)

The right of Fraser Beath McEwing to be identified as the Author of the Work has been asserted in accordance with the Copyright, Designs and Patents Act 1988.

All rights reserved. No part of this publication may be reproduced, stored in a retrieval system, or transmitted, in any form or by any means without the prior written permission of the publisher, nor be otherwise circulated in any form of binding or cover other than that in which it is published and without a similar condition being imposed on the subsequent purchaser.

Fraser Beath McEwing
A Toast to Travel
ISBN: 978-1-925707-86-1
p388

About the Author

A writer and magazine editor for most of his career, Fraser Beath McEwing has been published in many leading Australian magazines and newspapers.

His experience in the Melbourne textile industry led him to become Managing Editor of Rupert Murdoch's *Australian Fashion News*. In 1972, he founded his own Australian fortnightly fashion industry newspaper, *Ragtrader*, and ran it for twenty years.

Fraser Beath McEwing is also a fiction writer. His first novel, *Feel the Width,* was published in 1994. It took a satirical look at the Australian fashion industry of the 1960s. His experience in the early 1990s with network marketing formed the basis of his second satirical novel, *Cafe*. His *Adam Exx trilogy* delves into speculative fiction. Back in the real world, his book *Why Does My Dog Bark?* takes readers on a journey of discovery about the reasons behind human behaviour.

In addition to being a writer, Fraser has been a textile wholesaler, furniture importer and retailer, a champion squash player, a competitive tennis player, and a pianist. In 2012, he became a classical music concert reviewer for the Sydney Symphony Orchestra and built up a wide audience. He is a board member of the Theme & Variations Foundation that assists young Australian pianists in achieving their goals.

Also by Fraser Beath McEwing

Feel the Width

Cafe

Adam Exx Book 1 Genesis

Adam Exx Book 2 Exodus

Adam Exx Book 3 Leviticus

Why Does My Dog Bark?

Foreword

Travel companies want your money. There's nothing wrong with that (I too want your money when you buy this book), but the companies practise a certain amount of deception that flows on to their brochures and travel editorials. They paint a picture of everything being simply lovely. All promises will be kept and you will return with memories fizzing like a Berocca tablet in a glass of water.

Yes, travel does deliver some lovely experiences. Of course, I like them, but I am just as attracted to absurdities, stuff-ups and grim realities. I've worked hard to smooth out the bumps of my life at home, but when I travel, I want the bumps back again for a while.

This is what *A Toast to Travel* is all about. It's warts-and-all recollections of places I've visited rather than a confectionery of endless wonder. For instance, it is the discovery that the bricks making up the walls of the Kremlin in Moscow are not bricks at all, but an artificial coating painted to look like bricks to hide what is underneath: other bricks. It is the proclaimed health benefits and collection challenges of cow urine in Delhi. It is the disappointment that the illustration in my fifth-grade history book was wrong. The Colossus of Rhodes (of which there was a detailed drawing) never straddled the harbour entrance but stood at attention on a column. After it fell down during an earthquake in 226 BC, hacksaw wielding thieves demolished the wreck and flogged the copper.

I talk about cruising too, when an entire seaworthy suburb pulls away from a wharf on an adventure that promises to resemble not having left home at all, except there is far more to eat and drink, punctuated by hasty visits to famous places crowded to overflowing by cruising colleagues.

I can't remember when I started reviewing hotel toasters — or even why. But they have become a regular inclusion in my travel reports. You only encounter hotel toasters at breakfast time, when guests can get cranky at the slothful speed and efficiency of a poorly performing toaster, and have arguments over whose piece of bread entered and emerged first from the glowing interior. I have invented a standard hotel employee called the toast captain (actually I met a real one in Asia) and a feature writer called Derek Breadchamber, hotel toaster critic for *The New York Times*. Derek has become a world authority on hotel toasters. I also take pictures of the toasters when I report on them.

Travel has become mandatory for retirees. Not so long ago, men obligingly died soon after their farewell work party, but now, over-ripe husbands and wives have money and time at their disposal. What better way to spend both — before their children get hold of it — than boarding planes, trains and evermore bulging ships to see sights that are in danger of being worn out by too many visitors?

Contents

About the Author		iii
Foreword		v
CHAPTER 1	India – 2020	1
CHAPTER 2	Russia – 2019	37
CHAPTER 3	Sicily and Malta – 2019	71
CHAPTER 4	South Vietnam – 2019	89
CHAPTER 5	Thailand – 2018	109
CHAPTER 6	Greece – 2018	119
CHAPTER 7	Italy – 2018	145
CHAPTER 8	New York – 2017	173
CHAPTER 9	Orlando, Cuba and Boston – 2017	203
CHAPTER 10	Myanmar – 2016	237
CHAPTER 11	Khao Lak, Thailand – 2016	271
CHAPTER 12	Malaysia – 2015	283
CHAPTER 13	North Vietnam and Cambodia – 2014	323
CHAPTER 14	Thailand and Hong Kong – 2013	347
CHAPTER 15	China – 2013	363
CHAPTER 16	Update – 2022	375

CHAPTER 1

India – 2020

Covid had buggered up our travel plans. We were far from alone. It had buggered up everybody else's travel plans as well. All that anticipation, all that ouch-but-we'll-do-it money still sitting in bank accounts like baby birds that refuse to leave the nest. Our suitcases were going mouldy. Our travel insurance lapsed. Our travel agent closed – temporarily, we hoped. Pictures of aeroplanes parked on airport runways and deserts like cars at a football match. We could have been watching a science fiction movie – except that when we came out of the theatre, that's how the world really was.

Sure, we'd travel again – as long as we had enough time left. Nobody would crunch the numbers, but the next trip for some elderly travellers would be ghostly – really. I hoped we would not be among them.

Luckily for me, I have a means to revisit the past. I've documented all the travel we've done over the last twenty years.

Of course, I have photographs, everybody's got those, always too many. But my photographs cannot recall what I was thinking or tasting or smelling at the time. The written word does.

We went to India in February 2020, just as the news that a virus called Covid-19 had shown up in China and was likely to be troublesome. We didn't know how seriously to take the speculation that it might develop into a global pandemic. We were tempted to cancel our trip, but in early February, Covid didn't look too threatening. Nevertheless, we arrived at Sydney Airport with enough medicine to stock a modest pharmacy — along with gloves, masks, sanitisers, and a jar of Manuka honey which my wife, Michelle, believed could be poured down the throat of a dead person and they would immediately sit up and ask where they were.

Michelle was told by our travel agent that you could spend up to four hours at Delhi Airport standing in the immigration arrival queue. The best way to avoid this for those, like me, with hip replacements, resulting in an inability to stand for very long, was to seek what is politely called wheelchair assistance. My ego resisted, of course, but hell, nobody I knew would see me as a cripple in India, so I agreed to an anonymous two-wheel experience when we arrived in Delhi. My condition was that Michelle had to endure the same indignity. She probably deserved it more than I anyway, since she had painfully dodgy disks in her back. The airline had its condition too: if we needed wheelchairs, we had to begin our wheel-a-thon in Sydney. We reluctantly lowered ourselves into the surprising comfort of the wheelchairs, weighed down by our carry-ons as ballast.

I'd never been wheeled before, except lying on a gurney

in a hospital on the way to hip surgery. I wanted to steer the wheelchair because the robust but unskilled wheeler cut corners and grazed fixtures. We were kind of tipped out at the Singapore lounge where we pleaded that we be allowed to walk to the departure gate when called. It took some persuading for Wheelers One and Two to agree, but they reminded us that once a wheelie, always a wheelie, and we'd be force-wheeled, whether we liked it or not, for the rest of the trip.

At Changi Airport in Singapore (where the captain of the A380 asked everybody to remain seated while a 'sick' person was removed, gulp) we were met by a team of wheelers revving up their chairs and calling our names. Escape was impossible. I felt quite uncomfortable as my wheeling lady puffed and grunted, especially up the carpeted slopes of the huge airport. Her task was made even more taxing because my chair had a broken wheel bearing which made it seem to continually hop over an invisible rock. Close to exhaustion, she let me off at the airport Crowne Plaza Hotel. I should have been pushing her. The whole idea had only been to avoid a stand-up at Delhi Airport, but we were now locked into the wheelchair community.

We escaped the Crowne Plaza next morning by stealth on foot and took the flight to Delhi, only to find team-wheelchair waiting for us in the riotous Delhi arrival hall, where coronavirus testing stations had been set up like a shanty town, with clerks trying to understand hastily devised declaration forms and firing red temperature lasers at the heads of anyone they could see. I was immediately captured by a wheeler but there was no wheelchair for Michelle. She had to claim a miracle cure for her back and walk beside her crippled husband as we dived into the squawking throng. I must say it wasn't so bad being pushed, with the pusher emitting urgent honking sounds as we went to the front of queues and were spoon fed at the immigration desk. Once outside, the pusher was reluctant to let me out of the wheelchair, despite my requests. We continued into the darkness and on to the carpark, where the suspension of the wheelchair was no match for the teeth-loosening potholes. Was he going to kidnap me? No, he was just trying to secure a bigger tip. I was generous, but he still went away muttering. I decided no more wheelchairs unless I became an amputee.

We were back at the airport early next morning, full of apprehension at having to board the local Indigo Airlines flight to Udaipur. Righteous military-style security men divided males from females for an aggressive examination of bodies and bags. But after that, the tide turned. Instead of steep metal stairs up to the plane, Indigo used a much better three-stage ramp. And in spite of the appearance of utter confusion, the plane left on time and arrived un-crashed at a small, well-appointed airport, where a theatrically dressed driver from Leela Palace picked us up in a BMW. He drove us through scruffy towns until we reached Lake Pichola where an elaborately decorated boat took us to the Leela Palace Hotel. Our superbly appointed traditional room had a balcony looking out on the lake which had been hand dug in the thirteenth century and was replenished by monsoon rains. In parts, it had been picked and shovelled to a depth of 15 m. Despite the Leela Palace's ability to render us bankrupt in a short time, Michelle suggested we stay there forever.

Before we set out into the dusty mayhem of Udaipur there were a few facts about the Leela Palace Hotel worth noting. It had eighty rooms and a staff of 360. The imbalance became evident at dinner when we were beset by teams of waiters who couldn't do enough for us. They stood around ready to applaud our every mouthful, chew and swallow. The head chef appeared regularly to give a passionate account of what he was about to cook and then returned later to see if we'd liked it. And they all wanted to talk. It was hard for Michelle and me to get through a two-way conversation without some helpful interjection from one of the folk-costumed team. Room service usually brought two helpers per task. The entire place was being continually swept, cleaned and tidied up. When we arrived or left to take the *HMS Leela* across the lake to the downtown wharf, a small band secreted in a nook to one side of the main entrance door struck up with wild enthusiasm.

While our room was a model of elegance, comfort and superlative lake-viewing, we were well down from the top level of opulence at the *Leela*. One of the many effusive house staff took us on a tour of the hotel and showed us the royal suite, comprising a giant bedroom, formal dining room, lounge, kitchen and multiple bathrooms. Every room was enhanced by silver embellishments and works of art. Various serving persons were included. The price? AUD$12000 a night. This room rate, the receptionist reminded us, was 'dynamic', meaning that serious guests could make a lower offer.

Every night in the internal courtyard, there was a deafening Indian traditional song and dance show. I couldn't relate to it, although when two lady dancers jumped onto the stage balancing flaming pots on their heads, and then gyrated at quite a speed, I was engaged by the danger of immolation.

Our first venture into town was to the Winter Palace, a sprawling series of grand buildings that used to be home to successive kings – called *maharanas* by the locals, and ranked one stripe higher than *maharajahs*. The royal family survived Indian independence from Britain in 1947 but was stripped of political power. The current king lived in nearly-a-palace at the far end of the building chain. He was still very wealthy and revered.

The Winter Palace was the largest palace in Rajasthan and the second biggest in India. It sat on a lake hillside and was cleverly fortified. In all the conflicts that India had endured, the Winter Palace had never been breached. I could understand why. The narrow stone staircases alone would deter attackers because the steps were of different heights and some as steep as ladders. Because the home team knew the layout, they found it easier to defend. There were also myriad secret passages which were still being discovered.

The former kings lived well and entertained themselves by shooting farmed tigers from the safety of rifle towers and being carried about in elaborate carriages borne either by four hearty men or an elephant. And speaking of elephants, one of the favourite games was to position an elephant either side of a wall, have them lock trunks and conduct a tug of war. Whichever elephant pulled its opponent to touch the wall, won a pallet of vegetables. Apart from games and physical work, elephants also went into war. Horses were no match for them until somebody thought of fitting horses with mock elephant trunks to trick opposing elephants into thinking they were attacking baby elephants – which was against elephant ethics. One famous painting of a battle showed how the king escaped – even though his horse had one of its legs cut off by a sword wielding elephant. The horse continued on three legs, jumped a river, and saved the king before nobly dying.

The Winter Palace, also called the City Palace, showed plenty of old household wares, many introduced by the Brits when they ran India. One was a fan – but driven by steam produced by boiling water which heated up the room so the fan could cool it. That didn't appear to make a lot of sense, but it looked impressive. While visitors were ogling in disbelief at wind-up portable gramophones sitting in wooden cases, I felt old when I remembered they had been popular when I was a child.

Meanwhile, out on the street, holy cows wandered, dogs were fed for good luck and traffic demonstrated it was never meant to be in those narrow, dusty corridors. Local buses had ladders at the back to enable people to clamber up and ride on the roof, where there was nothing to stop them falling off except finger nails and balance. Our guide commented, 'The motorbikes have become minibuses and the buses have become trains.'

The Hindu religion dominated this part of India. Our guide, a young Hindu man called Rajiv, told us there were three main Hindu gods, but beneath them stretched a huge family tree of gods estimated to number, according to him, about 33 million. I asked him if their names were all written down somewhere. He said no; in any case, no book could be big enough to list them all. Moreover, it was unlikely any one person knew them all or even where to find them. I couldn't work out how he'd arrived at 33 million, but he was adamant that this was the correct number, verifiable in Hindu texts.

Rajiv was twenty-two and engaged to a girl he met by accident at a wedding. Normally, parents arranged marriage for their children who accepted that they may never love their spouses. Our young man was an exception, although he still had to seek approval from both families. His courtship was mostly conducted by phone. They occasionally met in secret where they talked, but no touchy-feely. 'I have too much respect for the girl who will be my wife,' he said earnestly. They planned to marry in two or three years when the groom's bank account had grown to match his libido. They would then go to live in his father's house which already held a battalion of relatives. He was studying to join the police force in the specialist tourists' branch. Being a guide with excellent English gave him a good chance to be accepted.

The Queen's Garden was the only public park in Udaipur that charged admission. It used to be closed to all but the queen and her ladies in waiting – who would frolic about in the shrubs. All the gardeners were women, too – and that hadn't changed – but rather than hoe and weed, they had taken to forming up in smiling quartets and charging for photographs. The gardens had two impressive fountains and a big tree that had a bend in the middle that suggested it was a metaphor for erectile disfunction.

Knowing the Indian penchant of taking machines beyond their use-by dates, we chanced our luck on the cable car that climbed a junior mountain, from where we were given a 360-degree view of the city, lakes, palaces and houses. The tallest building stood out at fifteen storeys; the rest only managed two or three. We looked down on the king's former Pleasure Palace sitting on a created island in the remarkable hand-dug lake

— one of an interlocking system of five that flowed in sequence. When the king felt randy, he would summon the *HMS Orgasm* and go to the island where a selection of ladies awaited his majesty's pleasure.

After the cable car returned without falling into the ravine, it was time for us to go into town. With a straight face I asked our guide if the Old Fruit and Vegetable Market, which we were scheduled to visit, sold old fruit and vegetables. 'Oh no, sir, it is all fresh,' he replied seriously. 'Nothing old. Only the name of the market.' We joined the honking motorbikes and mini vans, brilliantly saree-ed women, road repairs, all mixed in with clothing, dust, spices, barrows of vivid vegetables, tiny lemons, mountains of chilli and everybody in a frenzy. Yet there was order to all this. Somehow it worked, underpinned by friendly good humour. This was where the locals shopped, and they understood the chaos code.

One product we would never see in an Indian food market was beef. It was illegal to sell it in India. The cow was sacred because it was considered a micro-receptacle of the Hindu gods, all 33 million of them. Our hotel (voted in 2019 by Conde Nast as the best leisure hotel in the world), and whose menu went on for many pages of delicious options, never mentioned beef.

Hotel Toaster Report

Since the Leela had been elevated to Conde Nast's podium, I entered the breakfast dining room with high expectations of its toaster. It would surely be a bejewelled work of art topped by a silver elephant expelling perfect toast in record time from beneath its raised trunk. But no. There stood a battered Jaipur Juggernaut, its front scratched, and topped by a collapsed chef's hat. Full of apprehension, I put in two slices and waited, but they failed to reappear. They had finished their journey stuck deep in the outward-bound tray slide, joining other slices that would never see the inside of their disillusioned owners' mouths. I had to use tongs to get my two slices out and they were barely warm. I spoke to a distraught toast captain who was going to resign if management didn't make an urgent replacement. Derek Breadchamber would be horrified to know this, and may need therapy.

We declared a rest day for our last at the Leela Palace, but our plan was short-lived. The chef, who had taken special delight in cooking for Michelle (an accomplished cook herself), made her a couple of dishes that changed the course of our rest day. She awoke complaining of severe stomach cramps and found it difficult to walk. Her pulse rate had gone wild too. She rose from bed and immediately brought forth an award-winning, out of control, fire hydrant-worthy upchuck that covered the floor, the wall and me – as I sat at my computer. She had food poisoning. She finished the expulsion in the bathroom basin – which immediately clogged up. Being a qualified cat poo cleaner, I tried to apply my skills, but it was beyond me. We called housekeeping and a team of uniformed cleaners arrived, continually whispering their sympathy, along with a plumber, and a housekeeper who became mother and brought Michelle lemonade and other vomit cures. The staff couldn't have been more helpful as they went to work restoring us and our room to former order.

CHAPTER 1 India – 2020

Leaving the Leela Palace was sadder than I had imagined. The staff lined up like family, with hugs and good wishes. I had anticipated a wounding bill for all the room service extras that Michelle's sickness had required, but none of it was charged. We left the Leela, resplendent across the misty lake, with hope of returning, our bank manager's pale face notwithstanding.

Apart from a magnificent place to stay, a couple of points stuck in my mind. One is that the Leela made the best hot chocolate of my long drinking experience. Number one used to be at an upmarket food store in St Petersburg, but now the Leela had shot to the front. I asked the chef how he made it, thinking he may reveal a secret powder additive. He told me: 'Very straight forward. I like to share my knowledge because goodness will come of it. First you must obtain a block of dark chocolate, sir. Then break it into pieces! Prior to that you must have prepared a ganache comprising chocolate and cream. Then melt the chocolate pieces you have broken and mix them with the ganache. Then add milk, sir! Heat it all up and pour into a suitable cup.' That might have explained my love for the Leela's hot chocolate and the likelihood of me running out of belt holes if I stayed any longer.

The other was the Leela toilet paper. If bank paper was about 80 gsm, then the Leela toilet paper came in at about 20 gsm. This was too indelicate a subject to discuss with management or even other guests, when I would have to say, 'Lovely place, but what do you think of the bum fodder?' Then I'd have to go into awkward detail.

At Udaipur airport I laughed at the poor buggers who had booked on the budget Spice Air to go to Jaipur. They faced a squashed-up hour in a little prop plane. We had booked with Air India — and paid a fair bit more in spite of the fact that the Air India Jaipur flight didn't have a good punctuality record. The bus drove us out on the tarmac and what did we board? A little prop plane for a squashed-up hour. Same as Spice Air.

We'd come down a few notches when we arrived at the Jaipur Holiday Inn. It was situated opposite a massive roadworks construction site where an overhead railway was being built. Consequently, the view was not beautiful. Next door was a shopping centre with a McDonald's. We'd arrived late in the day and wandered in for a careful box of chips and a hopefully harmless chicken burger. Michelle was still getting over her food poisoning ordeal and I was coming down with a cold. The restaurant suddenly filled with little kids who rushed to fill up the tables and waited expectantly for a burger and a cup of water each — but only chicken or vegetable burgers. Beef and pork were *verboten*. The kids came from a nearby orphanage. Many were barefoot, and most needed a good bath. I was curious as to how they spent their time during the day and found out when we left. One little girl from the group, accompanied by her younger brother carrying a baby, were back on the street begging. This was their occupation, widespread in Indian cities.

We wandered into the shopping centre only to find most of the shops in darkness. An assistant in one clothing shop that was open explained that there had been a mass dispute with the management over rent and most of the shopkeepers had legged it. The massage parlour was still operating however, revealing a severely glowing red interior through the partly open door. It was about as inviting as an abattoir.

CHAPTER 1 India – 2020

We were supposed to visit a palace and observatory, but the next day the dreaded lurgy attacked me. My temperature went through the roof and would not respond to Panadol. Michelle decided it was time to call the doctor. He arrived late in the afternoon, carrying the obligatory black bag and doing an impersonation of Peter Sellers impersonating an Indian. He looked down my throat, thumped my back, asked my age and weight – but didn't take my temperature. Then he unzipped a bulging pouch from his bag and tipped out a mountain of packaged pills on the bed. With his special surgeon's scissors, he cut off the required number of pills from their sheets and doled out five lots for me, along with a set of hand-written, virtually illegible instructions. Michelle then made the mistake of mentioning that she'd been sick too. Ah, a chance for a double consultation with only one visit. He examined her throat and went back to his pile of medications for some more cutting, allocation and illegible dosage instructions. Although we had a travel insurance plastic card ready and loaded to pay, the little doctor lusted after cash, about AUD$200's worth, which we'd have to try and claim back later. Before we started pill popping, Michelle looked up the medications on the internet and discovered that most of them were for complaints we didn't have. One combination antibiotic was illegal everywhere except India. It was certain to make us feel worse rather than better, the entry warned. Subsequently we threw away all the doctor's pills and used those we had brought with us in Michelle's portable pharmacy. The doctor's visit had succeeded in scaring off my fever and we were ready to resume our schedule. I suppose it had been worth calling him.

After having recovered from the doctor's visit, we had to squeeze a two-day schedule into one. Our guide talked like a thirty-three-and-a-third record played at forty-five. His knowledge flew at such a rate that I had to buy a book called *The Holy Cow* to make sense of even some of it. India had an almost infinite system of interlocking hierarchies headed by three major Hindu gods, Brahma (the generator), Vishnu (the operator) and Shiva (the destroyer). If you took the first letter of these descriptions, it spelled GOD. Was that significant? 'Probably,' the guide replied vaguely. From there, the hierarchy ran down through another thirty gods and goddesses. That totalled thirty, not the 33 million that reside in cows, as our last guide had told us.

Then there was the caste system which was officially outlawed but is still observed in matters like marrying within the caste — of which there were four major ones. After Brahmins (priests and teachers), our guide was in the second layer, the Kshatriyas, or warriors, which was why he wore a moustache, he told us. Beneath him were the Vaishyas who were traders but lazy and happily fat. At the bottom were the Shudras who swept streets and cleaned toilets. But the caste system was far more complex than that, because each caste had layers of subdivisions.

There were many religions operating in India, and they all had different takes on gods and castes. Many were branches of Hindu and others of Islam. In some places, the Hindus and Muslims got on well, but in others they continually fought. I couldn't understand how anybody knew where they fitted in. They probably just put their heads down and ploughed on, guided by family traditions.

CHAPTER 1 India – 2020

Traffic was as confusing as religion, especially in Jaipur. There was a huge number of road rules, but nobody obeyed any of them and the traffic was too overwhelming for the cops to enforce them anyway. The general idea was to avoid collision but take the opportunity to fill any space on the road or footpath that was vacant – even for a moment. Don't be a sucker by keeping to your lane, was one mantra. Keep your finger on the horn button was another, because blowing your horn might cause a slight hesitation of the vehicle near you whose space you can capture. And it was okay to drive on the wrong side of the road if the right side was too crowded. The millimetre was the unit of measurement favoured for traffic manoeuvres.

On our way to the Amber Fort, we passed through old Jaipur which used to be called the Pink City, but was painted terracotta when the contractors thought that was close enough to the pink it had been painted in honour of Prince Albert, Prince of Wales. Prior to being pink, it was painted yellow because there was plenty of yellow paint available at the time. The Amber Fort and palace were highlights of the day. They were 400 years old and once the home of the royal family. Incidentally, according to our guide, there were 565 states in India and each had a royal family, most of which were still wealthy even though they no longer had political power. That equated to 565 kings, each probably believing he was more important than the others. It was also likely that the guide didn't know what he was talking about.

Back to the fort. It was surrounded by a 16 km wall which followed the contours of the steep hills around the palace. It was not unlike The Great Wall of China, but about 4000 km shorter.

Within the Amber Fort was a temple to the goddess Kali

in which a goat used to be sacrificed every day and witnessed by the king, so that when he went into battle, he would not be squeamish at the sight of blood. These days the goats had been spared, but in their place bottles of whisky or rum were sacrificed, but not spilled. Rather, they became the property of the temple officials who consequently spent much of their time drunk while in charge of a holy place.

Not yet palaced out, we dived back into the clogging traffic for a visit to the City Palace. The royal family still lived there. For a sizeable fee you could poke about in their spectacular private lodgings or, for a huge sum, take tea with the king. Why did the royal family allow such an invasion? 'To make money, 'our guide blandly responded to my stupid question. Even though the king owned plenty of city real estate he must have been short on folding money.

One of the historical exhibits at the City Palace were two 1894 silver jars – the biggest silver objects in the world. It took 14 000 melted down silver coins to make one – each weighing 345 kilos. They each held 4091 litres of Ganges water (hopefully cleaner than now) and were taken to England by Maharaja Swai Madho Singh when he visited for the coronation of Edward VII in 1902. He didn't trust the pommy H_2O. The jars had lids, wheels and ladders to make them accessible.

After a buyer-beware visit to a textile shop and a jewellery pretend-wholesaler we sought refuge in the Holiday Inn which had a Valentine's Day special of all you could eat and drink for about AUD$35. We tucked into some cheek-curling hot curry doused by beer after which I made for the dessert table where everything looked attractive, but in the mouth had little substance or taste. Then I spied some tall glass containers full of brightly coloured meringues. I took two green ones and was well into the second when the chef came running in to tell me they were very old and only there for decoration. I was eating the display. But they tasted better than the rest of the stuff on the table.

Hotel Toaster Report

The Holiday Inn breakfast was a boisterous affair with everybody loud and busily loading in the calories. Toast was not high in the popularity stakes, as demonstrated by their Skinnymini Double Knobber. This demonstrated an Indian preference for narrow loaves of bread. The first pass produced only warm bread but by the end of the second pass a satisfactory transition to toast had been achieved. This was far from the worst toaster I'd seen and certainly better than the broken-down contraption at the Leela Palace. I asked the toast captain to tell me about the origin of the Skinnymini, but his understanding of English led him to conclude that I was on the spectrum.

In most countries, when you want a well, you dig a deep, roughly round hole and keep going until you come across water. Then you need a long rope and a bucket to haul it up. Not so in eighth century India when the Chand Baori stepwell was built in Rajasthan. We stopped for a look on our way to Agra — by arduous car. In Chand Baori's case, the dig was about 60 m square at the top and it went down a dizzy thirteen storeys on three sloping walls, with the fourth forming a sculpted temple-style building that reminded me of an Escher drawing. To get the water, all you needed was a team of strong young women who had to descend using 3500 steps, fill their buckets and carry them back to the surface on their heads.

The site was remarkably well preserved, although the distant water was a suspicious dark-green and there was a fence to stop people who might take on the dangerous descent but not have the capacity to come back up without the assistance of a winch.

The main reason we went from Jaipur to Agra by car was to stop at the World Heritage listed Fatehpur Sikri, a walled city built in 1586 for the emperor Akbar and was the capital of the Mughal Empire for about ten years. Made from red sandstone, it took 36 000 people twelve years to build, but the emperor only lived in it for four years before he became fed up with the political wrangling and called in the removalists. From that point on, the place was deserted for 400 years, but did vandals destroy it, or squatters move in? No. Only vegetation was interested in occupying it until 1903 when Lord Curzon, the British Viceroy, said something like: 'It's too bad that this damn fine place is choked with weeds and other unsightly undergrowth. I'll requisition a few pounds and do a spot of the old restoration thing.'

Fatehpur Sikri was likely the most under-visited-yet-outstanding example of antiquity in India. Almost fully restored, it illustrated the rather nice life Emperor Akbar led. The city was home to around 700 people, 600 of whom were his concubines. Between those and three queens – each with her own palace, the emperor got plenty of sex – even if the women didn't. He slept in a huge, elevated bed, accessible only by a draw-up silver ladder. This not only gave him privacy while he worked his way through the concubines, but made him much harder to murder while asleep. Untimely death was more matter of fact than it is now. Those found guilty of a capital offence were executed by an elephant called Hirn who, on command, stamped on their heads as they lay on the ground. This elephant was much respected for his one-hit skill. A monumental tower in his honour stood in a field outside the city wall.

When the emperor wasn't busy being entertained or siphoning the python, he tried to start a new religion called Diney Elhai that encompassed all the popular religions he could think of. But his religion was highly complex, had too many competitors and not enough congregants, so it collapsed.

Another significance of Emperor Akbar is that he was the grandfather of Shah Jahan, who commissioned the building of the Taj Mahal, principally what we'd come to see in India. We took a room at the Agra Double Tree Hilton which promised a hotel view of the Taj. Well, if that little smudge through the smog was the Taj, the claim was genuine. The hotel was full of rowdy, rude, oversize tourists – in contrast to the staff who tried very hard to be pleasant.

Michelle wanted us to see the Taj Mahal from three different aspects: dawn, dusk and from across the river. For the first tranche we were picked up from the Double Tree at 6 am for a quiet drive through the streets for a Taj dawn experience. And so did about 20 000 other people. They formed a huge queue to witness the Taj dawn which unfortunately became the street dawn instead. The grumbling queue shuffled along, went through pointless but elaborate security checks and finally filed through the grand twenty-two-domed tower gate to behold the Taj Mahal – now washed in a rising rose-gold light. The sight grabs the heart, like a dream that has become a reality. I forgot the trample and the selfish selfies. I was in the presence of wonder. The closer I got to the building, the larger it seemed to grow, its white marble with intricate Islam-inspired inlays simply hard to believe.

The Taj's Islamic architecture was typified by precision and symmetry, built around the number eight. It was 80 m high and all the columns were eight sided. I was surprised to discover that the Taj Mahal had four identical sides, so that no matter where you stood, it looked the same: no front, no back. Either side of it were other identical buildings – almost as grand as the Taj itself – although made from reddish local sandstone to lessen the rivalry. One was a mosque and the other a guest house.

The Taj was not made from solid marble, but bricks and mortar covered with marble tiles. Because of pollution and zillions of clammy visitors it was continually being cleaned and covered with protective coatings. In case of earthquake, it was built over a huge, hidden water pit to cushion a tremor, while its four minarets were constructed so that they would fall outward and not into the building. In times past, visitors were allowed to climb the circular staircases right to the top inside the minarets until a woman fell out and killed herself – along with the public permission for the climb.

The Taj Mahal was commissioned in 1632 by the Mughal emperor Shah Jahan to house the tomb of his favourite wife, Mumtaz Mahal; and was now also the tomb of Shah Jahan himself. It took twenty-two years and 22 000 people to build it. Reproduction coffins were displayed on the ground public floor, but the real ones were below, and only rarely open to public gaze.

Wanting yet more Taj, we visited what is nicknamed the Baby Taj, also finished in white marble, and the last resting place of Ghiyas Beg who became Emperor Akbar's prime minister and was a highly regarded fellow. His tomb was built before the Taj Mahal and was not as grand or magnificently domed. But it still had Islamic beauty and symmetry with four identical gates and four identical gardens.

Since this was a day of tombs, we pressed on to Emperor Akbar's tomb. He had lived rather nicely in Fatehpur Sikri with his three wives and 600 concubines and had plenty of self-esteem because he grabbed 119 acres of prime Agra city land and began building a lavish mausoleum for himself in advance of falling off the perch. The massive project only took eight years to complete because Akbar died earlier than expected and therefore needed to move in. His son, Jahangir, pressed the fast forward button so the emperor could be laid to rest promptly. But Akbar was destined not to stay there permanently because the whole building was ransacked during an attack by Raja Ram Jat, who took all the valuables including Akbar's bones, which he burned. Enter Lord Curzon, the British Viceroy again. He had a soft spot for Akbar and ordered the restoration of the tomb and the massive gardens where today there are deer, monkeys and squirrels among the livestock.

And speaking of livestock, I discovered some cow rules. There were heavy penalties for striking a cow unless in self-defence. Most cows wandering the streets were owned by non-farmers who sent them out so that other people were obliged to feed them because they were holy. When a cow was too old to give milk, it went into government funded cow care for a happy retirement. While you were not allowed to eat beef in India, you could hoe into buffalo, goat, sheep or chicken.

Agra was so much more than the Taj Mahal, wonderful though the Taj was. For instance, we visited the Agra Fort, a massive construction over 97 acres built in 1565 by the very busy Emperor Akbar. It was home to successive royal families, their servants, religious advisors and 5000 soldiers to guard the premises. They had some help from a double moat, the larger one filled with hungry crocodiles. It was a remarkable engineering and architectural feat as well, with naturally powered heating and cooling systems, and beautifully decorated buildings with carpeted floors, luxurious cushions and exotic curtains.

My imagination was captured by an innocent-looking doorway with steps that led down to an escape tunnel in case the fort was breached and the royal family had to do a runner. The tunnel ran for 50 km and was big enough to ride a horse through. There was also a branch down to the river in case the escapees preferred a boat getaway. The long tunnel came out at Akbar's, Fatehpur Sikri, the walled city we'd visited on the way to Agra. Along the tunnel were ventilation and light shafts to enable rapid travel.

The one personal outrage of this visit to the Agra Fort was right at the beginning while we were waiting to buy entry tickets. One of the team of freelance helpers offered a wheelchair to convey me up the slope inside the drawbridge. How insulting. And on my birthday, too. Then the penny dropped. Singapore

Airlines had obviously sent out a general wheelchair alert to all tourist destinations in India to look out for Fraser the cripple and wheel him about.

My birthday was a day to remember — and not only for good reasons. After my wheelchair humiliation at the Agra Fort, we returned to our hotel room which was filled with an acrid smell. It was coming from next door where an untrained lad was applying a polyurethane coating to some woodwork using a folded rag. In Australia, if you use polyurethane on your floors you have to stay out of the house for three days. Consequently, we staggered about gagging before going down to reception to threaten World War Three. Nobody knew what we were talking about, but they still put on puckered-face concern. We took the manager up to the room, where he bravely didn't flinch as he took in a toxic lungful. 'It will clear in twenty minutes,' he croaked. Michelle had other ideas, like demolishing the hotel. The manager then hit on a solution. Send the rag lad away and place a small fan in the corridor outside our room — but the door would remain closed so as not to disturb the fumes inside. No, that won't work, we chorused. We want you to place four air purifiers in our bedroom (the windows could not be opened, incidentally) and we will return in two hours after our Taj II visit. Two hours later we found two modest fans in the room that had only succeeded in better distributing the stink. We packed up in a flurry and changed rooms to a badly worn version of ours, one floor below. The manager and three staff tried to help us but got in the way while he recited another stanza from the hotel apology guide and offered recompense of two free lunches. We didn't do lunch. 'What about dinners?' I asked. 'So sorry sir, but already charged and cannot be reversed. Electronic locking, you see.' When the lunch compensation failed, the hotel presented us with a small, decorated marble plate which we planned to take home to give to somebody who has everything except a small decorated marble plate.

Although it felt like a recurring dream, we trekked back to the Taj Mahal for the second tranche of the viewing trilogy – this time to witness the sun going down over the mausoleum. While there was not the vanishing-point queue to get in as there had been for the dawn viewing, there was a massive crowd inside once we passed through the grand gate and stood to again take in this remarkable building. In the hour before sunset, the Taj firstly became luminously white, then pinkish, and finally a failing grey as it gave up its splendour to darkness. The crowd comprised about 90 % amateur photographers, which included us, all trying to get the definitive dusk shot which must include the reflection pond, of course. Many photos ended up accidentally being of people taking photos of other people taking photos. But, in the end, we got what we wanted and trudged back along the tiled roadway being frantically prepared for a visit by Donald Trump.

Hotel Toaster Report

The Double Tree Hilton had a rare memorial model named after the famous hotel toaster designer Toastarius Maximillian, better known as Toast Max. He invented the sloping delivery tray. In one of his many compelling books on hotel toasters, Derek Breadchamber (hotel toaster critic for *The New York Times*) said that Toast Max should have received a Nobel Prize for his work on delivery tray technology. Prior to that, the toast simply fell out of the toaster on to the floor where it was sometimes accidentally trodden on.

Our last day in Agra was, as usual, unusual. Being a fashion industry writer, I wanted to see where the average locals bought their clothing. We went into a big shop that I calculated was the equivalent of Lowes in Sydney. So definitely not upmarket. While the styling was uninspiring, the prices were rock bottom. I tried on one shirt in XXL that looked okay, only to find that I could hardly do up the buttons. This was definitely a shop for skinny Indians, but where did the fat ones, who appeared to be in the majority, shop?

I gave up in favour of visiting what had been recommended to Michelle as a must-see embroidery museum. Ho hum, I thought. This will be boring. It was anything but. The embroidery was simply astonishing, much of it made by embroidery students and for sale. There was also an exhibition gallery showing the work of some of the great Indian embroidery artists. One huge work stopped me dead. It was a biblical scene of Jesus tending his flock of sheep and cradling a lamb in his arms. It was the final work of Padmar Shri Shams who took eighteen years to finish it and then went blind. He died in 1999. His work took on a three-dimensional quality as I stood before it.

Our last stop in Agra was a third scheduled visit to the Taj Mahal, but this time from extensive but dried out gardens across the river. Legend had it that there was a plan to build a replica of the Taj, but in black marble. An opposing story was that the plan was to build a big pond with a black floor so that the reflection of the Taj would be black. In the end, only the gardens and some foundations were completed – leaving the real intention a mystery.

When there were no suitable flights available, we decided to travel from Agra to Delhi by car. A Toyota SUV came for us at about 11 am after we'd had a spirited discussion with the hotel cashier at bill time about being gassed. Michelle's overview of polyurethane's effect on human lungs won us a dinner credit if ever we returned to the hotel. Then it was into the near-impossible traffic along the road Trump's motorcade would take on 24 February 2020.

Trump's Indian visit was to include Agra where the Taj Mahal would be closed for the day to all but his official party. All the streets on his route were cleaned and planted with fresh mature trees. The existing dusty leaves were hosed down. Fences were painted to hide rust while spaghetti tangles of electric wires were taken down and replaced with orderly bundles. A work force of thousands made footpaths to replace the homely dust-to-mud. New, fancy electric light poles were erected. People were restrained in a curfew when his motorcade passed and kept right away from the streets he might have glanced at. The entrance roadway to the Taj Mahal had been tarted up and there was a smell of fresh paint everywhere. In other words, Donald would see Disneyland instead of Agra.

The same type of farce had been enacted when President Bill Clinton visited some years before. He commented that Agra must have been a ghost town because there were no people living there. However, when he returned for a private visit after his presidency, the place had miraculously become over-populated and surprisingly filthy. On that occasion the only concession made to him was a few accompanying cops while he strolled around wondering at the change.

As we approached Delhi, the traffic made Agra look like a quiet country town. Coming into downtown Delhi there was a sharp left turn with a traffic light perched up high in the trees, which we didn't notice until we were virtually past it. Fifty metres further on the cops had set up a well-manned trap. I suspected they worked the traffic lights and when they switched them to red, the next cars to arrive were guilty of a 'serious travel offence'. Our driver was summoned for a dressing down and a fine of 5000 rupees (about AUD$115 – a huge sum to a local, poorly paid driver). We could see our man in earnest conversation with one of the cops who were dressed like soldiers to make themselves look more menacing. Our driver came rushing back to the car to borrow 500 rupees from us. He'd done a deal for an 'on the spot fine': pay now thank you, all forgotten. On your way, sir!

All over India cricket was an obsession. As soon as we said we were from Australia, Indian men started talking cricket. They all mentioned Shane Warne, Glenn McGrath and Steve Smith, but above them all, like a Hindu god, sat Ricky Ponting.

My last visit to India had been twenty years previously when the most popular car was the Ambassador – in reality, a Morris Oxford unchanged for about fifty years. Now they'd all but disappeared, mostly replaced by the Suzuki Swifts, followed by small Toyotas. Chunky, aftermarket bumper bars were fitted to most cars for obvious reasons, with dents on them like notches on Don Giovanni's bedpost. Serious motor accidents were relatively rare in the inner cities. There simply wasn't room for them.

Buying from small Indian retailers followed a set pattern. The first announcement of the price was delivered quickly, with the shopkeeper averting eye contact. The buyer's response, which was routinely half the asking price, had to be accompanied by a scoff and one step towards leaving. The shopkeeper then put on a face that looked as though he had a stomach complaint and muttered his best price. The response was to offer about 10 % less than that and flash the money. The shopkeeper grunted and wrapped up the purchase in a barely-there plastic bag. The deal done, the parties parted happily dissatisfied.

Guides often took tourists to government approved, clean, air-conditioned, neatly and profusely stocked shops where the tourists were ripped to shreds and the guides were paid commissions. But if you could rough it in the people's markets where you dodged honking vehicles, cows, buffeting crowds, shit, dust and yelling, you could experience genuine Indian retailing.

If weddings were banned in India, the economy would collapse. They generated giant waves of work for caterers, musicians, animal keepers, astrologers, holy persons, tailors, drivers, turban fitters, planners, photographers, venue operators and transport services.

Most marriages were still arranged by parents. They used to be paid for by the bride's family but now the crippling costs were shared with the groom's family. Our first guide in Delhi, Gotam, barked out staccato information to us as we moved about because he was continually distracted by his mobile phone. He was trying to organise his wedding on the run. He told us he had to decide on a band (mostly comprising blaring brass instruments and deafening drums) costing between AUD$600 for an outfit that was only roughly in tune, to the best band in Delhi that would set him back AUD$2000. The photographer was asking AUD$1800 for a combination of still and video shots. Gotam had to hire a dressed-up white horse for an outrageous sum even though it only had to carry him about 200 m. He recalled his friend who put his young nephew on the horse and rode in a car beside it because he feared falling off. Most of the official clobber was hired because of costs. It was only meant to be worn once and discarded anyway.

Gotam was only counting on a small wedding of about 500 people (they had to be invited in family groups) but a wealthy wedding could have thousands, with exotic animals like elephants and camels accompanying the horse-mounted groom on a noisy tour around the city. In addition to the wedding ceremony, several lead-up parties had to be thrown. It seemed that nobody eloped or jumped the sexual gun before matrimony. It was pay up or remain single.

While the Taj Mahal was a unique building it was not quite as unique as most people thought. It followed a pattern of Mughal architecture that was established well before and after the Taj was built. Our Delhi tour revealed at least two other mausoleums that were in the same style as the Taj Mahal. One was Nawab Safdarjung's tomb. Built in 1754 (the Taj Mahal was built in 1631), it looks like a smaller copy – but made from yellow Jaipur sandstone without the intricate inlays of the Taj. It too had a reflection pond, symmetrical gardens and four gates. Also like the Taj, one of its sides was all the same. Both this tomb and the other nearly-Taj were accessed by such high-rise steps that many unathletic people just took a look, shrugged, and walked away.

The 'other' Taj was even more look-alike in structure: Humayun's tomb. Humayun was the second Mughal emperor and his final resting place was built eighty years before the Taj Mahal. The concept was a reverse of the Taj in that it was built by a wife to honour her husband who had departed this world at forty-eight. If the government had painted it white (over the red local sandstone) they could have saved Donald Trump going to Agra. Humayun's tomb was a UNESCO World Heritage site, along with its symmetrical gardens and grand gates. The Taj's magic was probably in its marble whiteness and scale. Humayun was 50 m high whereas the Taj was 80 m. Humayun's had no minarets against the Taj's four balancing 'bedposts'.

Indian guides all had their own interpretations of history and facts about the country. Language also played a part in misleading the visitor. An early guide told us there were 565 states in India with a corresponding number of families with royal blood. Yesterday, Gotam got it right with twenty-nine states and only about twenty-five royal families headed by revered maharajas (not allowed to be referred to as kings) who generally had money, cultured British accents, but no political clout. Another example: at the Gandhi memorial, Gotam told us that, following Hindu custom, Gandhi's body was cremated at this site (he had been shot by a fellow Hindu in 1948, aged seventy-eight, for trying to settle differences between Hindus and Muslims) and the ashes taken away to be tipped into the Ganges. We overheard an opposing guide telling his group that Gandhi's remains were still at the site in a box beneath an eternal flame. Incidentally, I had to ask Gotam about the Ganges becoming polluted with ashes and body parts that hadn't burned too well. He said that the designated tipping places were strictly controlled, and the surviving body parts were sieved out and used to make electricity. Just how that was achieved, he couldn't say.

We visited the enormous Delhi Red Fort built by Shar Jahan in 1639. It took a nifty nine years to finish, including the obligatory moat with imported crocodiles. It was more a walled city, housing the royal family, grand meeting buildings, staff and military quarters. There was also a mosque to save the finicky young prince from going outside to pray with the commoners. When the British colonised India, the viceroy probably said: 'Now look here, we need a bit of jolly old British architecture inside the fort for our chaps to sit and tell these local fellows what for.' And so up went a long London-looking three storey building inside the fort grounds for the chaps.

Rather than walk the congested trading streets of old Delhi, we were advised to take a rickshaw. We chose a battery powered one rather than make some poor bugger pedal us along. I thought that walking may have been more enjoyable until we got into the thick of it. Agra's market streets had nothing on this. There was fruit, vegetables and flowers being sold on the roadway, people delivering, people buying, buffalos pulling carts, motorbikes, dogs, muddy puddles, overhead electric wires in a tangle like a kid's fishing line, and everybody yelling.

Hotel Toaster Report

The Shangri-La Eros Hotel offered one of the grandest breakfasts I'd ever seen, catering for European and Asian tastes. Yet when it came to toasters, all it had was a single Skinnymini Infuriator. This model gets its name from its dimensions which only took in one slice of bread at a time. With that level of intensity, you'd expect a speedy throughput, but it still required two passes.

Not that staying in the Shangri-La Eros was irksome. Incidentally, 'Eros' might have indicated some exotic sexual services, but it was just the opposite. The management didn't even want the male henna artist to go into our room, even with me present, to do Michelle's hands because it may have been 'improper'. A threesome with a male henna artist?

The hotel was set in New Delhi among embassies, mansions, government buildings and big business. The streets were wide and tree lined. This part of town denied the poverty and squalor nearby and charged accordingly. For instance, Michelle's tummy bug had made her cautious about eating. All she wanted was a simple bowl of fried rice for dinner. I'd already eaten, so all I wanted was a drink. The Shang's fried rice cost about AUD$19 and my crème de cacao – which covered the bottom of the glass to a depth of 1 mm, meaning that with one sip it was gone – cost AUD$12. Total about AUD$31. But by the time the add-ons had done their job the bill was AUD$40. The government gobbled 18 % GST, plus a 10 % service charge, and to express its abhorrence of strong drink, it popped on a further 20 % alcohol tax and called it VAT. This did not reflect poorly upon the Shang but illustrated the actual cost of living it up in India.

India was not really a country that welcomed tourists, despite all the nice Taj Mahal images in travel agents' windows. For a start, filling in a visa took hours of research to find out where your grandfather went to school and the name of every country you have ever visited since you were born. Once that was sorted, you might have wanted to buy some rupees in Australia so you could at least tip helpers in India, but that was forbidden. If we were caught with rupees coming into India, they would be seized and so would we. Delhi airport resembled a cattle sale yard and people were treated accordingly. After that, wherever you went somebody was imploring you to buy goods and services you didn't want, and demanded that you explain why you didn't want them, after which the price came down and it all started again.

In many ways it was a wonderful place to visit, but you paid a price — and then a bit more.

We had two more must-sees for our final day. The first was the Swaminarayan Hindu temple. Because it was opened as recently as 2005, visitors often dismissed it because it wasn't old and falling down. The fact was that visiting this temple was like visiting the Taj Mahal or the Red Fort just after they had been built. It had to be one of the most spectacular buildings in the world. It was made from sandstone and marble without using any steel or concrete. The huge stone blocks, all carved in intricate detail, were not held together with cement but limestone paste — which lasts much longer.

Security was excessive at the temple. No cameras, edibles,

phones or electronics allowed. Shoes off to go inside. In addition to the main temple there were vast gardens and other buildings – all in the name of Swaminarayan (1781–1830), whose followers believed he was God on earth, physically perpetuated by a succession of latter-day Swamis. The current one had millions of followers and millions of dollars from donations. Although all this was encompassed by the Hindu faith, it seemed to stand alone, in that it worshiped one mystical man who professed to be Hindu.

The temple and its surrounds made up a thriving business as well, with catering and souvenirs. A package ticket included a series of animated scenes of the Swami's life as we moved on foot through a series of theatres. The figures were quite lifelike as they blinked and moved their mouths, arms and hands. In the final scene a mechanical Swami delivered a message of peace, compassion and non-violence and then rose from his chair – like I'd seen the mechanical Abraham Lincoln do at Disneyland.

From there we took a theme park-like boat ride through caves that told us what historically smart people Indians were, claiming the discovery of most of the scientific, chemical and astronomical studies that were then later 'reinvented' by the West. About the only invention not claimed was the wheel. I thought we may have gone down a steep slide and a splash to finish, but no, this was a gentle cultural experience and we clambered out of the boat while the next two thousand people waiting to board shuffled forward.

Our last stop was the Bahai temple. I had seen it previously and wanted to share it with Michelle, but when we saw a queue that would take an hour to reach security and then another hour to wait for a ten-minute peep inside, we decided to take a picture through the fence and leave it at that. It certainly was an impressive building that looked like a rearrangement of the Sydney Opera House's sails into lotus leaves.

On the way back in the jerky, crawling Sunday traffic, our guide expounded the benefits of cow shit. Apart from the blessing imparted by it, being holy, it was dried and burned as household fuel, emitting a fetching and purifying odour, he assured us. Cow's urine was even more highly regarded, since it could be refined for many medicinal uses, including some anti-cancer treatments. The main problem was in collecting it. You had to follow the cow around with a bucket and then be nimble enough to place it in the catchment area when the cow got that certain look on its face.

CHAPTER 2

Russia – 2019

Why weren't airlines ordering any more Airbus A380s? After boarding one in Sydney, aimed in the general direction of Singapore, I had the answer. They were just too big for people, to say nothing of airports and runways. In business class there was an accepted expectation to run the seats across in the one-two-one configuration so that everybody had an aisle next to them. Because the fuselage was so fat, it took fat seats to fill it. They were actually sized at one and a half persons per seat. Two thin people could comfortably occupy one, or an adult plus young child. Or maybe three small children, well behaved. Only exceptionally obese people would consider the seats fit-for-purpose. Perhaps the Airbus designer of the A380 had looked at the world epidemic of obesity and calculated this was future-proofing air travel. But diet and fitness were fighting back, leading to the downsizing of aircraft.

Travelling in the A380 had therefore given me a vivid memory of something that would pass into history. One day I would sit down with my great-greats and hold them spellbound telling them about the now defunct whoppers of the sky. I would probably not mention the A380 male toilet feature for fear of offending somebody. It comprised a confronting, full-length mirror behind the bowl, inviting appendage assessment. Most young men emerged with a certain jauntiness whereas older men looked downcast. Newer, smaller aircraft didn't have room for such furnishings, thank goodness. In those, you had to brace your head against the sloping wall and devote your full attention to imitating a helicopter landing on a helipad.

Changi Airport was trying to become a tourist destination in its own right. Short stays were encouraged, with well-appointed, hotel-style accommodation within the airport or attached to it. We booked at the Crowne Plaza Hotel, built specifically for the flop-needy traveller. Moderately priced, it was absolutely soundproofed, even though it was within sight of departing jets.

The major feature of Changi Airport had shifted from simply shopping and eating to visiting Jewel, a nature-themed entertainment and retail complex. Linked to Changi's three passenger terminals, the centrepiece was the world's tallest indoor waterfall, named the Rain Vortex, and surrounded by a terraced forest setting where every leaf and twig was real.

Jewel included gardens, frivolous and more earnest theme-park attractions, a hotel, and more than 300 retail and dining facilities. It covered a total gross floor area of 135,000 m², spanning ten storeys – five above-ground and five below. Its attractions also included the Shiseido Forest Valley, an indoor garden spanning five storeys. The Canopy Park, at the topmost level, offered more gardens and places to lean and stare in disbelief at what man had created.

It was almost worth coming to Singapore just to visit Jewel. While the crashing water and verdant valley pulled in the crowd, the shops pulled in the money. All the important brands were there, including the biggest Zara store I'd ever seen. We passed a newly opened store selling massage chairs and, being desperate to sit down, decided to test drive the chairs. Michelle settled into hers and immediately began purring. I settled into mine and was immediately assaulted by angry, twisting fists that wanted to turn me into gravel. The trimmed and toned Chinese sales girl said that I was only on level one out of seven, adding that even seven was not aggressive enough for her. I briefly wondered at the demands she might make of her boyfriend.

Next stop was Moscow and my first glimpse of Russian hotel toasters. Derek Breadchamber who, as you know, was Hotel Toaster Critic for *The New York Times*, wrote some scathing stuff about Russian hotel toasters. This would be my chance to see if it was justified.

In line with all service industries, airports were trying to get machines to replace people.

We now had passport recognition scanners which, in my case, always failed to find sufficient resemblance between my face and the one on the passport. Singapore immigration, desperately needing to know who was coming and going, had added the double thumb print to the passport face test for those wanting to get out of Singapore. It should work without the intervention of humans, but didn't when I tried to leave for Moscow.

The passport scanner took several runs at my passport and

gave up. Then I was loudly told by a female official, brandishing a telescopic pointer, that I must press my thumbs down on a glass panel. This I did, but not hard enough, she yelled, tapping her now extended pointer on the machine from a considerable distance. Fearful that she might give me six of the best with the pointer, I pushed with all my strength, but failed again. She grew exasperated and pointed me off to a counter occupied by other exasperated officials who passed around my passport as if it were a turd, tried again to face-match, failed, and then tried more thumb pressing. After that, too, failed, they shrugged and reluctantly let me out through a glass gate. This seemed to be happening to a number of people trying to depart. One American man at the counter, also in an identity crisis, was trying to get his passport back from an official who couldn't recall having been given it in the first place.

It appeared that there were more people required (especially immigration officials who were dressed up like drum majors) to show travellers how to use the labour-saving machines than if they had no machines at all. The machines would be perfected eventually, but playing laboratory rat for their failures did not appeal to me.

Because Michelle had joined us up as members of the InterContinental Ambassador's Club in Moscow, we won an automatic upgrade when we booked a room. Since we were only staying one night on this leg of the odyssey, we booked an entry level room with the expectation we would ladder up one notch. Instead, we went up like a Saturn rocket and finished on floor eleven with a Cinemascope view of Moscow from a massive suite with two bathrooms, three TVs (one to view from the bath), two toilets, drawers to burn, and a lounge with sprawling couches and a partners desk. We expected a knock on the door and a family of ten claiming shared occupancy.

Moscow was an impressive city, with buildings of girth and substance — rather like the people — wide streets and a driving style that prompted ridiculously high speed when there was a gap in the gridlock. Some cars were doing short bursts in excess of 120 km/h in the middle of the city.

We were scheduled to leave the next morning for Suzdal and Yaroslavl with the promise of some hotel toaster revelations. The InterContinental's toaster was away at the panel beater but was expected to be back in service by the time we returned.

Apart from our promised Mercedes turning into a Toyota, we were pleased to swap the city for the Russian countryside, aided by a word-loaded guide, Helen, and driver, Roman. We were headed for a walled monastery called The Holy Trinity Saint Sergius Lavra, about two car hours north of Moscow.

This monastery was said to be the spiritual centre of the Russian Orthodox Church. It pulled in multitudes of pilgrims, herds of obedient Asians and nosey tourists like us from all over the world. The patriarch of the church visited regularly and blessed the devout from a balcony in the official residence — in much the same way the Pope did in St Peter's.

If you wanted a microcosm of Russian Orthodoxy, this was it. Within the walls were several ancient cathedrals, residential training for monks and priests (some female), lashings of gold carvings, frescos, paintings, mysterious echoing choirs and stunning gold onion domes. Priests and monks took visiting groups on explanation walks. There was even a spring gushing water said to possess healing powers. The story went that a monk, some centuries ago, got his sight back following a few splashes. The water was generously pumped to a decorative gazebo for anybody to use. I put some on my troublesome back, ready to become a convert.

The leading attraction at the monastery was the earthly remains of the church's founding saint, St Sergius. He was a thirteenth century monk who, as a child, was the school dunce until he was told by an old monk praying under a tree that a miracle awaited him at home. There he found that advanced literacy had been bestowed upon him and he could now read. He then became a holy academic and eventually, after a lot of wandering, established the monastery.

Legend had it that St Sergius could tell the future. He accurately predicted when he would die and began making his own coffin – a privilege reserved for the high priesthood – six months before he needed to get into it. After he was laid to rest and buried, he was canonised, which meant that the priests had to dig him up again and take him out to be placed in a special glass-topped coffin in one of the cathedrals. Instead of a very smelly, partly decomposed corpse, they lifted the lid to find his body in mint condition – proving to them that he was a saint.

People queued up to kiss the glass top of the coffin which resided in a spectacular carved canopy of silver and gold. Other saints, whose glass-topped coffins were placed around the cathedrals, also came in for a lot of kissing. A cloth was provided to wipe away the saliva, or most of it, left behind by previous kissers.

St Sergius's original wooden coffin went on display after he was taken out of it, but visitors began to cut off small pieces to take home as souvenirs that might bring them good luck. This forced the priests to cover the wood with protective metal and put it all in a glass case. Devotees kissed this as well.

The monastery was closed after the 1917 revolution when religion was suspended, but Joseph Stalin ordered its reopening and restoration in 1947. Stalin was both a cruel dictator and civil hero rolled into one. It appeared that today's Russians had not decided how to categorise him.

We spent the night in a weird Suzdal hotel in which guests were assigned a room in one of the many copies of ancient merchants' houses that made up the estate. It gave the impression of a ghost tour. Breakfast rewarded me with a rare hotel toaster sighting. There were also hard-boiled eggs on offer, one of which I bit into to find I was trying to eat the shell. This was my first life experience of a totally white eggshell. Our guide, Helen, remarked if she got a brown shelled egg like those in our supermarkets, she would think there was something wrong with it and throw it out.

Hotel Toaster Report

The two toasters at the Suzdal Hotel looked like mother and son. They were in excellent condition, probably because they didn't have much toasting to do. The available bread was so stale it was nearly toast before it was presented to the toaster.

Russia was a far more religious country than I had expected. There were publicly supported churches and cathedrals throughout the countryside. Russian Orthodox dominated, and was probably the world's most ornate religion in terms of gold carving, icons and frescos, just edging out Greek Orthodox. It also appeared that Russian Orthodox won the dressing up category with the best clergy crowns (some topped with antenna-like crosses) and glittering, richly coloured robes. Catholicism won easily on statues and stained-glass windows; there were none visible in Russian Orthodox, nor was there any organ music; singing was all *a cappella*. Apart from some Church of England passable brassware and a bit of fancy get-up, the Protestant divisions didn't rank highly in terms of grand appearance. My Methodist boyhood never got past timber pulpits and black cotton dustcoats for ministers. We were told that God liked austerity.

I discovered that Russian Orthodox had some other interesting practices, too. In most towns there were two churches for the locals, one summer and one winter. The summer one was bigger to provide ventilation, while the smaller winter one enabled the faithful to huddle together like penguins to survive the devastating cold during a service — in which they were obliged to stand. Pew building was therefore not a popular craft.

After three days of holy places, we were feeling somewhat over-frescoed, but a surprise awaited us as we walked in the gardens in Yaroslavl, heading towards the Cathedral of the Assumption — a huge and beautiful building, only nine years old, and paid for by the local property tycoon. A young man approached us on a scooter and told us he was a member of a male quartet that would sing for us, no charge, in rooms beneath the cathedral. Half an hour later we were seated in a small white stone theatre when four ordinary looking blokes in jeans sauntered out from behind a partition. The tallest one said they would begin with the Russian Orthodox version of the Lord's Prayer. From their first note I was transfixed. I had never heard more uplifting singing – almost to the point of tears. Then they sang a folk song about the Volga River, which flowed past the cathedral. That had the same effect. They asked for nothing more than that we might buy their CD if we liked their singing. I couldn't get my money out quickly enough.

Since we were on a guided tour, our meals were part of the package. That didn't apply in Moscow where we ate a magnificent first night dinner in a Georgian style restaurant we stumbled upon near our hotel. But on the road, we stopped at prearranged quaint little country eating houses that served especially awful food. After two dinners and lunches that tasted like recycled newspaper, we went into revolt. We changed to ordering à la carte and paying. Eating Russian food suddenly became a pleasure. We vowed not to be seduced by quaintness, frilly curtains and artfully placed knickknacks. Russian restaurants clearly resented providing set menus for tourists.

One of our stops was at a reconstructed village showing how the people lived in the eighteenth century. The houses were all authentic, having been transported from other parts of Russia. The whole village was made of wood, including the churches. Living conditions were both difficult and formalised. A typical couple would marry in their teens, a wooden house would be built for them by villagers and they would set about begetting their first child as quickly as possible. After that, the sleeping arrangements became so un-private that I couldn't see how they could go on begetting. And with winter temperatures as low as minus forty degrees Celsius, if you went outside for a pee in the night, you stood a good chance of turning into an ice-block held upright by a solidified urine support.

Although we never doubted their beauty, we found ourselves overfed on frescos. Most of them depicted events from the old and new testaments, with various historically important figures standing around looking vacantly pious. My favourite, however, was an action fresco: Adam and Eve being evicted from the Garden of Eden. They looked as though as they had fallen behind on the rent and the winged angel property manager was telling them to bugger off.

Hotel Toaster Report

I was disappointed by the offering at the Radisson Hotel in Yaroslavl. The toaster cowered ashamedly among bread baskets and butter buds. I identified it as an early Fourslicenov. I remembered it ranked very low on Derek Breadchamber's list of significant hotel toasters.

On the way back from our countryside excursion, we visited a museum dedicated to Russian astronauts. While Yuri Gagarin was the most famous, the museum told the compelling story of Valentina Tereshkova, the first woman in space. She took a solo flight of about twenty-four hours in 1963. Using now primitive technology, she went aloft without knowing what to expect. Taking off, she promptly half-filled her space helmet with vomit, then felt even sicker when she discovered that a miscalculation had her headed for a permanent place in the firmament with no return ticket. Ground controllers got out their slide rules and gave her new coordinates — which she followed. It worked and she came back. She was born in 1937 and was still living, now a revered and active celebrity.

Returning to Moscow, we found our InterContinental Hotel room had suffered a downgrade with now only one bathroom featuring an out-of-control heated toilet seat that obliged short sittings only, but a separate lounge and plenty of storage. The wardrobe was equipped with two gas masks. Was a gas attack imminent? Nobody we asked in the hotel knew what they were for and most didn't even know they were there.

As we awaited the arrival of our guide to walk us around the city, I prayed we'd get a middle-aged, large Russian woman with a bad leg who would prefer trains or taxis to walking. But instead, Oleg appeared, young and wide, with athletic thighs and calves. Not only that, he was a professor of philosophy. He'd done his doctorate on 'the nature of honour' and had written two books on the subject. Tour guiding, he told us, was his hobby. The earnings came in handy too. His knowledge was staggering, all delivered with humour. We walked, with hardly a break, for six and a half hours, rendering my lower half numb by the time I fell through the front doorway of the hotel.

Most of our time was spent in the Kremlin, along with a grand-final sized crowd of eager people. Oleg's bulk proved to be invaluable as he bulldozed lighter-weight visitors out of the way, us in his wake. Once past the elaborate airport-like security, we made for the Armoury — not a place of weapons but a whole range of exotic memorabilia covering several centuries.

This was regarded as Russia's leading museum. And for all its overwhelming presentation, only 7 % of its treasures were on display. The rest were stored in the basement with plans to build additional museum space to show more of them.

We walked past a spectacular line-up of elaborate old carriages, several used to transport Catherine the Great around Russia. One early design had the obligatory four wheels, but they were fixed, meaning that the carriage had no steering. When it needed to turn a corner, two powerfully built servants had to jump off the back and lift the carriage, including occupants, around to face the new direction. Both steering and suspension came later.

Other items included clothing and formal household goods of royalty and nobility, plus diplomatic gifts from all over the world. Napoleon once gave the Czar a superb hand-painted porcelain dinner set, but the Czar never used it because close examination revealed that Napoleon had already used it for his dinner and the Czar didn't accept second-hand goods.

Outside the Armoury stood the world's biggest bronze bell, weighing 200 tonnes. The first attempt to forge it in a huge fire-pit built on site failed, and the forger was so mortified he had a heart attack and fell down dead. His son stepped up and had another go which succeeded, but only sort of, because it rained during the casting and a chunk of the bell fell off. It was therefore never rung, but if it had been, it was calculated you could have heard it 23 km away and those close to it would have experienced no sound but simply bodily, low frequency vibrations. When I'd visited Myanmar two years previously, I had crawled beneath the second biggest bell in the world – but that one rang, and did so mightily.

Next to the Armoury was the diamond room. Michelle, who is partial to a well-cut sparkler, went weak at the knees as we passed glass cases holding some of the world's biggest and rarest gemstones and royal jewellery. And just to top off the wealth, other cases showed famous, massive gold nuggets. The whole display was genuine and priceless. Oleg remarked that there were more security cameras in the building than bricks.

Within the Kremlin compound was a big square in which we stopped to watch a parade of soldiers done up in nineteenth century, somewhat ridiculous, uniforms. There was also a brass band and a team of soldiers on horseback. The whole troupe put on a grand show of rifle twirling, bayonets attached. The absence of one-armed soldiers was a testament to their skill. There were horsey tricks and goose-stepping formation marching. At one stage the soldiers fired their rifles, giving the crowd a fright, but not the horses, who greeted it with ho-hum.

The huge wall around the Kremlin looked as though it was made of billions of bricks. Actually, it was, but the real bricks were behind a protective coating that was painted to resemble other, better-looking bricks.

Red Square was not red, I was disappointed to find. In Russian, 'red' meant 'excellent'. It was dominated by the famous St Basil's Cathedral, the most photographed and symbolic building in Russia with its unmistakable onion domes.

Our guide, Oleg, had a theory about why Russia appeared to be a pumped-up version of Europe; why the buildings were grander and bigger, the roads wider and the people more deeply passionate. He believed that Russia had always wanted to be considered part of Europe but hadn't quite made it. To prove its Europe-worthiness it had unconsciously magnified its appearance. Since Oleg was a philosophy professor, I took his point of view seriously.

Oleg generously made us walk for only five and a half hours the next day, with the concession of one coffee stop. He took us to Russia's leading art gallery, the Tretyakov, concentrating on paintings by Russian artists from the eleventh to early twentieth century. I was staggered by Oleg's knowledge of art. He seemed to know the history and significance of every painting in the vast gallery. Not only that, but the character depictions formed historical pathways of their own that Oleg could explain.

The gallery was built in 1989 and designed to provide perfect light for viewing the paintings, while its air-conditioning system removed moisture as well as maintaining an even temperate of twenty-three degrees Celsius — certainly better than the brass monkey weather outside.

The biggest painting in the gallery was called *The Appearance of Christ to the People* by AA Ivanov (1806–1857). In photorealistic style, it depicted a group of people who had just been for a baptismal swim while Jesus, at some distance, walked towards them along a road. Besides being huge, the painting came with a story. It took poor Ivanov twenty years to complete, but only a minor part of that was spent wielding his brushes. First, he made some sketches to decide the painting's layout and how many people it would show. Then came the time-consuming part. He had to find models for every one of his figures. To do this, he went crowd mingling and, when he saw a face or body he fancied, had to convince its owner to sit for him. Since the painting showed quite a few of the people getting dressed after their dip, this posed an additional challenge: 'Excuse me, sir, you have just the buttocks I want. Would you mind . . .' He probably collected a few black eyes in the name of art.

Another painting I especially liked, by I. Levitan, showed a log bridge over a river. As I entered the gallery, the logs appeared to be at an acute angle but as I walked past the painting they straightened and then went towards the opposite angle. Oleg told me it was no accident. Great artists like Levitan could do that — like the eyes of a face that follow you around a room.

Near the art gallery stood a stylish apartment block that was built in the 1930s as part of a government move to house artists together in condominiums, according to their specialty. This block was for writers, one of them being Boris Pasternak who wrote part of Dr Zhivago while a tenant. But the idea of an artists' residential-bundling didn't take off and it was abandoned. I could see why. I imagined a building full of fashion designers. They'd be throwing one another through the windows after the first week.

Some of the greatest attractions in Moscow were the metro train stations, mostly built on Stalin's orders after the end of the Second World War. Each one was in a different but spectacular architectural style. There was lavish use of marble, stained glass, chandeliers, frescoes, ceiling mouldings and statues. The regular locals had probably grown used them, but to the visitor they were breathtaking. The metro system itself was ranked as one of the best in Europe. Trains ran every two minutes and went like the clappers. They allowed only fifteen seconds for passengers to get on and off. Oleg said it paid to be pushy — if you wanted to live.

Hotel Toaster Report

I hesitated to call the contraption I found at the InterContinental a hotel toaster. It looked like a dual slot domestic model, except the bread descended automatically into the slot with the speed of the sinking organist finishing his gig in an old picture theatre. Then you were left with five unnamed buttons to guess their function. Once the buttons were mastered and the toasting completed, the slow ascension left the hot toast just short of the top of the toaster so that you had to toast your fingers to get it out. I hope that my very good friend, Derek Breadchamber, never reads this. He would not be pleased that I was wasting my valuable assessments on pseudo domestic toasters.

With the thankful prospect of less walking than the previous day, we set off by car to Izmailovsky Park – but not to be at one with nature. This was a kind of tired theme park, with Disney-like examples of traditional Russian buildings, a market, and the famous (claimed by the brochure) Vodka Museum.

Tourist markets were the same around the world, with a tsunami of stuff repeated *ad nauseum* down long rows of stands. There you could buy gifts for people back home who would say they loved them and then store them in a cupboard to be given to somebody else who would say the same thing. That applied here, with the exception of chilblain saving hats, one of which Michelle bought after the usual price tussle with the storekeeper. I noticed the appearance of remarkably low-priced cashmere scarves. Although they felt exceptionally soft and smooth, I was certain they were made from bamboo, not cashmere as claimed on the label. They fitted well with the other scarf deception, printed silk which was actually polyester microfibre.

It was not hard to tear ourselves away from the market to keep our appointment with the Vodka Museum curator, a hugely tall man with a barrel belly and legs that seemed part of an independent machine. It was as though his legs decided where he would go, as he strode around tidying his museum's exhibition of bygone vodkabilia. He'd set up three tasting stops as he delivered his lines in Russian which, sometimes after a loud argument, were translated by Oleg into English. The history of vodka was therefore hard to follow, as was the exhibition which featured a very unlifelike waxwork of Catherine the Great (placed there because she could take on the men in vodka drinking) with a pageboy thrown in for good measure. There were early metal utensils for distilling and storing vodka, and hundreds of old bottles bearing vodka labels, some of them claiming the contents to be 96 % alcohol. These were not intended for drinking, but as a solvent for cleaning or lighting fires. However, that didn't stop people from drinking the stuff. It may have encouraged a period of prohibition in Russia from 1914 to 1924. From examples like Boris Yeltsin, I had the impression that Russia was a country of alcoholics, but that was far from the case. There was now zero alcohol tolerance for driving and a growing disinterest in drinking among upcoming youth. According to Oleg they were into health, fitness and religion.

Back at the museum, our first sample drink was honey mead (5 % alcohol), the forerunner of vodka, then raspberry vodka (25 % alcohol) and finally, with me sitting down by this time, straight vodka (40 % alcohol). Since Michelle doesn't drink, I polished off her shot glasses and felt extremely partial to a lie down by the end of the history lesson. Speaking of which, there was a static display set up in a room to show conditions in a 1930s special hospital for alcoholism recovery. The two drunks lying in the beds looked authentic enough but the exotic nurse with cascading blonde hair gave the impression that getting blotto could have benefits.

On religion again, Oleg told me that there were two divisions of Russian Orthodox – old and new. The old stuck to the original biblical texts even though they had gone through multiple language translations and were now accepted as inaccurate. The new had taken the original texts and translated them straight into modern Russian. The two divisions didn't get on, didn't mingle and many of their rituals were different. While congregations in both had to stand for the two-hours-or-more long services, even the elderly had to get up and down for required kneeling. Painful, yes, but the more pain you suffered, the more respect you were showing to God. Only the patriarch was permitted to sit during a service.

We visited the Moscow State University, a magnificent, typically musclebound Russian building, where Oleg did his post graduate degree; he pointed out the window of his old room. Then it was time to part. I had loved his intellect, staggering knowledge and good humour. He was also off-beat. He told us of a time when he had to leave his apartment to take a three-month trip for work. The problem was, he had two cats and couldn't afford to board them out. He solved the problem by calculating and buying enough dry cat food for three months and also devised a system of slowly running water in his kitchen sink. The cats could come and go into a small walled garden via a cat door.

'When I returned, the cats were okay,' he recounted, 'but their personalities had changed. They were angry and didn't seem to know who I was.'

Many of Oleg's ideas would stay with me. For instance, the fact that man's technology had disrupted the course of nature, eventually to bring disastrous consequences. And that the realisation of nuclear fusion providing infinite, free energy would probably send civilisation out of control because it would circumvent natural process. And one of his lines: 'Each step is determined by the one before.'

The train from Moscow to St Petersburg was up there with the best in Europe. It loped along at 250 km/h, with comfortable reclining seats and a choice of combination meals served by pretty, but grim-faced, young female cabin crew. A screen showed the outside temperature got down to zero but whizzed back up to a steamy six for arrival in St Petersburg. I think I saw the speed-handle captain (indicated by his railway decorations) stride through, full of importance and purpose.

On first impressions, St Petersburg looked like the old low-rise section of Paris, but wider and grander. And the same went for our hotel, the Belmond Grand Hotel Europe. It resembled a palace where the last update was a hundred years ago but every detail had been kept in perfect condition. Our room was as tall as it was wide, with a huge tiled bathroom where the underfloor heating could not be reduced to much below fire-walking pit temperature. The hand-held shower, although the size of a little, old-style telephone, had a surprisingly generous output. After a shower I could dry myself by either using the monogrammed towel or rolling across the hot floor. We slept in the biggest bed I have ever seen — just short of boxing ring size. It would have held five people with ease. Maybe there would be a knock on the door and a couple of staff members would hop in with us.

Breakfast was served in what may once have been a massive ballroom, with stained glass windows and a loudly played grand piano on a stage. The food selection was vast, including that provided by a rotund, always smiling, omelette-ier. I couldn't believe the big bowls full of salmon caviar. We could spoon it out without qualm or question.

Hotel Toaster Report

Known as the Extremesky Tallboyavitch, this toaster had a mean little in-feed, a funereal speed journey low on fire power that then fed into a totally inappropriate delivery portal shaped like a cathedral. It also wore a chef's hat, probably awarded to it by the great grandson of Ivan the Terrible for terrible services to toasting. An English lady in the waiting line remarked, 'I say, it is taking rather a long time. I suppose we English invented toast but they don't understand that too well here.'

A major reason we wanted to visit St Petersburg was to see the Hermitage (local pronunciation 'errmitarrge') Museum. Its several buildings fronted the huge Palace Square featuring a granite tower made from one piece of stone weighing 600 tonnes.

The square also provided a venue for people who dressed up in bygone garb and offered to pose for photographs, after which they nailed the hapless photographer for whopping modelling fees. Professional pickpockets practiced their art in the square too, taking care to pay off the cops who controlled the territory. The journalist in me wanted to sit down with an accomplished pickpocket and report on training, skill levels and sprinting speed. Our guide shrugged his shoulders: 'Part of the culture, I guess,' he said.

The Hermitage Museum held the second largest art collection in the world, to say nothing of sculpture, installations, porcelain and historical jewellery. If you spent three minutes to look at each exhibit it would have taken three years to get through them all. And that didn't include the enormous number of pieces in storage. Art aside, the museum buildings themselves were breathtaking. Each gallery stopped us in our tracks with its grandeur and soaring architecture. They were palaces restored or recreated.

The effect of all this was overwhelming. I quickly became numb to yet another wave of exquisite beauty festooned with gold. It was like drowning in honey. The Museum of Contemporary Art brought me down to earth a little because I loved the Impressionist school, Monet in particular, of which there were many fine examples. And Michelle picked out a few pieces in the Diamond Room that I should remember if I win multiple lotteries.

Each day, tourists descended on the museums like stampeding cattle, many from the cruise ships that tied up at St Petersburg. Nobody wanted to miss out on taking selfies backdropped by the main attractions. Intolerable overcrowding was now the norm in the most sought-after tourist attractions like these. Part of their popularity was probably from a real fear to see it before it is loved to death.

Few countries have indulged in worse and more persistent persecution of Judaism than Russia. Today, out of a population of 146 million, only 200 000 admit to being Jewish even though there is now religious freedom throughout the country. Many others either denied it out of ingrained fear or didn't know they were Jewish because successive wars had destroyed heritage records.

Nevertheless, there was a vibrant Jewish presence in St Petersburg – which we wanted to experience. With Nadia, a delightful local Jewish guide to help us, we made visits to three places.

The first was to the Russian Museum of Ethnology, where artefacts, clothing and religious objects were presented in glass cabinets in chronological order. Two eighteenth-century figures, who were supposedly getting married, set off a discussion over a single male boot on display next to them. Apparently, if a husband wanted to divorce his wife, he took off one boot in the synagogue and threw it out the window – known colloquially as giving the missus the boot. And if your brother died and you were a single male, you had to marry his widow even if you couldn't stand the sight of her. Furthermore, any kids from that union were considered to be the offspring of the dead brother.

Our second stop was at the Grand Choral Synagogue. Built in 1893 in the Moorish style, it was currently the second largest synagogue in Europe. It had a capacity of over a thousand people, although, even on high holy days, was little over half full. It relied on donations from wealthy benefactors to keep it running, along with its team of rabbis, but didn't ask its members for money. Being orthodox, women sat upstairs. When we visited, workmen were moving the pews back inside after a wedding had been conducted outside in the courtyard the previous day. With St Petersburg daytime temperatures well under ten degrees Celsius it would have been one very cool wedding.

Our third stop was, in many ways, the most remarkable. It was at the St Petersburg Jewish Community Centre. That didn't sound too remarkable until we realised that this poly-funded organisation has been able to attract people of all ages and branches of Judaism that didn't normally see eye-to-eye, plus people who were simply curious about the religion, and make a happy mix of them. The facility had schools, an auditorium, a gym, pool, library, offices and a kosher-style restaurant where pensioners could get a free feed. Old folk were encouraged to spend time at the centre so they could meet up with people from their own era, many having lost their families to emigration or the Holocaust. Nikita, the young man who showed us around the centre, said he did many jobs there, one of which was as judge in chess competitions among the elderly. Apparently, the oldies had regular run-ins, some of them physical, over breaking established chess rules. 'Chess is an emotional game,' Nikita said. 'Advancing years don't take the edge off wanting to win.'

Another St Petersburg showpiece was the summer palace of Peter the Great, or *Peterhof*. It had been called the Russian Versailles – although it hadn't looked too good in 1944 when departing Germans blew it up, but restoration work began almost immediately and now it was back in pristine condition.

To get there, we boarded a 1980s so-called hydrofoil which looked like an aircraft fuselage after wing amputation. It sat low in the water, promising to get up on its foils and skim across the surface once the smelly, shuddering engine fired up. But it didn't, because once the speed passed a certain point the nose lifted which meant the passengers couldn't see properly. To prevent a mutiny, it ploughed through the Gulf of Finland chop like a grumbling old man until it arrived at the Peterhof wharf.

Peter the Great's reception plan was obvious. Guests would arrive by ship, then small boats would ferry them up a hand-dug canal and deposit them at the base of the palace where they would be humbled by the spectacle of the grand buildings, exotic fountains and gleaming gold baroque statues.

There were some 150 fountains and spectacular cascades throughout the 100 hectares of ordered gardens, but pump technology was not nearly developed enough at the time to drive them. There was a much cleverer solution. Twenty kilometres away, an elevated lake system piped water, in ever diminishing sized pipes, down the hillside. By the time it reached Peterhof it had picked up the enormous pressure required to drive all the water features of the palace. Moreover, because there was plenty of water in the lakes, the fountains could run all summer without a break.

We hadn't come to see the palace, except from the outside. The big attractions were the gardens, the fountains, and the bath house that adjoined the palace. The bath house building also housed the palace kitchen to cut down the risk of a spreading fire if the dripping caught alight.

In the bath house, the *banya* (Russia sauna) used hot cannon balls to provide the required heat. In winter you could hot up and then go outside for a therapeutic roll in the snow. Before Peter's time it was customary for men and women to be in the banya together but eventually they had to be segregated because there was excessive sexual activity which led to guests giving one another doses of the clap.

A lady could take a shower – cold, unfortunately – by going down some steps into a sunken, open top room, sitting on a stool and being pelted by an ornamental shower rose that hung from the ceiling.

Another way to have water fun was in a hexagonal swimming pool with a central shower ball on a pole in the middle and, for good measure, a number of geysers that came up through holes in the wooden floor. And then, of course, there was the common marble bath – often covered with cloth to save one's flanks coming into contact with the cold marble.

We finished the day with 'dinner and a show' at the Belmond Hotel which, we had been told by our guides, was arguably the best in St Petersburg, and certainly the best located, sitting in the middle of the concert and designer districts. The grand dining room had been cleared so that only sixteen tables were spaced out over the whole area and the stage had been extended to accommodate the loud pianist, string quartet, two singers and two dancers. They gave a classical program of second-eleven standard while waiters speedily crisscrossed in the style of the Ministry of Silly Walks. The food was exceptional. We both had beef cheeks – avoiding the menu page which offered Beluga caviar at five hundred Australian dollars for a smear. The classical experience was enhanced when I discovered that

Tchaikovsky had stayed in the hotel twice: first in 1877 with his wife, and then nine years later when he returned more happily solo, and waltzed into Johann Strauss.

Almost up to pussy's bow of palaces, we took a final lunge at the summer palace of the first, not the great, Catherine, about an hour by car south of St Petersburg. It resided in huge gardens in the suburb named after Russia's leading poet, Alexander Pushkin. His bronze likeness slouched, searching for a rhyming couplet, in one of the public parks now afire with autumn leaves.

The 300 m-long palace was in the ornate baroque style, with room upon room decorated with paintings and gold leaf covered carvings. The building, gift wrapped in gardens and ponds, was a present from Catherine's husband, Peter the Great. The main reception room was massive, with windows on either side positioned to take advantage of the twenty-two hours of sunlight per day in summer. Extensive use of mirrors turned the large into the enormous. Even though this was supposedly a highlight of any trip to St Petersburg, it had a feeling of being too pristine to be authentic. Everything looked new, everything glittering. The famous amber room, where all the wall and ceiling panels were made from pieces of amber, was only completed, as a reproduction, in 2005.

I did like the portrait of Catherine's daughter, Elizabeth, who was obsessed with clothing. She ruled as Empress of Russia from 1741 to 1761 and left behind fifteen thousand dresses and a rich dressmaker when she died. The Australian fashion industry needed a few Elizabeths.

We realised we had become hard to please when the summer palace left us underwhelmed, but it was undeniably a powerful magnet for tourists. The mornings were restricted to ticketed tour groups — which included us — but in the afternoon the floodgates opened and in streamed all the rest who couldn't book tickets but would not be able to go on living until they had visited the palace. Their queues filled the park's pathways to vanishing point and on a typical day they could wait for four hours just to get inside the door to join the jostlers. Some of the tour guides called the queues the Chinese wall, indicating the number of tourists now coming from China. It again occurred to me that the world was nearing saturation point with tourists trying to see the most famous sights. The weight of numbers was not only making visiting an ordeal, it was also destroying the very places and objects they had come to see.

After talking to locals about vodka, some interesting conclusions emerged. In general, Russians didn't like it. Even though it was virtually synonymous with Russia, they found the taste and the smell offensive. That's why the way to drink vodka was to fire each shot straight down the gullet. It used to be a tradition to hold your nose while you were drinking it to avoid getting a whiff of it, but modern vodka had been largely deodorised. Nevertheless, no sipping, no staring into the glass while you make a whirlpool and no commenting on its colour; it was clear anyway. Down the hatch, breathe in, say 'ahhh' and try to smile — was the way to drink it. Vodka's only purpose was to induce inebriation, we were told.

I bought a bottle of cherry/plum vodka for private swigging. With a mere 20 % alcohol, it took a while to scramble the senses. A shot of it helped me through an organ recital in the blazingly-lit concert hall across the road from our hotel. I paid for a program, only to find it all in Russian. Apart from some Bach, I didn't know what I was listening to and obviously wasn't meant to. All I could conclude was that the organist knew how to push and pull the stops.

We stayed around town for our last day with our guide, Vlad, and driver, Extralargeski. Vlad talked about the frantic apartment building projects on the outskirts of the city. When Russian developers put up a block, they made it a whopper. A hundred thousand people could find themselves living on a small footprint, many having to park their cars on the street. This led to crushing traffic congestion, since every apartment would have at least one car. If you arrived home late at night by car you may have to walk kilometres to get to your address — that is, if you could pick it out among the thousands of identical doors. If there was an emergency, help couldn't get through. Even so, there was a desperate housing shortage in and around the city, with corresponding escalating rental prices.

If you wanted to rent an apartment, you had to pay a bond equal to one month's rent, plus one month's rent in advance, plus the equivalent of one month's rent to the agent as commission. If you engaged an agent, all you got was a list of probable vacancies from a database. You then trailed around yourself to check them out and if you liked one you called the agent and grovelled. No such thing as an open inspection. The power was firmly with the landlord and agent.

The Russian experiment with communism had an odd effect. When the revolution came in 1917, many of the places of great opulence and historical significance were either wrecked, neglected or used for government purposes. Now that communism had gone and Russia was trying to get back to very approximate democracy, what did tourists want to see? Not the austere leftovers of Soviet Russia but the old, totally over the top opulence found in the palaces, monuments and churches. Gold, glory, schmaltz and famous tombs pulled in the tourists.

We stopped at a mammoth statue of Catherine the Great in a city garden. Beneath her feet were smaller statues of the men who won battles for her both in the field and in the bedroom. Cathy was partial to quite a bit of nookie, so the story went. She had at least twenty documented lovers – but not all at once.

Across the road from Catherine was, to me, the most attractive building in St Petersburg: the Kupetz Eliseevs food hall. In 1903 two wealthy Eliseevs brothers talked the city fathers into letting them build the last new building allowed in downtown St Petersburg. Since then, there have only been restorations permitted – no building. The brothers wanted to sell classy food but the fathers didn't like the idea. This was a cultured part of town, so no grubby retailing. The brothers came up with an alternative. How about if we put a beautiful comedy theatre on the first floor? The fathers stroked their beards and nodded. The brothers stipulated that patrons had to enter the theatre via the shop which stocked the most exotic food known to man. When we visited, an invisible pianist played a small automatic grand piano near the front of the store while high up, near the ceiling at the back, waxworks of the brothers waved greetings to their customers. The windows featured moving cartoon figures, all engaged in comic moves with food. I had the best hot chocolate in my long tasting experience of the genre and a combination honey cake/halva that could have become addictive. Although prices were high, they were not excessive, and certainly in keeping with the quality.

Godly urges called us to St Isaac's Cathedral just when I thought I couldn't be stirred by another church. I was wrong. It was soaringly magnificent – being the second tallest Russian Orthodox church in the world, made all the more impressive by the heavenly singing of a choir as part of Sunday worship. A well-whiskered priest, dressed gorgeously in purple with matching crown, was conducting an intricately choreographed service.

Our final look at Russian Orthodox cathedrals was the church of The Saviour of Spilled Blood; the blood in this case had belonged to Alexander II who was terminated there. Again, the building was awe inspiring but hard to digest along with all the other magnificence we'd seen.

We came down to earth when we rolled the dice with a mussel dinner at a Belgian style restaurant not far from our hotel. While the mussels were junior in size, they were submerged in a superb bisque. My connection to my surroundings was progressively reduced by the fruit beer which turned out to be a needful anaesthetic when the bill arrived.

Taking a river cruise and seeing the city from many different angles emphasised the far-sighted decision to keep the building height limit down to about seven storeys. The original reason was that nobody was permitted to have a building taller than the Czars' palaces, except cathedrals – because God had the right to unlimited height. In the city, we could see the dome of St Isaac from virtually everywhere, but away beyond the city limits, and therefore with no height restrictions, the tallest building in Europe was being completed. It was the Lakhta Centre, its eighty-seven storeys reaching 462 m into the sky. It looked like a giant rocket ready to launch.

I thought we were lucky with the weather, since the rain had held off, and the temperature deceptively encouraged us to sit out on the open deck for the hour excursion. By the time I returned to the wharf, I had seized up with cold. However, that didn't deter us from observing St Petersburg from the water – firstly from the canal and later the Neva River which was exceptionally wide in parts and went down to 24 m – just where they needed to build a bridge. The Russians had been happy to employ the world's best engineers, designers and architects for their big projects and gave them credit for their ingenuity. Even though smiling wasn't popular, I detected a layer of kindness beneath the clamped jaws. Let us not forget that Russia lost 27 million people in the Second World War. Imagine the entire population of Australia being wiped out – and that still not being enough. Even today, every family had early deaths on its tree.

We passed a First World War battleship, the *Aurora*, tied up in the river and resembling a fierce old dog that had lost its teeth. It apparently survived the most unsuccessful sea battle Russia fought in WWI. When Russia joined in the Second World War the navy cranked up the *Aurora* for another go but it was like entering a T Model Ford in a Formula One race. After failing to threaten anybody it grumbled home to its rocking chair in the river where it was lovingly maintained by naval cadets.

Don't leg it before you egg it, was the advice to Australian travellers. That meant a visit to the Fabergé Museum, luckily only a ten-minute walk from the Hotel Belmond. The museum was on the bank of one of the canals that Peter the Great, founder of St Petersburg, envisioned to resemble a city like Amsterdam. Most of the canals were subsequently filled in but a few had survived, now used for brief tourist trips in crouching boats made to fit under the low bridges without decapitating the customers.

The Fabergé Museum had on exhibition some of the famous Easter eggs, along with many of the other precious personal Fabergé products like snuff boxes and jewellery. The exhibition was overcrowded with plates, vases and exotic tableware from the eighteenth and nineteenth centuries plus quite an extensive collection of Russian paintings. The building in which the exhibition was housed used to be a palace, then it was meticulously recreated as a museum.

The Fabergé jewellery business was started in 1842, supplying a wide range of clients from royalty down to mid-market. By 1872 Carl Fabergé was in charge and began making the famous Easter eggs, almost exclusively as gifts between members of royal families. Besides their exquisite craftsmanship and precious materials, each egg contained a surprise. Some opened to reveal tiny items inside. Two of them opened at the top and a bird popped up, flapped its wings and sang. Others doubled as clocks. It took a master craftsman at least a year to make one egg. The full collection was dispersed around the world, with pieces in museums or private hands. The largest single collection, of ten eggs, was in the Moscow Kremlin Armory.

My personal experience with Fabergé was in my youth when I discovered Fabergé Brut aftershave. It was supposed to disarm women's sexual hesitancy, although not the ones who sniffed me. It became the world's top selling aftershave, but was not made by the Fabergé jewellery company. It came from a licence arrangement with Unilever to use the name.

I spent some time admiring the art collection. Here were Russian artists little known outside the country, but whose work was up there with the best — in portraiture, landscape and Impressionism. One artist who I'd seen frequently in Russia was Ivan Aivazovsky, best known for dramatic seascapes. He specialised in showing sailing ships in trouble or breaking up on rocks while the sailors were doing badly in rowing boats trying to save themselves, but you knew the next wave would see them all in the drink and wishing they'd been taught to swim.

Leaving Russia was a greater challenge than arriving — especially because we were going to Malta. Only Air Malta offered a direct flight from St Petersburg and being well down in the pecking order, had to put up with the most inconvenient departure times, like ten to four in the morning. Rather than stay one more partial night at the wonderful Belmond, we booked into a Radisson right next to the airport to increase our chance of being on time for the flight. This hotel was designed by a kid with a Lego set where there were too many lime-green bricks. The bedhead had a band of light running around its perimeter and, of course, it continually changed colour. To turn it off, and save ourselves having seizures, we had to manhandle the heavy bed out the way. Having said that, it was a fit for purpose building, within bag-rolling distance of Air Malta check-in.

Inside St Petersburg airport we found another interesting way to create a transit hotel. Called a Capsule Hotel, it comprised rows of wooden boxes (like Great Dane kennels) with mattresses for floors, a pillow and a towel. You crawled in, maybe accompanied, and slid the door shut. I guess you'd use bathroom facilities in the airport. Cost was 500 roubles an hour: about AUD$13.

Leaving St Petersburg was so unnecessarily complex that it became farcical. First was a security check of us and our luggage just to get through the airport front door. Air Malta check-in fell into slow motion because the girl behind the counter appeared never to have done the job before. From there we joined another haphazard queue, continually violated by cut-inners, to check our passports. Once through there, we lined up again with no supervision, outside what looked like a line of portable beach cabins to again have our passports checked. Then all smiles and cooperation as we were ejected into the duty-free shops. St Petersburg Airport loved us after all, hoping we might spend some last-minute money. But when we were called to board our Air Malta cramped little A320, matters become vexing again because we were sent down a long stone staircase carrying, in our case, deceptively heavy cabin bags.

The flight took four and a half hours. We'd paid for business class, imagining flat beds, but instead we got skinny, fixed economy seats with an empty one in the middle to denote the wasteful luxury of business class.

Malta eventually materialised from a dawn sea; such a contrast to Russia. Below us were small, square-shouldered Mediterranean buildings. We were there for only one night because our car tour of Sicily would begin the next day as long as Air Malta got its ducks in a row.

CHAPTER 3

Sicily and Malta – 2019

Just when I thought Air Malta's A320 was irreducibly small for international flights, I discovered we were going to Sicily in a sawn-off version called the A319. It was about as comfortable as a school bus, but the ride lasted only forty minutes. Arriving in Palermo was a breeze because EU freedom of passage had done away with immigration queues. It should have been a perfect return to Italy, were it not for the over-friendly taxi driver whose meter suffered a speed surge late in the trip, aided by a conjurer's flick of the wrist to add another twenty euros to a fare already inflated by a fifteen euros airport tax. What the driver had not considered was Michelle's unblinking gaze fixed on his meter. When he wanted enough fare money to buy a new taxi, Michelle did her berserk act and went to take a photo of his licence plate so she could report him. He knew he'd met his match, shrugged his shoulders and halved the fare.

The Excelsior Palace, Palermo, would have made a perfect set for an 1890s movie. It had not been spoiled by upgrades for at least a hundred years and that included carpet and plumbing. In the traditional stone bathroom, there were two long cords with red knobs attached to the ends. These, we assumed, were for emergencies — for which help might arrive the next day, or thereabouts. Our room, on the first floor, came with an obstacle. Halfway along the corridor a substantial flight of stairs presented itself, down on arrival, but up, with coronary consequences, on departure. With no help in sight, we had to haul our cases via the unexpected stairs. On the plus side was an excellent bed and a nice view of a park. And if we didn't mind a flooding bathroom, the shower with its two mysterious ancient taps jetted out plenty of hot water once we'd won the hot and cold guessing game.

One major disappointment about the Excelsior Palace was that no hotel toaster had appeared at breakfast time. I carried out a thorough investigation involving senior management, but we had to wait until we moved to Marsala the next day for my first Italian hotel toaster report. Derek Breadchamber will be told about this serious omission.

Palermo really came alive on Saturday. City streets were closed to traffic, street vendors had set up their stalls and people appeared from everywhere, mostly beautifully dressed. It was dogs' day too, brought along by their owners for eating, drinking, mating opportunities and the occasional fight. That also described their owners' aspirations.

We set off down the traditionally European main street, with the help of Michelle's map reading, which lead us to the two leading churches, a famous bakery and a big fountain of naked statues that was said to disturb the overlooking nuns. Close by was the Palermo Opera House, completed in 1897. An audience capacity of 1380 people made it the third largest opera house in Europe. We took the guided tour of Teatro Massimo which covered the six-storey public interior, the grand marble rooms that surround the concert hall and then a look backstage. There it became even more interesting. Behind the set of the current production (including an onstage basin, toilet bowl and bidet which made me wonder whether actually using them was part of the drama) was a huge space with lifting machinery to facilitate multiple set changes. The floor of the stage sloped four degrees towards the audience to enable better viewing and voice projection. I thought four degrees wasn't much — until I stood on it. Then it felt very easy to stumble into the orchestra pit. The floor of the pit, incidentally, could be raised to stage height to accommodate a full symphony orchestra.

We were invited to go up onto the roof where we would get the best view Palermo had to offer. We were warned that it did involve some stairs and the last section was a bit steep. We found ourselves climbing open metal staircases in the semi-darkness and feeling like phantoms of the opera. The last climb was up an almost vertical metal ladder with a wriggle under a bar at the top as the final test. The view of the township, ocean and surrounding hills was spectacular, but with it came the dread of having to go down, this time backwards and feeling for each rung in the darkness. Returning to ground level, I felt I had done a strenuous workout and also frightened the daylights out of myself.

We had been joined by two old friends from the US for a motor tour of Sicily with the added benefit that Steve was used to driving on the wrong side of the road. He and his wife, Patrece, travelled the world, each with a backpack weighing only eight kilos. Our shoes weighed nearly as much.

Our hired car had been upgraded to a Jaguar SUV, ideal for the job but a tad wide, as we discovered. Putting our trust in the satnav, we set off along the coast to Castellammare del Golfo, but the satnav made us miss the marina turnoff and we ended up sharing a windy beach with one shivering swimmer. I wondered if the satnav was working properly but blamed the wrong turn on consensus error.

When we loaded the next address in Erice into the satnav, it guided us along a spectacular coast road to a ruined castle in the ancient town. The road had the most severe switch-backs I'd ever seen. Steve often had to do a three-point turn to get around them. But once at the top it afforded the best chocolate box view I could remember, with mountains, township and out to sea via saltpans where commercial salt mining was done. We then explored the ancient town, still occupied by people who probably hadn't changed their lifestyle in a century and may not have cared much about the outside world. There were the usual local handicraft shops and restaurants, along with La Pasticceria di Maria Grammatico a world-famous bakery started by a defecting nun, that sold confections straight from heaven-to-mouth for the teeming tourists.

We sauntered back to the car, parked near the castle, and put our next stop, Marsala, into the satnav. Because we were now actually on a one-way road, the satnav told us to go ahead rather than make a U-turn. We did, only to find ourselves obliged to drive on the same tiny streets we'd shared with walking tourists.

Instructed by the satnav, which we now mistrusted, we were swallowed by the cobbled labyrinth, with streets so narrow there were centimetres to spare as Steve crept past walls hell-bent upon reshaping our car. The tourists now detested us as we monstered puffing old people and women wheeling prams out of the way.

Driving a car through here, what could they be thinking? After a final squeeze through an ancient archway, we found a road and escaped the angry crowd. We were later told that driving where we had just driven was prohibited, punishable by heavy fines – or maybe hanging. Luckily, the copperoni were elsewhere.

Disappointed that we'd escaped Erice without so much as a fine, the satnav decided to prevent us from finding our next destination: Baglio Oneto winery resort. With microchip impishness, it sent us along increasingly unmade roads through scrubland until we had to stop in a paddock because we were about to go over a cliff. We did what travellers did before satnav. We found somebody who spoke English and humbly asked the way. It turned out we were about 5 km off target. The satnav hummed with satisfaction.

The Baglio resort took itself very seriously, with acres of tiled courtyards. Being an island in the middle of a vast grapevine sea, we were given no choice but to eat in the swept-up resort dining room with a silver service dinner at a spine-tingling price.

Breakfast the next morning was the most comprehensive so far in Sicily. We could drink champagne, crack walnuts or eat rolls containing surprise foods inside. And here was my first sighting of an Italian hotel toaster.

Hotel Toaster Report

I was not initially impressed by the design of the extended-leg, narrow gutted Marsala del Glowmou Mark II, but it turned out to be one of the most efficient hotel toasters of my long experience in writing about them. It was quick, simple and turned out, in one pass, crunchy toast as opposed to warm bread. That was not all to do with the toaster, either. The bread had been cleverly baked so that half the job was done before it arrived toaster-side. I emailed Derek Breadchamber that evening to share my exciting find.

We almost forgave the satnav for attempted murder when it guided us to our destination in Agrigento without a hitch. In total contrast to our accommodation so far, this was a recently built B&B run by a charming Italian lady. It had five immaculate, modern suites, all very well thought out: a model for the genre. Our stay finished with breakfast in the small, tiled dining room where a gleaming upright black piano stood as an incongruent addition to the furniture. The owner did not play it, she said, whereupon Michelle let it drop that her husband could produce a note or two. They then asked me to play, at breakfast please note, so I obliged, to earn my sausage and bread. This piano was a recent Kawai and I knew, as I opened the lid, that it did not want to be played, confirmed when I tried a few notes and found that it was defiantly deafening. If I tried to play softly there was no sound at all. I launched into *Summertime*, threatening to do structural damage to the house. Being unable to control the volume, I threw caution to the wind and laid into a bit more

Gershwin. They were all politely thankful when I finished. The echoes slowly died away, peace returned to the valley, the dog came out of its kennel and we fired up the Jaguar to see what mood the satnav was in.

We had driven through hilly country to get to Agrigento, past vineyards giving way to vast olive plantations. One of the main historical attractions was the Valley of the Temples, built by the Greeks. It was not in a valley at all, but high on a rocky ridge where is could be seen from great distances. It was the largest archaeological site in the world at 1300 hectares. There were the remains of seven Doric style temples, the best preserved being the Temple of Concordia which dated back to fifth century BC, around the time of the Parthenon in Athens. The two temples were similar, except that Concordia was smaller and dirtier than the Parthenon because it was built from limestone, now oxidised, rather than marble. Moreover, its roof was made of wood, mostly rotted away. So overall it was a bit down-market but there was still more of it intact than the Parthenon.

Our visit to the ruins — now UNESCO World Heritage listed and in the endless process of restoration — was blunted by persistent rain. It made the forlorn remains look even more so, to say nothing of the long lines of soggy visitors. Static displays near the time-wrecked buildings showed how the Greeks moved the massive column sections and stone blocks from the quarry to the building site. The large sections were too heavy to be loaded onto carts, so they encircled them in huge wooden wheels and rolled them along the lumpy and mostly unmade roads. Corners were a special challenge because there was virtually no steering.

On our way to Modica we made a stop at the Villa Romana del Casale, a large and elaborate Roman villa located about 3 km from the town of Piazza Armerina. Excavations revealed one of the richest, largest, and most varied collection of Roman mosaics in the world, for which it had been designated a UNESCO World Heritage Site. It was built in the fourth century, but by whom and for what purpose was open to debate. One theory was that its owner was a prosperous importer of wild animals for use in circuses, including the Colosseum in Rome. While the massive expanse of floor mosaics depicted lots of animals, there were other arresting images, such as a collection of female athletes limbering up. This was pretty risqué stuff for the time because they were dressed in what looked like 1940s two-piece bathing costumes, making it a mosaic version of third century *Playboy*.

Busloads of tourists added to the numbers as they joined us on elevated walkways that looked down onto the remarkable mosaic floors without shoes damaging them. The best business was being done by the toilet attendant who charged half a euro per piss, irrespective of quantity. I wondered how he would have reacted if I'd returned two hours later asking to continue, at no additional charge, my earlier visit during which I hadn't quite finished.

Back on the road, the satnav's mood had turned ugly again, especially at roundabouts where it loved playing deceptive exit games, sometimes sending us into charming but tiny country lanes barely wide enough for our car. We passed the usual olive farms and then came across extensive cactus farming. This enterprise seemed best suited to lazy farmers because they had to treat their crops with neglect, never touching them except to gingerly pick the fruit, which had become a local delicacy.

I was looking forward to Modica because it was said to be the home of Italian chocolate. It took only one bite to know it was unlike any chocolate I'd ever tasted: absolutely delicious, slightly aerated and a little crunchy, with a huge range of subtle flavours on offer. Seven blocks, enough to guarantee hives or maybe a bilious attack, cost us about twenty dollars.

Prior to dinner we boarded a little green train which pulled us through rainy streets for forty minutes. It showed Modica as a charming, old, traditional European town, with mouldering stone, shuttered apartment buildings and narrow, cobbled roadways.

We had booked dinner at Accursio, a Michelin Star restaurant, as a special treat. We chose the seductive tasting menu accompanied by unspectacular wines, presented with an exhausting narrative by the wine captain who stroked each bottle like a much-loved cat as he extolled its virtues, almost to the point of tears. At the end of the meal the *maître d'* appeared with the bill and a defibrillator.

We returned late and impecunious to our lodgings, the Torre Don Virgilio Country Hotel, its ten rooms made from stones and cement to give the restored ruin look. Our room was tall but tiny, with the smallest shower stall I have ever seen. Michelle had previously tackled reception for an upsized room but was told we already had one. Entry level rooms were even smaller, the receptionist said, with a typical Italian shrug. I couldn't see how, unless they specialised in accommodating very skinny people.

Hotel Toaster Report

From the best to the worst. The Blue Ticker model at the Torre was without doubt the slowest and most disappointing toaster so far. It had hand loading clamps and a timer that ticked for eons before sounding a ding to designate toasting over – and then only produced lukewarm bread. I'm sure the instruction book would tell you to load the bread, then go and do some odd jobs before the ding eventually hailed you.

Another two-and-a-half-hour drive brought us to our final destination in Sicily, Taormina, where the nearly three-star Hotel Condor offered us a superlative view over the sea from a spartan bedroom, but not much else. It did not provide drinking water but could probably suggest a doctor if we drank from the bathroom tap. Apart from local Italian programs, it charged for watching television. It was built on multiple hillside levels, as was every structure in precipitous Taormina, with a creaking, barely two-person lift offering buttons with minus floor numbers as well as plusses. Finding our room remained a challenge, even after we'd visited it several times.

A seven hour walk around the town was a delight, as it was for the thousands of other tourists who had come to marvel at the perched houses, attractive but expensive retail merchandise and restaurants that seemed to hang in the air at the top of impossible flights of ancient steps or were hidden away in secret stone burrows. When I could only get through half my diavola pizza I knew I'd eaten one too many, delicious as they were. A long love affair was over – for a while anyway.

Since we were in Taormina, we had to take the two-hour drive to indigestive Mt Etna – even if the satnav didn't feel like going there by feeding us into tiny, ancient towns with horse-width roads. Steve, who had taken on the difficult task of driver, often found himself having to take a second attempt to get around a hairpin or to let a mini-car squeeze past in a muddy country lane.

As we travelled upwards around the endless, ridiculous bends, suddenly there was no foliage, only sinister black mountains on all sides. In the distance, a dark, moving cloud indicated where lava was still spewing from the Mt Etna crater. Further down, where it had cooled and solidified, it had formed a frozen black sea of rock waves sitting in grotesque blobs on top of one another. Eventually this would become rich volcanic soil and produce an abundance of greenery, but for now it was a hellish wasteland reaching up to the horizon.

At the top of the roadway was the expected collection of tourist enterprises. Many were selling jewellery made from lava, which you could say was in plentiful supply – like billions of tonnes of the stuff. If we wanted to go up to the summit and paddle in the flowing lava, we would have to hike for four hours. After a discussion that lasted all of two seconds, we decided to give that a miss and began the serpentine decent.

Although our hotel was placed high on the hillside, there were villages much further up. One, called Castelmola, seemed to have its head against the sky. How could people build there, live there and take the necessities of life up there? The solution was, by road. A long series of rising knots delivered us by taxi into a charming little town straight out of a children's fairytale. But it had a side that wouldn't have suited a fairytale too well. Anybody who finds discomfort in reading about male reproductive anatomy should stop here – even though I am only reporting what I saw.

Led by the Turrisi Bar and Restaurant, the sweet little place was obsessed with penises. They stood, sat, poked out from, and were worked into every Turrisi piece of furniture, menu and plumbing. Penises were so frequent that we very quickly stopped noticing them. The shops in the town carried through the penis theme, selling pottery and novelties based on them. During the visit we became so immune to penis memorabilia that we might have unthinkingly brought some home as gifts or souvenirs. Apart from an awkward interview at Australian customs, our penis gifts would have been grossly misunderstood by their recipients.

Speaking of buying, what was the silliest item we could have bought on an overseas holiday where weight, space and packing was at a premium? Yes, a serving plate. Italy was one huge seduction by pottery and glassware. Softened by the local wine, we looked casually into a shop window in Taormina, saw a plate and fell in love with it. No, we reasoned, not that plate! The way around it was to go into the shop and find out it was too dear. We did. No, it wasn't too dear. We offered the vendor a lower price hoping he'd tell us to bugger off. He didn't. We bought the plate, filled with buyer's remorse but nevertheless sniggering at the fun we'd have if we got it home in one piece. The plate was square and appeared to be made from two fine layers of glass, between which slices of dried orange had been laid flat. We'd have a dinner party at home and, for dessert, with the guests' eyesight blurred by alcohol, offer around the plate spread with dried orange slices. When they reached the bottom layer, they would think they were going crazy not being able to pick up the slices behind the glass. We would fall down laughing.

The plate, however, was not what it had seemed. Rather than fragile glass, it was made of super-tough clear resin. We discovered the deception when we unwrapped it in our hotel room. If there had been a wipe-out plane crash, investigators would have found our plate as the only undamaged item in the rubble. Packing it was therefore simple. Instead of being the protected, it became the protector.

Sicily didn't want us to leave. The satnav threw a farewell tantrum with wrong roundabout directions to Catania Airport. We cursed short circuitry upon it as we left the Jaguar at the airport drop-off.

The departure hall quickly filled with travellers who rushed from one boarding gate to another as snap changes were made, Italian style, but no aircraft were leaving. The place was becoming dangerously overcrowded when the news broke that Mt Etna had thrown up and produced an ash cloud that threatened flying. Our flight was delayed, in fits and starts, for four hours until suddenly a gate opened and Captain Moses led his people out of departure lounge slavery. He smugly told us over the intercom that we were the last flight to leave that night. Then he took off, gunned the engines and got us to Malta in under thirty minutes.

We found Malta quite a tiny place, a British colony until its independence in 1964, with a population of less than half a million. It was a member of the EU and although the cost of living was relatively low, it had an unemployment level of only around 3 %. It was the most densely populated country in Europe and the fifth most densely populated in the world. In 2001, Malta became the last country in the world to legalise divorce. Our guide, a young mother, said that the unavailability of divorce had been holding back marriages and that the Catholic Church eventually had to cave in to stem the flow of defectors.

Christianity got quite a boost when St Paul was shipwrecked off Malta in 60 AD. He dog-paddled ashore and spent a few months organising a more seaworthy ship. His unplanned visit produced twelve churches around the country plus a constant stream of pilgrims, including popes, who'd come to walk on the hallowed ground — and presumably take a short, symbolic swim.

Since it was Michelle's birthday, I'd hired a motor yacht for the day, along with a youthful captain who doubled as engineer, food and beverage waiter. Our first obstacle was getting from the jetty to the boat via a wobbly plank that kept getting longer as the boat, keen to leave, eased away from the jetty. To lighten the fear of falling in the drink even before we'd started, we exchanged weak jokes about walking the plank as we tottered aboard.

Having passed that test, we moved through the calm marina out into the not-so-calm waters around Malta. The low, rocky cliffs of the coastline blended with the buildings — all in various shades of sand, with very little foliage. The British were blamed for cutting down most of Malta's trees, but after independence the locals hadn't shown much interest in replanting them.

We were headed to lagoon territory, a must for visitors to Malta, but quite a voyage through choppy seas. The boat had both sail and snoring diesel engine, slept six, had three toilets, a shower and a table below deck as well as one on top. We quickly learned the folly of going below while the boat was swaying through the waves. It produced instant sea sickness. Even on deck we all felt on the verge of a heave but warded it off with heavy sea-air breathing and eating the salad lunch and drinking chardonnay provided by the captain, now in the role of maître d'.

Eventually we reached nirvana — the Diamond Lagoon — where we anchored and swam in the bracing water that began as aquamarine and graduated to emerald and finally to Prussian blue as you looked down. Sensing this would be the highlight of the day, we stayed there for a couple of hours. Not far away was the better-known Blue Lagoon, where the high-density tourist boats anchored to allow the more enterprising of their passengers to swim and play water games. If you wanted to see overloaded boats, Malta was the place, remembering that this was the end of the holiday season and would normally be much busier and even more overloaded. Our captain told us that the locals liked the economic benefits of tourism but hated the intrusive, and often overwhelming waves of eager visitors.

The trip back to the marina was quite a bit rougher than the outgoing one. We fought off embarrassing upthrows and didn't even dare to look below, knowing that the porcelain buses were down there waiting to be driven. Later, even in the comparative safety of our hotel bed, we were returned to the motion of the boat as soon as we closed our eyes. I awoke in the middle of the night still riding the waves and trying to deal with something difficult to digest in the captain's lunch.

After a day of recovery from the birthday voyage and the captain's fare, we met up with our guide who took us to the old side of Malta, beginning with the walled city of Mdina, filled with beautifully preserved limestone palaces, churches and opulent houses owned and still occupied by old families or foreign embassies. There was also a solitary seventeen-room luxury hotel run by the Shipton family, well known in Australia. The value of the real estate was mind-bending, and properties rarely changed hands. The whole of Mdina was pristine, but with a falling population, then down to 230. Mdina's predominant claim to fame was that much of *Game of Thrones* was filmed there. Predictably, there was *Thrones* merchandise being sold along with the attractive glass products for which the area was originally known.

We made the obligatory winery visit to the Meridiana Wine Estate, established on an old WW2 air force base. Malta made quite good reds and whites, based on the principle that the more miserable the soil, the more the vines have to struggle and the more intense the grape flavours.

Malta was also known for its ancient catacombs – always dug outside the boundaries of the cities because the dead were capable of infecting the living if there had been a plague. We visited the catacombs of St Agatha, a martyr born in 291 AD and brutally treated for her choice to lead a strictly holy life rather than marry in order to forge family links. The catacombs named after her incorporated different types of stone tombs for more than a thousand bodies in two thousand square metres of digs. Many had skeletons still inside them and ancient paintings on the walls. Going into these catacombs was not for the claustrophobic, nor for those easily spooked by skeletons or the pervasive presence of death. The St Agatha catacombs were the largest in Malta but only a small section was open to the public. The rest lay in peace, obeying instructions on many of their tombstones.

We wandered the streets of Valletta, the capital of Malta.

They were typically preserved-European, confined mostly to pedestrian access, with plenty of cardio-challenging steps and tight alleys. In many ways, Malta was a version of Sicily, and that wasn't surprising, because that's where most of its people had come from.

The main church of the city was that of St John's Co-Cathedral, built in 1572, originally as a dignified structure inside and out until the baroque period came along in the seventeenth century and schmaltzed up the interior into one of the most elaborately decorated and carved places in Europe. As well as gaudy, it was overwhelmingly impressive. Admission was €5, which included the use of an audio guide with headphones not designed for the human head. My neck had to make sense of the muffled commentary.

We needed a plain cup of tea after all that unspeakable splendour and sat in one of the many open cafés to crowd watch. Our patience was rewarded by the arrival of a jovially dressed man pushing a white upright piano along the street. Closer inspection revealed that the piano had four rubber tyres to enable mobility. Its owner stopped outside our café, let the piano down to ground level with some well-practiced winding of handles and then peeled off the piano's panels. From inside the case he retrieved a folding chair, a box of his CDs for sale and a red top hat which he perched on the lid for gratuities. When he sat down to play, I thought we were about to hear a reincarnation of Horowitz, but unfortunately that wasn't the case. He was two levels of skill below me – which indicated how bad he was. That didn't stop me from feeding his red topper, because he'd shown me a possible future employment opportunity, maybe in Sydney's Martin Place.

Hotel Toaster Report

I assumed that the InterContinental Hotel, St Julian, would have had a better toaster than an old six-slotter veteran. But there it stood, in need of a good clean and possibly some panel beating. In one of his many books on hotel toasters, Derek Breadchamber mentions this type of six-slotter as causing the Great Toaster Affray of 2012 in Japan, when a dispute erupted at breakfast and bread was thrown. The toast captain stepped in and took control of the situation with a fire extinguisher. The problem was that the 'is-it-ready?' knob raised all six pieces of toast at once, with the outcome of one satisfied *toastor* and five enraged *toastees* who didn't like their toast being inspected by strangers.

CHAPTER 4

South Vietnam – 2019

Michelle and I went to Ho Chi Minh City to celebrate my birthday and for me to attend the biennial Hotel Toaster Exposition at which my very good friend and hotel toaster critic for *The New York Times*, Derek Breadchamber, was to give the keynote address titled: 'Hotel toasters that have changed the course of history'. I couldn't wait to hear him.

We travelled with Vietnamese Airlines in a shiny new Dreamliner which I could thoroughly recommend – with two reservations. The business class lounge that the company shared in Sydney with other modest airlines had made advances in unrequested weight loss by providing plates that were so small they hardly held any food. Not only could we eat very little, we used calories when walking for multiple refills. The other was that the Dreamliner's Vietnamese captain's command of English conveyed nothing more useful than to confirm that the PA system was working. I was sure his Vietnamese was impeccable.

Anyway, he did a feathery landing in Ho Chi Minh City which gave us a feeling that all was right with the world — until we queued up in the arrival hall with 5000 other travel-weary souls, all with the shits. The numbers had been grossly swollen by the end of Chinese/Vietnamese New Year — something that we'd failed to factor into our schedule.

As expected, traffic in Ho Chi Minh City was chaotic. The city had two million motorbikes, moving about in swarms that somehow dodged the larger vehicles which continually changed lanes for no apparent reason other than cultural habit. Wherever you went in Vietnam you couldn't avoid motorbikes. There were nearly fifty million of them, ridden by a population of around 100 million. The motorbike helmet business was booming. A green plus white stripe helmet designated the owner as being a member of Grab, the Vietnamese equivalent of Uber. You could Grab a motorbike or a lousy car or a better car. If you Grabbed a motorbike, you too had to wear the bonny green helmet as you clung for dear life to the back of the owner as he joined the deadly swarm.

Unlike many Asian countries still wedded to the US dollar, Vietnam wanted everybody to use the local currency, the dong. It might just as well have been called the ding-dong because I heard bells ringing when trying to equate it to Australian dollars. One hundred thousand dong dinged down to AUD$6.50. I left Australia a dong-millionaire after I changed money for the trip. My wallet developed a sudden carbuncle as I stuffed it in. I was sure it would un-stuff just as quickly.

We'd booked in at the InterContinental Hotel, but in an apartment (called a residence) rather than a room. For a rate less than a room, we were given a generous bedroom plus a big lounge with a fancy TV, washing machine, fridge, dining table and cooking facilities – which added up to double a room space. In future we'd be looking for deals like this – although I was waiting for a catch. Maybe we were sharing with a family that was yet to arrive.

Our first full day in Ho Chi Minh City was spent in the company of a guide and driver for a city tour. When walking on the footpath, we were warned to keep one and a half metres from the gutter because of kingfishers. This reference was not about wildlife but bag snatchers on motorbikes who rode in the gutter and pecked handbags from pedestrians in the manner of kingfishers plucking fish from the water. If you were securely attached to your bag, you would be taken for a ride – literally – until you eventually decided it was best to let the kingfisher have it.

We visited a Buddhist temple where the locals came to pray, presumably so that they would do better than other locals. Their supplications were augmented by the lighting of candles and the purchase of bottles of vegetable oil which were poured on holy candelabra. There was so much oil that it formed puddles and had to be collected and then, I suspected, recycled. Our guide glared at me for suggesting such heresy.

Since Vietnam became a unified communist country, religion was not encouraged. Buddhism was followed officially by about 12 % of the population and Catholicism came in a poor second. Our guide said that many non-affiliated people went to the Buddhist temples because they felt a need to pray to somebody and Buddha covered a lot of bases.

We visited the Independence Palace, once the home of the

president of Vietnam but now occupied by government workers and exhibitions to show how things used to be. There were many grand meeting and dining rooms, all set up as if to receive guests, but empty and frozen in time. The main meeting hall was, however, still in use. It could comfortably accommodate 500 people beneath whose feet lay a huge woven rug. I knew a little about fabric weaving and this rug was 15 m wide. How was it woven? Was there a 15 m carpet loom or was it so cleverly joined that you couldn't see the seams? When I enquired of Google, I was overwhelmed by rug suppliers wanting my money in exchange for goods, but no information on how the huge rugs were made. I concluded they were knotted by hand on a hessian base that could be joined and hidden beneath the pile. The biggest rug in the world was inside the Sheikh Zayed Grand Mosque in Abu Dhabi. It had 2.2 billion knots over an area of 5453 square metres.

The day before my birthday, when I was officially, but not actually, a year younger, we visited Saigon's biggest building, the Bitexco Financial Tower. The 49th floor gave an unparalleled view of the city. An unmissable feature of the building was a helipad two-thirds of the way up, looking like a huge, petulant lip sticking out of it, but it was actually useless because helicopters were not allowed in the city airspace. Neither were people allowed to walk out on the helipad. Some of them would surely jump off for one reason or another and that would disrupt the building's routine and make a mess on the road below. The lip sat there, inert, a lemon monument to the architect who probably adopted the same facial expression when it was mentioned.

We took the Heineken tour on the sixty-fifth floor where, for a hefty fee, we listened to a lecture on how beer was made followed by a jerky ride in a simulator wearing virtual reality helmets to help us imagine that we were turning into beer. Following this was a lesson on how to pull a beer – which we were obliged to gulp down because the next eager group was just behind us. Then on to a race car simulator in which I ran into the Armco because of my sudden intake of beer. We moved from Formula One into a make-believe pub lounge where I had to fast-guzzle three more beers before being returned to the street wondering what had happened. The parting gift was a bottle of Heineken with my name on it. Having lost some of my wits, I left my personal bottle in the taxi. I hoped the driver's name was Fraser and that he liked beer. We finished the evening at a nice-looking Vietnamese restaurant in the arcade near our residence. Unfortunately, nice looks were all it had. The picture of the food on the menu did not resemble that served on the platter for two. Maybe I should have blamed Heineken for anaesthetising my palate.

I awoke on my birthday with the promise from Michelle that I could do whatever I liked for the day – with some limitations. We had an indulgent breakfast and then set off to Ban Thanh Market where I bargained for socks ('But papa, we only have two pairs of blue socks, and I know you asked for three but why won't you take grey or black? Look very nice for you'), a pair of perfect shorts that didn't fit because it was my body's fault, a one-sized hat that fitted all heads except mine, and a plastic belt at a leather price ('But look here, papa, the belt reversible so you get two and only pay for one. Plastic? Shhh! Don't say loud because not good for other customer to hear'). The bargaining, which involved family hard luck histories, hopping about in anguish, fear of employer backlash and other blatant porkies, ended in me paying half the ticket price. We came away laden with limited-life products.

Michelle took me for a birthday dinner at the Vietnam House Restaurant, offering very upmarket Vietnamese food and run by the fellow who owned the Red Lantern restaurant in Sydney. This excellent degustation came with a bottle of wine which the waiter made a passionate show of presenting, but then poured just enough to cover the bottom of our glasses. He returned many times with practiced flourishes to repeat the dribble, even when we asked for a couple of fingers' worth. Needless to say, we left a portion of it behind for the staff end-of-day celebration. Michelle made mention that it was my birthday and we looked forward to a cake, candles and a kitchen quartet rendition of Happy Birthday to Fraser. Instead, Fraser got a tepid cup of coffee on the house. Nevertheless, it was a memorable birthday meal booked and paid for by Michelle.

Hotel Toaster Report

The InterContinental had a rare Double Veranda model with top furnace and bottom delivery tray. The dashboard was relatively complicated and should have had a toast captain in attendance, but the guests had to fend for themselves. The Double Veranda had an inherent fault called 'two-in-one-out'. I placed two pieces of bread on the crawler, waited while the people behind me became restless, and then only one piece of toast came out. The other had lost momentum on the U-turn and had taken refuge in a dark corner at the top of the slippery slide. There it might have stayed for decades but, being a student of hotel toasters, I coaxed it out with a long knife. I realised, with a shudder, that in inexperienced hands this might have caused electrocution. I tried to explain the problem to a Japanese man in the queue, but he looked out the window and pretended not to hear me.

As a birthday gift, Michelle had purchased a tiny plot of land in Scotland for me which brought with it the title of Laird. Had it been in England, I would have become Lord Fraser Beath McEwing, but because of my Scottish heritage I preferred Laird. Michelle also bought herself a similar plot so she wouldn't have to rely on me for her title. We could then, at our discretion, add Laird and Lady to all official documents, business cards and licenses.

On the night of our investiture, we waited for the Queen's message of acknowledgement and the official notice as to where I stood in succession to the British throne but it was not forthcoming. I blamed the Vietnamese Communist Party, which didn't believe in royalty, for a KGB type interception. In the meantime, I would have to be content taking my place in the Scottish House of Lairds.

With our guide, Randy (his name, not his inclinations), and a driver, we set out to the Mekong Delta region so we could appreciate its vast waterways from a nicely appointed, skinny boat as it glided down tributaries and across huge river intersections. In the narrower tributaries, the houses were built out over the taupe-coloured water, some of them slowly toppling into it. The river people who lived in them relied on the water to give and take almost everything in their lives. Consequently, I didn't want to fall into it, which would have been quite easy, as we found when we had to negotiate steep, crumbling stone steps and straddle rocking boat decks when we got on and off to visit places of interest. I asked Randy if anybody on his tours had done a splashdown into the virtual-cesspools and he said yes, because they hadn't obeyed his safety instructions. Had he jumped in to save them? 'No, not my fault,' he replied with a frown. 'So I throw in a rope. Like catching a big fish.'

We spent some hours in the Toyota where front seat occupants had to wear seatbelts but those in the back seat were not required to and could be legally catapulted from the car in the event of a severe impact. During our trip we heard how communism in Vietnam had gone from idealism to corruption. Five million party officials enjoyed luxurious lifestyles and wealth while the rest of the population had to pay through the nose for education and health services on near-poverty wages. Old people relied on their children to care for them. If there was no family help available, they simply died of neglect.

Randy upped the national motorbike count to 60 million, which I didn't dispute as we drove along in a sea of them. He said that riding the motor bikes for long distances was exhausting because of the heat and the carbon monoxide fumes. The way around this was to stop for a 'hammock coffee' every hour or two. You could stop at one of the numerous roadside open-plan coffee shops and, for one dollar, have a coffee. But for a dollar fifty, you could also hire a hammock to sleep yourself back to road readiness.

Even though the government did not encourage religion, it tolerated one that offered to swallow a few others. Cao Dai only existed in South Vietnam. We stopped at a multi-coloured temple that offered a one-god-fits-many religion. It catered to

Christians, Hindus and Muslims plus their offshoots, and was looking for more. The three religions were represented among the decorations, figures and artefacts in the church building, all overseen by a big, single eye which indicated that the universe was watching. Both men and women could become priests. Marriage was permitted, although casual fornication was not mentioned. It was doubtful that the applicants would have had time anyway, because the study required to attain priesthood was daunting. It had to cover almost infinite religious dogma – some of it contradictory.

Since vice-regal festivities or horse drawn carriages did not eventuate for our newly acquired royalty, we returned to the Toyota for a very hot tour of the city. Randy explained that, commercially, the city was broken up into specialist trading districts. Apart from upmarket shopping centres of chrome and glass dotted about town, where designer labels of many genres did battle, you saved time and money by heading your motorbike towards the product group you wanted. For instance, if you wanted a hi-fi system, you would go to the electronics district where there were blocks of retailers all in hot competition. We wanted to see flowers, fabrics and temples.

As a warm-up, we went to the History Museum set in an old, charming French designed building containing artefacts not only from Vietnam's history but much of Indochina's. The exhibit notices avoided mentioning the advent of communism, declaring Vietnam to be a democratic republic instead. I found the collection of Buddha related images the most appealing, and not necessarily those from Vietnam. My favourite was a very tall, very thin – assisted by being partly rotted away – woman who, in spite of her shape, was called a female Buddha. She stood about nine feet tall and had disconcertingly long toes.

On the way to the flower market, we dropped in at a Buddhist temple in full swing because this was the first day of the lunar new year. There was a swirling fog of incense as the believers crowded in to pray for good fortune. One of the favoured ways of doing this was to buy a coil of incense, looking like a giant mosquito repellant, and attach your prayer to it. It was then hung up in the roof, and when it burned out hours later your prayer fluttered down for consideration by Buddha. There was no guarantee that he would grant your request because it may clash with more deserving cases – which somewhat deflated the value of the investment in the incense. That didn't stop Michelle, who loaded in a number of prayers, some to my benefit I'd hoped, and had her coil hung up in a propitious position.

We visited another Buddhist temple later in the day and it too was smoked out in burning incense. Michelle had already done the coil prayer, so she turned her attention to the huge, highly decorated cylinders into which you thrust thick sticks of incense. Michelle lit up, waited until the flame had settled into a smoulder, and then planted it in the sand inside a holy cylinder. She made her prayer and we escaped into humid, but at least clear, air. Later we discussed what we could possibly ask of Buddha. We had enough of everything to live on, our country and way of life were the best in the world, we probably lived at the best time in history so far and, in my case anyway, I could not die young. What more could I ask of Buddha? Maybe a few more healthy years and a painless passing? I simply said thanks to the smiling fat man sitting cross-legged on his plinth.

If you wanted to buy flowers, either wholesale or retail, you went to the flower market district where there were hundreds of vendors with billions of blooms. Many of the flower sellers lived in unbelievably small houses or flats in the flower market district. A two-floor apartment I photographed was one doorway wide. There were plenty of others of this size. It seemed flower marketing was not a high profit business, and consequently neither was real estate.

Our next market district was textiles, and here I experienced bliss. I again forgave my father for making me work in a Melbourne weaving mill and for the many textile people who force-taught me for the twenty years I ran my newspaper, *Ragtrader*. I loved textiles, and buffeting down the narrow, cloth-clogged alleyways in this market was a homecoming. Not that I intended to buy anything. But I became so intoxicated by the smell and the infinite textures and colours that I emerged in a daze with fabric for two shirts and a pair of pants. When I went to Randy's tailor, she said I had supplied too much for my trousers and threw in two additional pairs of shorts. Usually, it was the tailor's son who got the shorts.

Across the road from the tailor, Randy took us into a little shop that specialised in Vietnamese chocolate and honey. The chocolate tasted like a laxative, but I bought a couple of blocks to help old granny at the back who looked as though she needed dental work. But the honey products held a stronger attraction. There were bottles of Mat Ong Len Men fermented honey liqueur. 'What's this?' I asked. 'Oh, wine,' the owner replied. 'Very nice. Made only from the honey.' It came in a whisky type bottle with square shoulders. 'How many per cent alcohol?' I asked. She tried to tell me what she thought I wanted to hear – because the label was all in Vietnamese and no percentage was mentioned. 'Ah, maybe five.' She held up her fingers. I looked disappointed. She laughed and held up both hands. 'Really ten,' she said. I tasted it and got hit by Muhammad Ali. 'Maybe forty,' I said. I had to buy a bottle. Surely it couldn't be all that strong. It called for further investigation. Back at the residence, I drank three fingers' worth and went down to dinner with two personalities, one spouting unfunny one-liners and the other telling it to shut up. Over a pizza, the sensible one got the upper hand and saved me from divorce and being thrown out of the restaurant. Beekeepers had a lot to answer for.

We shrugged off the city and headed for Can Gio Island, in the middle of a mangrove jungle. Randy said we'd get to see 'many specie' and should take bananas to feed the monkeys who could get very put out if you arrived banana-less. We bought these at a small food market where a lady butcher was washing her dog in the shop. The meat of the day lay in the open in the sun. Oddly, the flies didn't seem interested in it. Randy said the meat had been walking around only hours before and would be cooked before it could go off.

Along the way, we saw, in the distance, a tall stand of classy apartment blocks that turned out to be part of a satellite city built by wealthy Koreans on land that their government leased for fifty years from the Vietnamese government. The lease was due to run out in ten years, Randy said, but nobody knew what would happen then. It looked like a science fiction city where only rich people, mostly Korean business families and Vietnamese political fat-cats, lived in isolated western luxury while the rest of Ho Chi Minh City rushed around like busy ants outside. The only restriction on who could live there was how much money they had.

The Toyota took us across on a ferry to the island where there was a waiting speedboat. Well, that was the travel company's description, but the boat was no threat to the water speed record. We crawled under a low, flapping fabric roof and settled into back-modifying plastic seats as we hacked into the caramel-coloured chop. Getting on and off the boat was a major balancing act. However, we were grateful that it didn't sink or break down during the hours we spent on it.

The first stop gave us a long walk through the mangrove jungle where we had to use most of our bananas to keep the aggressive monkeys at bay. If you shouted at them to go away, they stopped and displayed their scary, full sets of teeth. That got us to a lake among the mangroves and a shallow boat in which we were serenely rowed to look at two small water fowl swimming and some bats high in the trees. Another breezy speedboat ride brought us to a jungle path that led to some listless brown Vietnamese deer in a bald paddock and crocodiles which we were permitted to feed from a protective cage with tiddler fish on nylon lines. The crocodiles would clearly have much preferred to eat fresh tourists.

We also saw the occasional small crab and dragon eel. 'You see, good specie!' Randy roared with delight. There were more monkeys too, friendlier than the others, but I was not game to test their amiability.

More pretend-speeding in the boat delivered us to the Toyota and lunch at a seaside, inappropriately called, resort where we sat and partook of tasteless fare. Randy had suggested we take a dip in the swimming pool rather than the dirty looking South China Sea across the road. Although we hadn't brought our swimming costumes, the pool rules would have kept us out of the water anyway. They stated, on a large official noticeboard, that we were not permitted to swim if we 'ran around and jumped straight in the water', that 'footwears, food and beverage are not allow to use in pool area', that 'children and adult who can't swim shouldn't swim', and that guests who were 'mental or have skin and eye infections are not allowed to swim', nor are those who are 'full or influence of drug, and liquor', and that smoking was not permitted while you were swimming – even if you could manage it. The final rule might have related to solicitors: 'Hotel are not responsible for any lost cases at the pool'.

We drove home in Saigon's peak hour traffic, which was the stuff of nightmares. At one point we had to cross two roads to visit a Buddhist temple Michelle wanted to see at dusk to see traffic chaos and religious calm juxtaposed. There was a service in progress where men and women, dressed in grey robes, chanted over a PA system that drowned out the traffic noise. This temple was relatively new, built on four levels and beautifully appointed with the accoutrements of Buddhism. But I preferred the incense smoke and decay of the old temples we'd visited previously.

If we'd had chalk, now cheese awaited. From the choke of Saigon, we were taken by basic but determined Vietnam Airlines domestic A321 to Nha Trang and thence by car to the Anam Resort. Here was white sand and turquoise water. Sea swimming was a delight not easily found in Asia. Our room was actually a villa, with its own four-strokes-and-you-reach-the-other-end pool, separate lounge, and a massive bed which looked across billiard-table lawns to the inviting, clean sea. The suite had lots of imaginative cupboards and places to recline, but not one drawer, obviously inspired by the popular people's market concept of laying all the goods out where you can see them. There were two televisions in case of a program-clash crisis, a wickerwork overhead fan, and a can of mosquito spray the size of a fire hydrant, sending a clear message to expect an airborne attack after dark.

The minibar was free and replenished daily, which obviated the inquisition at checkout time as to whether you had been fossicking in God's cupboard. If we'd paid proper attention to the timing of the freebies, we could have warded off starvation and remained drunk for no more than the room rate. On the other hand, if we liked a bottle of unremarkable wine with dinner, it cost between AUD$80 and AUD$160. The food was uninspiring, but going into town for a tastier meal was a losing proposition because it took forty-five minutes and cost more than paying for a meal at the resort.

The temperature in Nha Trang was five to ten degrees cooler than Ho Chi Minh City and there were hardly any motor scooters — resulting in the same feeling you'd get if bees had gone on strike. Behind the sandy seaside flats rose a substantial collection of junior mountains. The whole area looked ideal for resort development and that's just what an army of wealthy developers were thinking too, because there was a building boom underway.

We knew we were in multi-star accommodation when we looked at the spa treatment prices. In Ho Chi Minh City, a one-hour massage cost less than twenty dollars, but it came with a physical challenge. Lovely girls in the street implored you to take a brochure which looked photographically attractive but did not relate to the services offered. If you allowed them to trophy-ferry you into the establishment, you were confronted by multiple flights of stairs which closely resembled ladders. People with bad hearts or poor balance could expire before reaching the massage floor. It comprised multiple massage benches divided by floating polyester curtains, meaning that you could enjoy the audio of the bloke next door groaning through an assault by knees and elbows in the name of good health. Or maybe sounds emitted for other reasons.

Cut to the Anam spa and we were almost in hospital facilities, with whispering girls, tiled rooms, private showers and a variety of fragrant treatments which cost about the same as day surgery. The rule was that everybody must creep around as if riding on air cushions. Because our package included a couple of free massages, I did a warm-up with a body scrub comprising the application of special goop containing honey, sugar, lime and some mysterious herbs. My masseuse, who had the muscles of a daddy-long-legs spider, prepared me like a pork roast. But instead of the oven, I was sent to the shower to wash it off, followed by the application of a fragrant lotion. Then I was ready to serve.

Hotel Toaster Report

In Buddha's teachings on reincarnation, it said that if you lived life with a grumpy demeanour, you would come back as a hotel toaster, identifiable by skinny, black legs. The Anam had one. And it was still grumpy, or maybe arthritic, demonstrated by its painful slowness. To show its further professional disinterest, it dropped the toast right at the back of the delivery tray. Gullible users might have thought their toast had vanished supernaturally. No use looking around for the toast captain, either. There wasn't one, probably because the word had got around that the toaster was cursed.

We finally slowed down to the pace of sloths at the Anam, and found it dangerously addictive. Maybe we would never be able to speed up to normal life-pace again. Only two years old, the resort was not part of a big international chain. Rather than having a professional hiring and training policy, the management plucked staff from here and there, including LinkedIn on the internet. While politeness and helpfulness were prerequisites, a command of English wasn't. Miscommunications and lack of staff coordination brought some memorable outcomes. For instance, during the free-drinks happy hour at the beach club, I ordered a gin and tonic from one young waiter and while he was away getting it another two asked what I was waiting for. Even though I explained I had ordered with the first one, I promptly got three G&Ts. The same thing happened with my spaghetti arrabbiata – for which I requested extra chilli. Three different waiters, plus the manager, all went and told the chef to add chilli, so when it arrived, I could see it glowing from across the deck. I needed the multiple gin and tonics to put out the fire. On TripAdvisor, one contributor told how he ordered up a surprise nineteenth wedding anniversary gift for his incoming wife and when he grandly threw open the door, the room was empty. Because of a problem in understanding numbers, the staff had put the flowers and elaborate decorations in a room on another floor.

Down at the beach one day, the peace and quiet was broken by the yells of a drowning man. Apart from the noise he was making, it was hard to take him seriously because he was standing in waist-deep water near one of the floating markers that told swimmers to venture no further. The two young lifeguards, suitably attired in official yellow outfits with impressive signage, ran down to the water, one holding a polystyrene flotation device above his head like a tennis trophy. There was no indication that the lifeguards could swim either, because they waded out to the drowning man and walked him back to the beach. Wondering what all the fuss was about, I asked one of the rescue heroes the next day what had happened. After I repeated my question three times, slowly, like an elocution lesson, he looked at me for a long time, giggled to his colleague, and said, 'The sun benches all use up, sir.' Somebody later suggested that the drowning man had become tangled in the rope that tethered the marker which had been placed there to prevent drowning.

Another water hazard concerned our private swimming pool. While it encouraged us to jump in, there was no ladder to get us back out. There were steps at one end, but the risers were too high for all but giants to use. Those of average dimensions would have needed to imitate a slug and propel themselves, belly down, slowly across the steps and up over the top.

Hotel Toaster Report

I understood that, in order to get five stars, a hotel had to have two washbasins in each bathroom. What I didn't know was that it also had to have two toasters in the breakfast rooms. I found the second one when we tried out the smaller, upmarket breakfast room. This toaster was the daughter of the big one in the main breakfast room. Called a Justa (short for Justanotherfuckingtoaster), it had narrow hips and long, skinny legs like its mother. The Justa was ponderously slow with a final convulsion that tossed the toast to the front of the arrival tray.

I'd had a bad hair holiday. At home, my usual conditioner had been known to bring out hidden tints. But when its chemicals were combined with the resort's shampoo and the salt water of the South China Sea, an unexpected and unwelcome chemical reaction took place, resulting in a puce/copper head of hair. Even the massage girl was mystified by it. She tried pulling on it, thinking it was a wig.

In common with many Asian hotels, the Anam Resort took considerable trouble to train its staff in how to direct guests. Since language was a problem, hand signals became vital, especially the 'Over there, please' frozen forehand drive. To execute this properly, the arm had to be extended, elbow locked, the hand open and flat, and the thumb tucked down; up indicated disrespect. If the guest stupidly headed in the wrong direction, the other arm, deploying the frozen backhand drive, was brought into play with the same sweeping action, often augmented by a nod of the head and an inaudible disparaging mutter.

One morning I noticed a small gathering of hotel staff near the swimming pool, kneeling beside a large, flat, brown-with-white-spots plastic cut-out. There was also a pump on hand. I later saw the cut-out in its three-dimensional form at the beach. While there were many blow-up horses and birds to keep swimming kids happy, this was new: a blow-up giant pretzel. Its proud owners took it into the surf and, as one might expect, it proved unseaworthy. Its intertwining curves offered nothing to sit on, it had no fore or aft, and the waves kept capsizing it. I gave it one out of ten, with no chance of making the semi-final.

Ah, the limitations of perfect peace. While most people publicly proclaimed that was what they wanted, when they reached it there was creeping disappointment. The Anam was a busy hive of peace. The first days were sublime, the next few relaxing, and the final ones cried out for stimulation, like overhearing a spirited row between guests. This was a perfect place for recovery but, once over the annoyances of life, enough already. We craved tension and release. I was becoming philosophical, probably a sign that I was ready to finish with Anam and get back to join my fellow rats in the race.

In praise of Anam, it was a beautifully designed five-star resort, with unparalleled expanses of the best lawn I had ever seen, an outstanding beach, friendly staff that tried very hard to give good service, a spa with high quality massage, and plenty of shady places to sit and allow the warmth to penetrate. Michelle suggested that a better way to launch the resort would have been to lease it to an experienced hotel group for the first five years — because that's what it lacked: professionalism. I wasn't so sure. There was more to love in Anam's imperfection.

CHAPTER 5

Thailand – 2018

Since Michelle and I had taken only an eight-day drop-and-flop holiday in Hua Hin (Gulf of Thailand), I had decided to take a break from writing. But the start of it went so off the rails that it sent me back to my keyboard.

We'd booked a business class flight to Bangkok and back with Emirates, leaving in the evening and promising a flatbed for a sound sleep, induced by a superior meal and suitable liquids. We would wake in Bangkok. *Cap khoon Kaa!*

One of the nice touches with Emirates is that it sends you a classy car and driver for your trip, from home to the airport and back. An Audi A8 duly arrived and we set off. Our journey was halted at South Dowling Street while the world stopped for Prince Harry and his wife, Meghan, to scream past, accompanied by a team of beautifully groomed coppers in various white vehicles, including a helicopter. That added twenty minutes to the trip and should have been seen as an omen from the dark side.

We boarded our A380 and settled into our business class kennels. I downed a glass of champagne while Michelle checked that it was okay to plug in her CPAP machine (needed to deal with sleep apnoea) into the power socket in her seat. The cabin crew shook their heads and, after some discussion, pointed us to the exit. They declared Michelle a health risk because they would not allow her to plug her machine into the power socket, which might then cause breathing problems, culminating in arriving in Bangkok with a corpse. Backed by the captain's demeaning announcement over the PA system, we were both offloaded, even though my transgression was never specified. We were escorted back through the terminal, our unopened bags put through security checking in case we were smuggling goods from Sydney to Sydney, and then we were taken upstairs to a service desk for a robust debate. We were told to go back to our travel agent who had booked the tickets and that we were now categorised as a 'no show' which attracted an AUD$800 punishment — although we had not cancelled, or contravened the airline's website-stated policy, nor did we fail to board the aircraft on time. We slunk home, tails between legs, and tried to explain to our cats why we were back so soon. We slept that night in somewhat larger spaces than we had anticipated. The next morning, Michelle donned her travel battle suit and declared war. She was so scary that I escaped up the street for a haircut that I had intended to entrust to a Thai barber. When I returned, Michelle had us booked on a Singapore flight for that evening. We loved this airline, especially as the cabin crew specifically invited the use of Michelle's CPAP machine. The downside of the flight was that it went via Singapore, but not before it had stopped in Canberra to take on some politicians for their needful study tours. The upshot of our run-in with Emirates was a long-winded email exchange between Michelle and the Australian representative, and eventually a refund from the airline that covered some of our loss.

By the time we arrived in Bangkok, we were not sure what day or time it was. We were picked up by a driver for the three-hour car trip to Hua Hin. She had parked her Toyota 'all-purpose' in the airport carpark which was roughly a quarter of the size it should have been. The way around this was to double park so that cars in designated car spaces couldn't get out. This, in turn, was solved by leaving every blocking car in neutral with the handbrake off. It could then be pushed out of the way where it would block somebody else. If you were having trouble pushing, there were signs on the wall giving the phone number of official pushers who, for a modest fee, would come to your aid. I wondered how this worked in sloping areas when all the cars illegally parked would have rolled down to the lowest point. The pusher teams would have had to be numerous and strong.

We set off on another car ride, but although Prince Harry and Meghan were not around, we were again delayed, this time by pounding rain and crazy Saturday traffic. One huge sign that we passed near the city warned people not to place tattoos or draw additional features, such as moustaches or spectacles on images of the Buddha's face because it was disrespectful. I agreed.

Settled into the InterContinental at Hua Hin, we set out in search of a tailor to make Michelle some linen pants and tops in fabrics we'd brought from Australia. After the usual spirited debate about price, we went for a massage in an establishment

I'd fondly remembered from five years earlier. Time had not been kind to it. Gravity and mildew had gotten the better of the furniture. Michelle was allocated the beautiful young trainee for an hour's worth of feathery finger-fluttering while I got, as usual, somebody who looked as though she'd come out of retirement just for me. She set about giving me a punishing salt body-scrub more abrasive than a rubdown with a brick.

In an attempt to put the negative massage experience behind me, we found a welcoming Thai restaurant for dinner. While the food was superb, we had to wait for a long time to be served. I filled in by enquiring about Thai whiskey. The premier brand, at AUD$10 for a large bottle, was Hong Thong (sounding like budget Chinese footwear) and was a blend, although the label didn't say of what. I decided to try a nip, expecting something akin to fly spray. But I was in for a surprise. I was no whiskey drinker, but this was the most gentle and delicious beverage I'd tasted in a long time. It had 35 % alcohol against basic Scotch at about 40 %. I might add that it helped calm the toothache I was suffering as well as probably being the cheapest way to get drunk in Thailand.

We went on a food tour of little places tourists didn't know about because they didn't look like restaurants; they were hidden in the shanty hinterland and were mostly part of somebody's house. There were five stops. Two of the eateries were outstanding and we would return under our own steam. They all served authentic, local Thai food. I made a mistake at the first place by throwing a generous dollop of 'chilli jam' into my chicken and vegetable broth. Our guide cried out a warning, but not before I had disabled my respiratory system.

It took several bottles of water and some counselling before I could continue the tour. At another place, we had curried water fowl. That interested me. Did they wade through leech-infested swamps to capture the birds or did they farm them? I could not get the question understood so had to leave without knowing. The highlight dish (among many outstanding ones) was sticky rice and red beans cooked in a length of bamboo. It was hard to find in restaurants but you could buy it on the street.

Hotel Toaster Report

The InterContinental Hotel was a great place to stay in Hua Hin. Apart from more light switches than a piano accordion has buttons, the rooms were excellent, along with the food and extra-friendly staff. The only flat spot was the hotel toaster which I encountered at breakfast on our first morning. I did a double take. I'd seen it before! It was a Caution-hot single knobber with a green light as an optional extra. I rounded up the toast captain and he admitted that he'd bought it on hoteltoastersales.com. This was a little-known online marketplace for new and used hotel toasters. It linked to a network of hotel toaster repair shops around the world that recondition and, in some cases, panel beat and repaint used hotel toasters. The dishonest shops might take the front of one damaged toaster and join it to the back of another. Serial numbers were then filed off and the toaster offered for sale as an original. The toast captain said he thought he'd bought a new one, but when it began to prematurely turn yellow and show signs of rust, he wasn't so sure.

Hua Hin was a place where we expected to laze by a pool, swim in the gentle sea, or walk along the beach. Unfortunately, none of those eventuated for quite some time. Lying by the pool in the rain while your book turns into papier-mâché had little appeal, nor did walking along a beach through a downpour. And if we'd ventured into the sea, we would have joined a welcoming crowd of *jellyfisss* – local pronunciation with a long hiss at the end to emphasise the unpleasantness of the creatures. Hua Hin jellyfisss were particularly ugly. They were the size of frisbees and coloured blue so you could be cuddling one in the water before you realised it. Because jellyfisss had no brains, you couldn't reason with them. Like hammerhead sharks, there didn't seem to be a good reason for their existence.

Although we were rained in, massage – a principal pastime in Thailand – went on undeterred. Based on a recommendation from the food tour operator, we took-took a *tuk-tuk* to a modest establishment not far from our hotel. It was run by a friendly Thai lady and a staff of four rubbers. Three were youngish and there was one lantern-jawed veteran. Two were busy rubbing behind curtains when we arrived. Michelle, of course, was allocated Miss Very Attractive, while Fraser, as usual, got the veteran. At least this was to be an oil massage, with no abrasions like the last veteran's body scrub. I was nonetheless apprehensive, but my veteran turned out to be a real pro, still in good form. Since I couldn't see her (I was either face down in the bench aperture or face up with a towel over my eyes), the only items in existence in the universe were my creped body and her hands of firm rubber. The greatest benefit was to my neck, which had been sore and stiff for weeks.

CHAPTER 5   Thailand – 2018

While we were in the shop's waiting area, a man emerged post-massage from the curtained-off section and we got talking. He was a Belgian who had come to Hua Hin seven years ago on holiday. He had never been married and was quickly seized by a Thai girl with a view to hurrying him down the aisle before some other girl did. He bought a house for them but had to put it in his new wife's name to comply with foreign land ownership laws, which she knew in detail. He soon discovered that this was a marriage made in hell. Divorce followed, and she scored the house. However, he loved the Hua Hin lifestyle and so retired from his job in order to return. His capital having been snaffled by his then ex-wife, he rented a house and had a less ambitious Thai girl as a companion. His comment on Thai girls was that they all had bad eyesight. 'They call me handsome, so I know they can't see properly.'

When I unexpectedly developed a toothache, I saw three alternative treatments. I could suffer until I arrived home and see my long-trusted dentist, or I could go to a local dental clinic variously called Extractopan, Thripdrillers and Nohurtu, or I could take the Hong Thong spirits cure which would relieve me of caring about anything. Since the clinics were closed and my dentist was a week away, I chose Hong Thong. It not only banished the pain, but did not cause a hangover. My tooth liked it too, and eased up its campaign. A business was now staring me in the face. Some crowd funding and a simple change of label was all I needed. It would say:

'Hong Thong Painkiller. Especially good for toothache. Taken orally, this pleasant-tasting remedy is a natural molasses product. Warning: this medication can cause drowsiness or slurred speech. Users should not be in charge of vehicles, operate heavy machinery or sign important documents for 36 hours after the last dose.'

At the InterContinental, along with many Asian hotels, breakfast was a major event. There was particular pressure on the egg department to produce a variety of egg dishes quickly. The InterContinental's system presented an egg ordering chart in the form of a block of tear-off coupons offering a long list of egg solutions, plus additions or subtractions of ingredients. After taking some trouble to fill it in with the special egg-pen provided, it had to be presented to the egg captain who stared at it as though he'd never seen it before and then he handed it to an eggling (lower ranking egg cook) who prepared the dish. Gone were the days when you could march up to the man in white with the tall hat and ask for two poached eggs. We had progressed to automated times. In my case, I carefully formulated an omelette, presented the chart to the egg captain and waited at my table. Twenty minutes later, I was still eggless. Apparently, the new system had failed to specify the destination of the egg after cooking. I spied it sitting like an orphan on a shelf behind the eggery. When I pointed this out, everybody was very sorry.

On our last night before departure, we walked across to a new shopping mall called Bluport, which turned out to be quite spectacular. It felt like being in a Westfield of the future, with offerings from hastily-sewn, cheap clothes to expensive designer, along with a massive, high-class supermarket down one side. Why Uniqlo, the Japanese clothing and accessories store, was flogging furry and quilted jackets suitable to wear in Antarctica was mystifying. Apart from European tourists — and bear in mind that Hua Hin was not an over-popular tourist destination — who would buy such hot clothing in a hot climate?

The restaurant selection was overwhelming. We wandered from one to another, trying to judge the quality of the food by the expressions on the diners' faces inside. We had to accept that the billboards and lavish menus on the lecterns in front of the restaurants were not a reliable guide to the food. They showed pictures of dishes that only faintly resembled what was served. We rejected one restaurant that looked promising when its billboard offered tasty 'crap meat'.

We paid a final visit to the massagery. I'd grown quite fond of my veteran since she had brought such relief to my neck. She was a no-nonsense woman who went to work on me like a carpenter would on a block of wood. She tutted with dismay when she failed to get a click out of my fingers, not realising that she was up against arthritis which had taken me years to accumulate. She didn't give up easily though, as she put her considerable power behind further attempts. My toes were more vulnerable, being small, distant and defenceless. She nearly broke a couple as she bent her back into the task and I had to tell her to stop. But I emerged with another incremental improvement in my neck. The massagery favoured tiger balm oil as the rubbing solution. I suspected that was because it was cheap and overtook the smell of hirsute, unhygienic clients.

I did a final check on the egg department chart system at breakfast on our last morning and it seemed to be working well, except for final delivery by the waitresses. I saw one wandering around with four omelettes trying to find lawful owners. If no homes were found for them, they would be fed to the jellyfisss.

CHAPTER 6

Greece – 2018

This would be one of our longest times away, seven weeks in all, provided I didn't expire from over-eating spaghetti in some tiny Italian restaurant run by a rotund, aproned wife and failed tenor husband. This trip was to Yerp – how the upper classes of England pronounced Europe. We were headed for Greece and Italy. Michelle, my companion and champion organiser, had mapped out visits to legendary cities and other bucket-list places. There was also a cruise on a floating apartment block where I would be able to establish intimate friendships with nearly two thousand people.

Along the way, I intended to continue my insightful study into hotel toasters and those brave souls who have been placed on this earth to design and run them. I would be sending the findings to my very good friend and hotel toaster critic for *The New York Times*, Derek Breadchamber, and would be delighted in his responses.

Being at the pointy end of my life, Michelle had convinced me to fly at the pointy end of aircraft, hotel rooms, trains and restaurants so that my bank account would also head towards a pointy, and probably premature, end. I realised that as years raced past, they created an unspoken contest with the beneficiaries of Wills. On one hand, the Willers felt guilty if they spent the kids' inheritance – a feeling encouraged by the kids – while, on the other hand, the Willers told themselves that they earned the bloody money and were therefore entitled to spend it.

The kids might have been worried that we'd booked to fly from Sydney to Zurich first-class. They shouldn't have been. For years we'd been accumulating enough points to go, not just first class, but in Singapore Airlines' first-class suites. If Bill Gates ever had to lower himself to fly on a commercial aircraft, this was where he'd sit. A new A380, with the latest suite configuration, sat loading up on the tarmac at Sydney International Airport as we were ushered into the suites lounge where suites-trained staff administered extreme pamper.

The aircraft was similarly staffed. They were devoted, and deeply in love with the six occupants of these just-built studio apartments. The chair and bed were separate pieces of furniture. The television screen was enormous. The tray table was like a partners desk. The grog was the kind you saw locked in glass cabinets at wine shops. I warmed up on vintage Dom and downed a rare Vodka with my Beluga caviar. The bathroom may have been modelled on Lucille Ball's dressing room: all bright lights and space. However, this was an aeroplane and for reasons of design, habit couldn't help placing the toilet bowl on the curvature of the fuselage, meaning that urinating men had to retain balance by jamming their heads against the wall. Very short men would have had to sit down.

Taking off was a new sensation compared with other aircraft I'd flown in. The studio apartment had two portholes through which one observed the distant airport slithering past as the A380 gathered speed. But the engines didn't seem to deliver enough *oomph* to take off. There was no lung-emptying acceleration. It just rolled along in relative silence and then rose for no particular reason.

The suite also bestowed upon us a pair of Lalique pyjamas and a gift box of other Lalique treasures such as body lotion, soap, a tube of lip balm and a scented candle – which I was not allowed to light on the aircraft. I saved it in case we got a smelly hotel room. As a nod to glassware, my goodies included a very small, strikingly-blue fish that lived in a black bag. I didn't know what I was supposed to do with it. Maybe it was the beginning of a collection – like KLM's pottery canal houses.

The suite's chair was worth special mention. It was like a cross between a traditional dentist's chair and the kind they used in old movie electrocutions. One armrest opened to reveal a mini controller and a touch-sensitive screen to operate the chair and the television. I had to admit, I was not good at coordinating these high-tech devices but the crew, gathered around almost in tears because a suite's occupant was not experiencing overwhelming joy, didn't do much better. Prodding fingers came from everywhere. One arrow swung the television out from the wall but then turned the chair in the opposite direction, so I couldn't see the screen without kneeling and looking over the top of the chair. The reclining button didn't like me paying attention to the television either. And sometimes the television got in a huff and turned itself off altogether – especially if I got the chair right.

Still in the care of A380 suites, we spent some hours in the Singapore suites lounge, where everybody seemed compelled to whisper. No singing under the designer shower, either. We sat and dined to pass the time while waiters strode about with bottles of 2009 Vintage Dom, pouring it as though it was water. This was like being in intensive care without being sick.

At about one in the morning, it was time to quit the whispering gallery and board our next A380 suites to Zurich. We were ushered into a section of fourteen old-style suites. They looked like a line of half-finished children's fun train carriages being built by an apprentice carpenter. They didn't have the space of the new suites, but instead gave the impression that the incoming passenger was an intrusion. When bedtime came, an attendant asked us to go for a walk around the block while he re-configured the furniture. On our flight, there were only three out of the fourteen suites occupied. Hence, we were a little over-serviced. Plates, cutlery and dishes came and went after every move I made. At one stage, they took away everything except two knives and then served me yoghurt. I called the female attendant and gestured at the imbalance of cutlery, trying to indicate by pointing that I couldn't eat yoghurt using a knife without cutting my tongue off. She hurried away and returned with a third knife.

The next day, we took a step down to Alitalia business class from Zurich to Rome. Going through security in Zurich taught us something about what you couldn't take onboard an aeroplane in Yerp. Forget the Australian rule about only liquids of less than 100 ml being allowed. The security officer prised out every container in our carry-ons, made a pile of them, and then informed us that, in addition to the 100 ml per container rule, we were only permitted to take a total of containers that would fit into a small plastic bag — which she produced for the purpose. To her credit, she helped us squeeze in as much as possible, but we still had to leave behind various preparations essential to the preservation of our skin.

We were due to leave Rome to board the cruise ship, a floating apartment block I'd nicknamed the *FAB*. The organisers had put us up in the used-to-be-grand-in-1940 Mediterraneo Hotel, not far from the train station. Jet lagged and confused, we wandered the streets looking for a local nosh. The trouble with Rome was that it was full of Italians and not enough of them understood Australian English. However, we did find a little, English-friendly restaurant where Michelle scaled a spaghetti mountain and I wrestled down a cheesy pizza the size of a Ferrari wheel.

We got chatting to a couple at the next table and found they were from Bondi, not far from where we lived, and were booked on the same *FAB* voyage. How nice, we thought, as he told us his great love was to sing and that he used to have his own band but no longer gigged. I began to grow apprehensive when he said that whenever he saw a band, he always gave his vocal services for free — whether invited or not. From his pocket he drew a piece of paper with a long list of songs he could sing. They were all up-beat, feet-aboppin' howlers that I particularly disliked. He dashed off a few samples, much to the immediate discomfort of his wife, who told him to put it away — a comment usually reserved by women for other unwelcome male activities. I feebly muttered that my father used to sing Bye Bye Blackbird, which set him off again. As he stood to leave, promising that we'd jam onboard, I realised that we may have come across a Tourette's singer. Maybe this wasn't his wife with him, but a carer armed with a chunk of wadding and a syringe. We wrote down their cabin number so we could spend our time at the other end of the *FAB*.

Hotel Toaster Report

A big moment at breakfast: my first hotel toaster report from Yerp. The Roma Growler stood before me on three original and one prosthetic leg, its interior glowing and growling with expectation. A sign warned that it would only accept sliced bread. That must have had history. Did a past diner try to toast a chicken, or maybe a whole loaf of bread? I obeyed the sign in case the toast captain was watching, and posted two slices. Quite a bit of time and growling later, warm bread slid onto the out tray. Since it took another pass to make it into toast, I gave the Roma Growler six-and-a-half out of ten after deducting half a point for the prosthetic leg. Tough, but I'd seen Derek Breadchamber disqualify a toaster altogether just for unruly crumbs.

A special moonlight tour of the Colosseum, with dinner, had been organised by the *FAB* for its incoming sailors. However, it morphed into a very un-special tour of the Colosseum in hot afternoon light along with about half a million other people who had come for un-special tours of their own. I interpreted this as a *FAB* fitness test. Because most of our group were of advanced years, many with aids such as adjustable walking sticks, there was a possibility that some of them would be unfit for travel and expire during the voyage, their bodies having to be committed to the deep. Better to have them fail on a march around the Colosseum, which included a few sets of punishing steps. To their credit, our sailors survived, but then had to pass a final test of steeply-sloping cobbled streets and multiple stone staircases to get to the restaurant. Again, they came through and were rewarded with an excellent Italian meal, including wine. The next morning, we set out by bus for the port where the *FAB* awaited its sailors. Lurking among them was the Tourette's singer, but also the promise of other very interesting people.

If being bused from the hotel to the wharf showed one thing, it was the overwhelming popularity of supermini cars in Rome. Every big city was heading in this direction, I suspected, because there simply wasn't enough room for all those family-sized cars we used to think of as normal.

The supermini car was a cross between a quad bike and a car. Most models were so small that you had to sit on your own lap to fit in. The very smallest held only one person, but most took two, with no room for freight. They were parked on the simple principle of not quite enough room. Parking restriction signs meant nothing. And if there wasn't parallel room, park them sideways, or on pavements, or on corners. In stark contrast was the roomy *FAB*, squatting in port waiting for its 2000 paying sailors. It awakened my apprehension when, in Sydney, I'd seen similar vessels so huge they looked as though Circular Quay had arrived to tie up next to them.

Inside, the *FAB* public areas were as I had imagined, with powerfully coloured examples of every interior design extravaganza since the invention of the chair. But this is what cruising sailors obviously liked, and who was I to question it? Cruising was a demand-driven business. Speaking of which, paying for the cruise had many layers. Once the ship had encapsulated and collected the fare from 2000 fun-seeking sailors, its attention was turned to how further monies could be extracted. Each day, each passenger was charged US$15 for staff gratuities, whether they felt grateful or not, after which they would flick across some more money to express their further gratitude to those with whom they had direct physical contact. A 15 % gratuity was also added to every service and item purchased. When we queried this arrangement, we were reminded that, for example, we should be grateful to the person who puts soap powder in the ship's washing machine even though we will never meet and cannot tell whether the powder was placed with scowling indifference or with a smile for the pleasure of washing our clothes.

Surcharges aside, the ship was bristling with sphincter-clamping prices for services such as beauty treatments. There were special deals applying to eating and drinking too, where we could save by signing up now and regretting later. We were given a drink contract where anything under US$9 was free, but if we ventured into a $9.50 drink, we would be hit with the whole charge, not just the portion over our free allowance. All transactions, even when losing money in the casino, were charged to our multi-purpose plastic card. That meant we wouldn't know if we could be headed to debtors' prison until the end of the voyage.

CHAPTER 6   Greece – 2018

Our stateroom (it was a keel-hauling offence to call it a cabin), was excellent, along with our designated personal assistant whose smile started at one earlobe and finished at the other. We had generous space with a great television, a king-sized bed, plenty of cupboards, a full-width private balcony seven stories up from the water, and a decent bathroom with twin basins. The toilet was the airline-deafening, suck-and-pop type and there was a separate, straight-jacket shower fitted with a body-seeking curtain, plus a very small bath which was not recommended for large people whose buttocks could become vacuum-sealed on to the base.

The public areas were vast and varied, some charming, it must be said. If we couldn't find the solitude we craved, we could book a quiet *cabana* where, for a fee plus surcharge, we were cordoned off from the crowd. That contrasted to the two swimming pools. The large one was small and the small one minute. During most of the day, guests didn't actually take a swim, but lowered themselves into a family bath with hundreds of others. There was also a swirling thermal pool which didn't attract as many people because it charged per wallow.

We berthed at Naples with permission to go ashore, and the possibility of visiting Capri or Sorrento by ferry. We opted for some earthly experience in Napoli. Just outside the wharf, we found a tram that offered a hop-on-hop-off tour of the city – with a warning that if we hopped off, we would have to wait more than an hour to hop back on. Michelle developed a fear of seeing the *FAB* on the horizon, minus us. We decided to take a less risky journey, boarded, and then found that the tram was actually a bus impersonating a tram. It had a steering wheel and a shuddering diesel engine that gave a free massage as it trundled us around the city and climbed the picturesque hillsides. Naples, like many famous European cities, had too many cars and not enough money to restore its magnificent ruins. To its credit, like Paris, it had not allowed new high-rise buildings to dwarf its charm. There was nothing over eight storeys and most of the grand, Italianate buildings hadn't changed for hundreds of years. That went for their paint, too.

The schedule included two days at sea — a time when the *FAB* came into its own with fun and serious stuff to do while communication with the rest of the world ceased. The *FAB* put its best effort into keeping the paying sailors happily paying a bit more. For instance, we attended a detox and weight loss talk in the gym which gave good information but went down a plughole at the end when we were told the best way to revive our wrecked and wretched bodies was to submit to a body composition analysis. Fortunately for us, a machine and a dedicated consultant were onboard to take our measurements for a fee plus gratuity surcharge, followed by an up-sell of six months' supply of detox pills to enable us to conduct this essential process 'externally'. We were advised to eat five times a day, poo thrice, drink litres of water and pee profusely, exercise the heart and muscles vigorously, sleep at least eight hours — all of which left about ten minutes to make a living. We realised that detox and weight loss on a cruise were oxymorons, even admitted by counsellor Purebody doing the talk. After we received a grim warning that we were all eating and drinking ourselves to death, we gave the man a polite round of applause and resumed our march to the gallows.

CHAPTER 6 Greece – 2018

We were invited to the theatre for a fact session with Captain Jürgen Von Wilhelmsen III, who made himself available to lift the lid on how the ship actually worked. It weighed in at 50 000 tonnes, carried 1968 guests, 840 crew, got along at nineteen knots out of a possible twenty-three and was driven by two huge electric motors that swivelled to provide rear steering as well. When they were turned fully in the opposite direction and revved up, they could stop the ship in four ship-lengths. There were five massive diesel engines that generated all the electricity to run the electric motors and the rest of the ship's essential needs such as hair dryers and toasters. Three of the engines were at the stern and two were at the bow in case of a Titanic-style flood. Also at the bow were three electric motors either side, driving propellers to steer from the front. The ship produced all its own water by either reverse osmosis or evaporation. Uneaten food was ground up and fed to the sharks well out to sea while all the other garbage was sorted, recycled, and sold when in port. Water from showers, baths and laundry was recycled for use as grey water for the likes of washing. Sewage was also treated and went to the sharks who considered it a delicacy.

During our travels we'd connected with many people who, like us, were cruising through their savings, trying to spend the last dollar just as the grim reaper pressed the doorbell. These people, many of them retirees, were delighted by cruise ships that were so enormous they could reproduce what they left behind on land – which seemed a bit pointless to me. There were go-kart tracks, climbing walls, forests and streets – all to make you feel as though you weren't at sea. I thought our *FAB* was big at 50 000 tonnes, with a crew of 828 and nearly 2000 guests, but it was a tiddler compared to the biggest, *Symphony of the Seas*. That could take 6680 guests plus 2200 crew members for a total of nearly 9000 people. It had eighteen decks, twenty-two restaurants, twenty-four pools and 2759 cabins.

I must say I enjoyed the *FAB* (proper name: Holland America Line's *Oosterdam*) as an experience, but would I do it again? I didn't think so. I liked boats and I liked the sea, but moving along in a waterborne suburb was not for me – especially when contemplating going on something three times the size of the *FAB*. For the record, our twelve days covered 2647 miles at an average speed of fourteen knots and guzzled up 180 000 gallons of fuel. *Symphony of the Seas*' statistics would be jaw-dropping.

One of the highlights of the cruise was to sail into Santorini – really a huge, broken-up volcano that filled with water when one of its sides blew out a few thousand years ago. The area was still actively volcanic, the most dangerous threat being underwater. It currently provided hot currents to the Adriatic Sea, but might have blown at any time and again rearranged the islands in this magical part of Greece.

Man the lifeboats! Not because the ship was sinking but because the *FAB* decided to use its orange lifeboats to tender people ashore onto this neat, busy, but unspectacular island of Santorini. It also established the fact that the lifeboats were in good working condition. They seated 120 people each and were totally covered in, so in a big sea, you could bob about upside down if you needed to. Some of the lifeboats had windows but those that didn't would create the impression of travelling inside a giant plastic drink bottle.

Because there was no big-ship wharf, the *FAB* had to tender its eager sightseers ashore where they took buses up the rocky steeps of Santorini. The scarily-perched roads were never built for buses. In fact, the first car didn't arrive on the island until 1967. The width of the roads was meant to allow pack animals, such as donkeys, to pass when going in opposite directions. The same roads now had to accommodate big tourist buses that must creep past one another, with one on the death-fall side. If the roads were narrow, the streets and alleyways were even more so. Santorini was designed for its 15 000 permanent inhabitants who had built their stone-and-concrete houses along rocky outcrops. But the archaeological find of Akrotiri, a prehistoric city of great significance plus the sheer beauty of stark rock islands sitting in an indigo-and-emerald sea turned it into a compelling visitors' destination, especially for tourist ships. The amount of work tourists created swelled the population of Santorini to 78 000 during the summer, dwarfing the permanent residents. Then there were lucrative one-day visits from cruise ships like ours. Our day visit probably put 1500 people onto the rocky, burnt and bare island. We became a muttering, queue-burdened herd, going where we were told to view, taking pictures, wise-cracking, oddly shaped and variously dressed. Okay, we were a typical tourist crowd and the island handled it. But we were lucky, because there could be many ships in on the same day, and some a lot bigger than the *FAB*. The island could wake to the arrival of 30 000 people, all baying for the same services. Even our small crowd had to wait for four hours if they wanted to take the cable car down to the wharf. Falling would have been much quicker and going down by donkey much scarier, but most walked down pathways that were quickly reaching maximum capacity, and they were grateful to reach the bottom.

Although tourists brought money, they also brought chaos — surely not welcome by all of the permanent residents. There would come a day when we would have to win a lottery to go to Santorini. And that applied to many tourist meccas. The weight of growing numbers would eventually break the back of tourism as we knew it.

There was no such thing as a free pee in Santorini — or many parts of Europe, for that matter. Either you used a public pay facility known as a 'pee as you go' if you could find one or, failing that, you could do a deal with a restaurant on the arrangement known as 'user pees'. Because many of our colleagues were having trouble with their prostates and leakage problems, they quickly became skilled at making deals.

Each day there was an exertion symbol circulated for upcoming tours. A moderate exertion, with a two-leg symbol, pushed all but the young and fit into coronary territory. A three-leg symbol was for Olympic athletes or those who had decided on assisted suicide. The Santorini rating was only two legs, but the actual exertion was closer to three.

A welcome respite was lunch and a visit to the black beach — a strange place where the sand and rocks were black, but the water crystal clear. We also tasted the local wine, much praised by the tour guide because the vines had to struggle along without much water. Apparently, they sucked it out of the pumice stone which, in turn, sucked it out of the clouds. Normally, abused vines produced good wine, but that wasn't the case in Santorini. I went into the vineyard shop to enquire if there was anything better than the organised tourist tasting had offered. The sales girl became so enthused and long winded about their lousy wines that I bought a small bottle I didn't want, just to escape from the shop.

Santorini had 500 churches, many built by families and only used once or twice a year. Apart from religion, drinking and looking after tourists, the chief activity on the island was painting every building — and plenty of tree trunks — white every year. The paint importer was probably the richest man in Santorini.

When we tied up at Rhodes, I looked forward to seeing the Colossus of Rhodes, made in the likeness of Helios, the Greek god of the sun, even though nobody had actually seen him. According to what I had been taught in grade five history by Mrs Elliston at Murrumbeena State School, this huge copper statue had straddled the entrance to the harbour and the ancient mariners sailed in and out between its legs. Our tour guide immediately pulled the rug from beneath my expectations by pointing to two columns at the entrance to the harbour and telling us that they were positioned where Colossus was said to have had stood, but it was a load of bullshit because the Colossus had never been there at all, but up in the old, walled city. In case we were wondering, nothing of it remained because marauding Arabs had hacksawed off bits and sold them for scrap metal until there was nothing left. Back to the two columns at the port, they had statues of deer on top of them to celebrate the introduction of the animals to the island — going on advice from the local temple's oracle — to get rid of an infestation of venomous snakes by the deer kicking the life out of them. The snakes had been wiped out, but the deer were still roaming about in the countryside and were revered. However, going on other countries' experiences, where deer get the family bug and reach plague proportions, they might have to consider a few prides of lions to get rid of the deer. Then the lions would start to eat the people, who would wish they had the snakes back.

At the highest point of Rhodes is the Acropolis, and oi, what a trek! The bus dropped us off on a steep, downward-sloping street (not encouraging because, as Confucius remarked, every down has and equal and opposite up) that took us to the base of the walk up to the top of the mountain, involving hundreds of steps and paths, many worn smooth and slippery, with no hand rails and about twice the number of people using the track as it could safely fit. It was a nightmare walk, but the view from the Acropolis was spectacular, since it looked out over the whole of Rhodes. The ruins of the Acropolis itself were not so spectacular. They had a few restored columns to show where the old ones had been, and there were some ancient ruins of buildings on the way up, but most people were preoccupied with prevention of death by falling or dealing with extreme fatigue. Back at sea level, the old city was a delight, especially the Palace of the Grand Masters, even though the streets were loaded with tourist shops, their money vacuums turned to high.

Some old Greek customs were noteworthy. One was that sons were the preferred offspring because they would carry on the family name when they married. But daughters, even though they were expected to care for ageing parents, were a burden because, when they married, the parents had to provide them with a fully-furnished house. The groom contributed nothing except his presence.

Another was the housing tax dodge. When a house was completed, it attracted a property tax higher than an unfinished house. The trick was never to complete it. The accepted way to achieve this was to leave some steel reinforcement bars sticking out of the top of the concrete frame like rusty whiskers – which told the government that there was more to come.

The *FAB* welcomed us home with frozen daiquiris. As a result, we so liked the ship that we enquired about doing an internal tour of its vast kitchens. Our internal tour representative responded that the tour was no longer available because not enough people had wanted to take it. However, if we got a group of six or more starters, she might reinstate it. And it wouldn't only be an internal tour of the *FAB* kitchens. We would be shown the bridge, embrace the captain, inspect the engines, look through the crew quarters, and generally go where no other man or woman guest had gone before. 'Yes,' we chorused, 'we can get at least six starters.' The representative got out her clipboard in anticipation and then added, 'And the cost will be US$150 per person.' That killed the deal on the spot. Here we were, preparing to be ambassadors for the shipping line by spending a couple of memorable hours looking behind the scenes – and then having to stump up for the privilege.

Since it was mandatory to swim in Greek island waters, we took a low-stress day and went by official bus to a quiet little beach not far from the port. There it lay: whiteish sand, still, clear water, a civilised line of sun lounges and umbrellas, and a bar. We settled in for a restful half-day. Then the air traffic started. We realised that our dear little beach was on final approach to busy Crete Airport. As a balm to the roar of coming and going jet engines, we decided to take a swim. That prompted a grotesque dance into the water, because the first 5 m were all stones underfoot, and not necessarily smooth, and to top it off, the water was just this side of brass monkey. Once we got under, and properly numb, we grew accustomed to it. However, we had fulfilled the unspoken contract to go somewhere and appear to have a good time.

For our departure from Crete, a twenty-piece brass band assembled on the wharf and farted forth a medley of famous tunes, much to the joy of the *FAB* sailors who waved and clapped from their balconies.

We forsook the marshalling yard and bus method of exploration and hired a driver to whisk us around Athens for eight hours. He was a hand-waving, exuberant, continuously-talking local man who had come unstuck as a building developer when the market dived 60 % while he was in the middle of building a block of apartments. With local unemployment running at 26 %, he was happy to have a job driving people around. Something about the Greek male personality struck me. Every man was a manager. They all loudly told one other what to do, using exaggerated gestures. The women, on the other hand, simply shrugged their shoulders and got on with it.

As we drove out of the port, I noticed a high-rise building that looked bedraggled and deserted. The story was that when its construction reached twenty-three floors, it suddenly slumped sideways. The engineer hadn't calculated its weight correctly in relation to the subsoil and it had to be abandoned because it might topple over, especially if tickled by an earthquake. It had been sitting awaiting demolition for some years because the money to put it up had not included enough to pull it down again. It was in contrast to the Parthenon, built some thousands of years previously. Not only was the Parthenon a building masterpiece, but it was also a brilliant optical illusion based on the Fibonacci sequence. We got up close and personal early in the day before the regurgitation of passengers from an armada of busses. Michelle had been to the Acropolis before, but I hadn't, and I was spellbound by it. I found out that there were many acropolises. The word simply meant the highest point in a city. Early civilisations had built temples and castles there because it was easier to defend as the opposition came puffing up the hill.

With a big crane inside the building and piles of marble blocks all around, it looked as though the Greek government was restoring the Parthenon, but no. That was not allowed under the international agreement on antiquities. It was permitted to put pieces back where they used to be and occasionally introduce a bit of infill, but making new parts was forbidden. Ruins had to be left ruined. There was nothing more disrespectful than a new ruin, our driver commented dryly.

The most recent Olympic games hadn't done Athens much good financially. Many locals blamed them for sending the city broke. However, the city still played a part in the whole concept of the games. We visited a stadium that sent off the Olympic flame around the world. It had been restored to its original 1894 condition, and now held 75 000 people seated on haemorrhoid-inducing marble steps. The Olympic flame and all the fuss of running it around the world started in 1936 for the Berlin games and the man who thought up the flame idea was none other than Adolf Hitler. We couldn't find a marble bust of him anywhere.

We wandered around the old city of Agora where, in the marketplace, Aristotle, Socrates and other men brimming with challenging ideas, stood on a particular pedestal and addressed anybody who would listen. Since they were communicating in an era where there was only word of mouth for news, they pulled good audiences and had no need for commercial breaks.

While the old city was charming, we were told to beware of gypsies who were very good at relieving the gullible of worldly goods, especially cash. Our driver recounted a popular saying: 'If you buy an egg from a gypsy, when you open it, there will be no yolk inside'. Michelle took this warning very seriously and gave me lessons in positioning my man-bag as though it were a sporran. My Scottish ancestry made this feel comfortable enough, but I told her that I drew the line at wearing a kilt without underpants.

While many cruises were praised for entertainment, some with big-name artists, the *FAB* wasn't one of them. The main theatre had run a few song and dance compilations that had the senior sailors tapping their walking sticks and twitching their legs (although that may have been one of many medical conditions), but none of the singers would have turned a chair in *The Voice*. Then there was a troupe of traditional Greek dancers, led by a female singer who was a semitone flat for much of the time as the dancers hopped here and there, done up in old-world garb. The pianists were okay and the classical quartet often went shmaltzy with early American plantation hoe-down jollity between an occasional nice piece of Schumann. The juggler did some good balls, batons and knives, but his stand-up lines only got polite laughs. The best act was an illusionist who used mime to introduce some old and some original magic. 'How does he do that?' continually echoed around the theatre, with the occasional, 'Godammit! Now honey, that's darned clever.'

This cruise used to make Turkey a stop, but because it more recently threatened to annihilate passengers, who then couldn't be surcharged, the peaceful island of Argostolion took its place. Apart from a grotto and a lake, not much else was remarkable. The main street had all the expected shops and cafés. And there was the Little Red Train, the kind you see at a country fair to keep the kids happy. In our case, it kept the adults only semi-happy. For €5 each, they piled aboard the open carriages and were carted up the main street, bell clanging, around two corners, past the fire station where a line of clapped-out fire trucks looked like it hadn't been disturbed in years, around another corner and back up the main street to the start again. Here, another crowd of tourists tried to get in before the arriving lot got out. The journey took all of about ten minutes. We maybe should have taken its competitor, the Little Yellow Train, that charged €7 but added a few more corners and back street buildings. In the afternoon, we took a taxi to the back of the island and sat on a highly-organised beach with various levels of reclining equipment, a bar, bracing water and a user pees system. Argostolion was a calm, well-greened place, but I would have preferred to take a chance on some exciting gunfire in Turkey.

Korfooo! as our American sailing friends pronounced it, was a bit of a fizzer. Michelle and I had been coughing for a few days and it reached a point where Michelle decided to stay state-room bound while I went out and 'did' Corfu. Trouble was, Corfu did me. Alone and without a map, I strode away confidently to the right of the wharf, following the coast, with the plan to circle inland and end up in the old town, far left, which was supposed to be charming.

However, once I moved away from the coast, I became lost in a maze of streets. I found a highway and caught a random blue bus, paid the fare and it did a nice trundle through the burbs with a lucky finish in the old town. After enjoying a leisurely walk along the gracious, tree-shaded streets, I stopped to sip lemonade in a narrow alley restaurant, redeemed a user pee, and asked the waiter for directions to the port. 'Ten minutes. Down the street and turn right,' he said. He lied. I found myself headed towards a mountain that I took for the one behind the *FAB* when, in fact, it was the one on the other side of the island. Needless to say, I got lost again, this time deeply so. I followed some touristy-looking people into a bus station with green buses but was told I needed another blue bus that stopped across the road and it must head in the opposite direction to my walk. I waited at the bus stop for half an hour. No blue bus. Then, I spied a taxi sitting under a tree. I pleaded my case to the driver. 'Blue bus? Rubbish! You would never have got back to your ship on the blue bus,' he said to establish his superiority, 'but today God sent me to find you.' I had to love Greek philosophy.

If we wanted to eat extra upmarket on the *FAB*, we went to the Pinnacle Grill, via a surcharge, of course. There, on the drinks menu, cocktail subsection, we found the revered name of the master mixologist. He had a degree in general and specific mixing, and was qualified to mix other products such as paint, cake ingredients and two-pack glue. My new friend, Bob (a retired photography professor), told me that was no surprise, because American universities offered degrees in all kinds of subjects. For instance, you could become a bachelor of driving instruction. At the Pinnacle Grill, where nothing was actually grilled, I ordered Devon sole. When the waitress brought it, she instructed me not to start eating it until I got a boner. I was mystified by this exciting prospect until a nervous waiter appeared and announced he was the boner, but this was his first time. A virgin boner. With a few flourishes he removed the bone from the sole – well, most of it anyway. I was sure he'd do better next time.

It was worth getting up at dawn to witness sailing into Kotor, surrounded by towering, wooded mountains diving straight into the sea. The *FAB* was able to run close to the shore so that we could watch the city, with its typically Mediterranean buildings and houses, and its people, waking up to another day in paradise. Most of the buildings huddled near the shore because of the construction challenges up the mountain sides. One quite substantial house had slithered down the slope during a heavy rainstorm and now clung to the rocks like a surreal work of art.

Of all the ports we visited aboard the *FAB*, Montenegro impressed me the most. With its huge hillsides that finished in picturesque villages, this was probably the place I'd come back to first. We hired a driver for a four-hour excursion which took us over (and through) the tall mountain that dominates Kotor, and then on to the capital, Cyrillic, where there was the Presidential

Palace. The President didn't live there and it wasn't much of a palace anyway, in spite of a couple of fancy-dressed guards in the doorway. The more impressive mausoleum housed the bones of the last royal family. Montenegro has had bits of it taken away and returned, but now was an independent, democratic country with a relatively tiny population of 624 000 and dropping. It gained independence in 2006 and its culture was a blend of its neighbours: Croatia, Serbia, Italy and Turkey. It couldn't afford armed forces but relied on its membership of NATO to be looked after like a little brother. UNESCO also had a say in how the country was run and insisted its heritage be preserved.

Our driver, Nicholas, was born in Montenegro. He drove his taxi during the tourist season and became a deck officer on a container ship for the rest of the year. He was passionate about his small country and wanted to increase tourism – already its main industry. Sensibly, there was a big road building program under way, with some of the major projects being managed by the Chinese. The Riviera-style foreshore had already become a playground for the rich and famous, who could hide away from public stare. We walked past a row of private motor yachts some probably costing millions of dollars. Tennis star, Novak Djokovic, although now a Serbian citizen, was born in Montenegro. When he married, he booked out the famous Saint Stefan Hotel, the dearest venue on the strip, and invited his guests to stay there for the nuptials. The hotel sat on its own peninsular, joined to the mainland by a single, narrow road which could be patrolled to turn away the uninvited. But the hotel buildings themselves were far from spectacular. They looked more like a military garrison or a prison.

Nicholas told us about some dietary practices in Montenegro. Olive oil was a staple remedy for many ailments. True believers took a shot of it every day. If you were planning to do some heavy drinking, you should down a tumbler of olive oil before you started, he advised. His grandmother, who reached the age of ninety-two, was not only an olive oil enthusiast but started each day with a shot of homemade grappa with unspecified alcoholic content. She also favoured eating smoked pork or goat. A specialty was cheese made from donkeys' milk. Not being notable milk producers, the cheese made from donkeys' milk had become an expensive rarity.

CHAPTER 7

Italy – 2018

It was time to visit Venice before it sank. The *FAB* glided up the Grand Canal and ejected us, with practised theatrical regret, into one of the world's most famous cities. Our hotel, Savoia & Jolanda, sent a man-in-a-Merc to meet us. He carefully placed our cases in the trunk, drove 20 m and got them all out again for a transfer to a water-taxi. We entered the scramble of rocking boats on the churning, greenish canal and were deposited outside our hotel, which was right on the main drag, just down from the legendary St Mark's Square.

I'd forgotten about European hotels, but it all came back in the tiny lift in which a sign incorrectly claimed that it could hold 'four persons'. It should have gone on to elaborate: 'four pygmy persons without luggage, or three American persons without luggage, or two Russian persons without luggage, or four luggage with no persons'.

Michelle had forewarned the management that we were 'two

big persons' which is why we needed a big room. But a big room in Venice means it has to be filled with big furniture so that it affords the occupants no more walking space than a small room. The furnishings of our room included two gigantic lounge chairs with gilded surrounds, a huge bed with a gilded bed-head, a glass-topped coffee table that would seat eight around it, a very tall, very skinny desk with colossal, gold cabriole legs plus a too-low gilded chair to go with it, and a giant, ancient-style couch in gold velvet that could sleep two people. The lighting came from a multiple collection of glass wall chandeliers with a profundity of bare globes. With such finery, who needed drawers or wardrobes? There were a few after-thoughts, but the room was meant for people who spent most of their time in there naked. The bathroom, newly renovated, placed the towels in a rack in direct firing line with the open-ended shower cubicle. But hey, we were in Venice, where art and design took precedence over practicality.

While Michelle went on a retail discovery tour, I went to the Basilica Della Salute to hear a vespers organ recital. The Basilica was magnificent and so was the sound of the organ, but the priest had inserted a mass into the middle of the recital. He was done up in bright green-and-gold vestments which provided a fine counterweight to his solemn Latin intersession. After it was over, he popped out for a change into standard clerical black, and quickly retrieved his religious equipment – indicating to me that they were in danger of being souvenired by atheists. The organ concert then resumed – on a wonderful instrument built in 1782 and still able to stir the soul. I left to catch my first *vaporetto*, a public water bus, but I didn't have a ticket – which was only available across the Grand Canal. I needed a ticket to get a ticket. The only solution was to become a fare evader pretending to be part of a squabbling family that seemed to have plenty of tickets. Luckily, I didn't get caught.

Apart from tourism, the best employment prospects in Venice appeared to be in rising damp eradication, marine engine repair, marine varnishing, and waiting with attitude on tables. Captaining a gondola was on a higher level, requiring a certificate in single oar steering and paddling, a horizontally striped shirt, a flat straw hat with rear tassel and a passable tenor voice.

Hotel Toaster Report

Derek Breadchamber named the Grande Clampo di Venezia as the most advanced hotel toaster of its generation. It had no in and out via a belt. Instead, each slice of bread had to be placed in its own hand-operated clamp which was then inserted into the unique open-fronted infernotron. Once the time dial was activated, toasting began immediately. Unlimited inspection capability enabled exact browning. I emailed Derek that evening and sent him a photo that I expected would appear in *The New York Times* cooking supplement.

We shared alfresco breakfasts with the aggressive pigeons of Venice. As soon as we stood up to get some more food, they hoed into what was left on our plates. The locals tolerated them far more than visitors like us who were not very successful in shooing them away because the pigeons only understood Italian.

A following three-hour walking tour of Venice with our guide, Antonio, was well worth the €90 each, since it cobbled together a secession of must-sees — even if it did finish with a glass blowing demonstration followed by a hard up-sell in a glassware showroom.

A few other stops were memorable. The Basilica St Marco ranked high among the world's most awe-inspiring buildings. As well as being huge and dripplingly ornate, the mosaics that adorned its ceilings, walls and floor carried four tonnes of gold. The floor, like the rest of Venice (it was built on a swamp) was showing patches of subsidence and would eventually sink unless technology saved it. Another staggering building, also on the square, was the Doge's Palace. It had the biggest hall without supporting columns in Europe and the biggest painting in the world in which thousands of figures all seemed to be writhing in anguish — which went for many of the religious paintings by the Old Masters. Our guide pointed out that the most acceptable female form of the fourteenth century was small-breasted but otherwise plump — just the opposite to today's aspirational female body. One building that especially appealed to me was a spiral tower, officially known as the Bolovo Staircase, hidden in a side alley near Campo Manin. It reminded me of an Escher drawing of something rational but impossible.

One of the drawbacks of sightseeing in Venice was the long queues, with listless security screening added, to get into the most interesting places. And this was far from peak season. However, because Antonio was a registered tour guide, he had 'skip the line' privileges. Trouble was, 'skip the line' could also be purchased by ordinary tourists for a premium so the 'skip the line' line would eventually grow into a tiresome line of its own, prompting a next generation of impatience-savers called 'skip the skip-the-line line'.

I was having some personal issues with my developing beard. First was a terse email from George Clooney asking why I was trying to impersonate him in Venice. I noticed in the recent royal wedding coverage that he had a carefree stubble similar to my own, although George's had a tad more salt. I was going to discuss with him how he dealt with the problem of hair ends pressing back into the face at about week two of the start-up growth period. But now I couldn't ask him because he was upset with me. In bed, I felt as though my face was lying against a new doormat. I even dreamt about doormats instead of hotel toasters.

The streets, alleyways and canals of Venice must have been designed by a maze builder with a grudge, because everybody became lost most of the time – even the locals. When we tried to find the opera house, we went past the same shops three or four times, in spite of having a map. We even went to Google Maps on our phone, where the stupid voice told us either we had arrived when we hadn't, or that every direction we took was moving away from the opera house. It was like black hole physics. When we came upon it by accident, we'd been walking for hours and had missed the tour we'd come to take. Instead, people dressed up in their opera finery were going in for an afternoon performance of *La Traviata*. We went to the box office and found that 'last minute' €200 tickets were now reduced to €50. Nodding, I reached for my money, but then the ticketer saw that I was wearing shorts – which would offend the sensibilities of rack-rate paying opera buffs in the stalls. The best she could do was hide my offensive lower legs away in a shared box on level two for only €20 each. Up we went, to be enclosed in a small, open-fronted stable with the two seats at the front occupied by full-paying horses, with the two of us behind them on crane-your-neck high-chairs. But all that aside, we were in for a treat.

The Venice Opera House, or *Teatro L Fenice*, first built in 1792, had a habit of burning down and being rebuilt; the latest incarnation being in 2004. Inside, the opera house was jaw-dropping, with a massive stage, floor level stall seating, and then boxes rising four levels in a semi-circle of gilded reliefs – like La Scala and just as ornate, but smaller. From the first trembling strings of the familiar overture, I was spellbound. I remembered Antonio, our guide, telling us that only the best singers won a gig at *Teatro L Fenice*, which explained the extraordinary voices of the three leads, Francesca Sassu, Matteo Lippi and Julian Kim. They were supported by a top rate orchestra, with no musicians stuffed in a pit beneath the stage as they are in many opera houses. I came out uplifted, almost enough to forget that in my bag I had a pair of YSL sunglasses, bought in a stupor during our lost period, that were as ridiculous in design as they were in price. Michelle posted my folly on Facebook. That said, I loved them and, in any case, I was approaching the pointy end of everything.

We had planned to visit the Jewish Museum and synagogues by placing our trust in Google Maps on our not-so-smart phones. They went on the rampage again – but we were not the only ones suffering. There were people everywhere, dizzily staring at their phones and cursing. It struck me that you could book into one of the hundreds of elegant, hole-in-the-wall Venice hotels, unpack, go out for a meal, but never find the hotel again.

Back into random directions, we aimed at the opera house we'd visited the day before, hoping to see another opera at a last-minute price. The stars were aligned. We found the opera house where Google Maps said it wasn't and then my trousers allowed prime seats for €50 each. We sat down to a memorable performance of Donetsetti's *The Elixir of Love*. Again, these were top singers and an outstanding cast in a magical place.

For the record, there were about 65 000 permanent residents in Venice, but the city was obliged to swallow another 60 000 visitors every day. No wonder we sat at breakfast and watched a river of people streaming past on their way to St Mark's Square. They looked like escaping refugees, headed for the square to create massive queues. I wanted to go up in the huge brick tower in the square. It had 1000 steps, which were thankfully not in use. Instead, intending tower climbers had to make do with a lift which did not relate to the numbers wanting to use it. I persevered in the long, shuffling queue, but disappointingly the view from the top was restricted by the massive thickness of the walls, preventing viewers from seeing what the pigeons could see without queuing up. After waiting in a long queue to descend, I did another St Marco must-see by sitting down and drinking a beer at one of the tables. There was no cover charge, but instead, a €12 'music fee' to listen to languidly played hits from last century and before. Those not in the party mood, but wanting just to sit down, lowered themselves onto the rows of marble steps, little realising that by so doing they were in breach of the laws of Venice that say, 'Thou shalt not sit on a public step'. The step cops spent their days shooing them away as they did the pigeons, and then, like the pigeons, the illegal sitters fluttered around and resettled once the cops had moved on.

We returned to non-sinking ground when we reached Bologna, famous for Italian food.

The best way to experience it was to go on food tours. They were typically led by megaphone-armed young women who were slim because they grew tired of food and walked off what little they did eat. We had some sympathy for them when we saddled up for a second food tour before we'd recovered from the first. There was method in our madness, however. Because we were trying to get from Bologna to Modena – not on the train because we had too many cases to manage – we found a food tour that would pick us up in Bologna, take us on a gastronomic journey, whiz us out to the Ferrari factory and then drop us within a short cab ride to Modena.

We joined an affable group of fourteen chompers in a swanky Mercedes bus. The chomp captain, on this occasion, had a clear voice and very pleasant manner. She told us we would experience boutique production of parmesan cheese, prosciutto, and balsamic vinegar. All these products were available from the supermarket at competitive prices, but the chomp captain declared them fake. The genuine articles took time, were strictly quality controlled and were mostly in the care of small families dedicated to traditions and methods refined over generations. Consequently, what they offered was rare, tasted entirely different to the commercial versions, and were priced accordingly.

At the parmesan cheese factory, we were told that the production of the cheese must begin within two hours of the cow being milked, which happened twice a day and produced about twenty-five litres of milk per cow. Because the cows were not religious or members of trade unions, they didn't take weekends or scheduled days off. Therefore, cheesemaking was a continuous enterprise. The cows didn't wander around in paddocks like they did in Australia either, but lived a quiet barn life and were fed on the best quality, eco-friendly hay. The cheese had to be aged, tested and approved before it could be branded and offered for sale as first quality. My favourite was twenty-four months old, but some connoisseurs liked them much older, imparting an eyebrow-raising finish.

Our encounter with traditional balsamic vinegar radically changed our understanding of what it really was and what went into making it. Far from a humble salad dressing, it was an ancient cure for many illnesses. In that part of the world, when a daughter was born, her parents filled at least five wooden barrels with raw balsamic vinegar as a gift to her. By the time she married, the vinegar would have matured and would provide her future family with what is regarded as medicine. Boni, the producer we visited, was run by a fourth-generation son who had stock of balsamic vinegar going back 150 years. We could buy a 100 ml bottle of this rare vintage for €500 – putting it on the same footing as rare, vintage wine. And like wine, vinegar came from grape juice – in balsamic's case, boiled for twelve hours. Young Mr Boni said that the processes were so different that he would rather top himself than produce wine. We did a tasting of some old vinegar that was simply superb. It led us to buy a 100 ml bottle of thirty-year-old balsamic for €60 – cheap if it cured the lingering cough we'd picked up on the *FAB*. We planned to take a teaspoonful each night until cured.

High on balsamic vinegar, we visited the Ferrari factory in

Maranello, just out of Modena. The management wouldn't let the curious in to see the production line but there were plenty of compensations. The factory employed about 3400 people and delivered 840 new cars each year – all made to order after a waiting period of one to two years. There was a test track next to the expanding factory buildings and you could buy yourself a test drive accompanied by a works driver (who I assumed had an engine-off switch hidden under the dashboard) in a new Ferrari for a substantial outlay. Since I hadn't brought my international driver's licence with me, I was not allowed to drive one of these sculptured, angry beauties, but for €100 a works driver would undertake to scare the daylights out of me for fifteen minutes. I declined their offer and went to look over the museum instead, where iconic Ferraris were lined up in an awesome exhibition. One room was devoted to Ferrari racing cars that had competed in every Formula One series since its inception and had won more races than any other make. The company founder, Enzo Ferrari, only made and sold sports cars to fund his racing – and that still seemed to drive the company. Enzo was a cranky old bugger, with a short fuse and given to a good shout-off. He exercised his celebrity by refusing to visit other celebrities; they had to come to him. And they did.

While we associated red with Ferrari, its symbolic colour was actually yellow – as in the prancing horse badge. It was incorrectly allocated red by the organisers of the first Formula One race and has stuck with it ever since. One of the sad moments was seeing the racing car in which Michael Schumacher won his last race.

If we'd had the money and the inclination, we could have

bought a superseded Ferrari racing car, stored it at the factory, where it would be kept in mint condition, and pop out to take it for a spin around the test track when the spirit moved us.

Ferrari employees were not permitted to order new sports cars. They were for external customers only – who had to wait anyway, poor things. Formula One race drivers were allowed to buy a new Ferrari, but had to pay full price and wait their turn.

Hotel Toaster Report

There could be no report of the Modena Best Western Hotel toaster, because it didn't have one. The tall, always-smiling waiter told me the epic story at breakfast:

'We did have a toaster, but the guests kept leaving bread in it which caught fire and set off the fire alarm many times. Then one day, as I am peddling my bicycle to work, I see a toaster flying through the air. With the fire bell ringing again already, the owner of the hotel had lost his temper, grabbed the toaster, and threw it out the window.'

As Derek Breadchamber remarked in his definitive 2016 book *Duties of a Successful Toast Captain,* a toaster was no better than the toast captain in charge of it. Toast smoke was regrettable, but fire was unforgivable. He made the point that a careless toast captain should be sacked or at least busted down to 'dish pig'.

Lerici was going to be the beach resort part of our trip. We took a car from Modena for a two-hour country drive to Lerici, supposedly a charming, quiet part of the Italian Riviera. Our hotel was advertised as close to the beach where, for a modest amount, we could hire umbrellas and sun beds for some seaside indulgence. We understood that the hotel had its own pool if we didn't feel like getting sandy and salty. None of that was true. The car dropped us off at a pool-deprived hotel perched on a hillside with a wonderful view of distant harbour and beaches best accessed by hang glider. Before guests became angry about having to become mountain goats, they were reassured that there was a shuttle bus on demand — as long as it was not on demand elsewhere. It would take us to a selection of beaches where, for up to AUD$300 a day, we could recline, shaded, at a beach club. The alternative was to bake on the sand, or the more plentiful rocks, at no charge.

While Michelle unpacked, I took the long goat trail down to the main square — which I had to say was delightful once I arrived, but the return trip challenged my cardiac capacity. Next time I would bring oxygen with me.

Apart from many restaurants, which we planned to explore, there was a grey castle on the harbour headland and a main street spa that offered, among other services, the removal of hair from your buttocks or a total chocolate body massage. I wondered who ate the chocolate after the massage.

One advantage this hotel had over most others I'd stayed in was a free minibar, conservatively stocked with basic hard and soft drinks and replenished every day. Thus, we wouldn't face that inevitable question at checkout time when the cashier leans across the marble reception desk, suddenly injects you with sodium pentothal, switches on the lie detector, looks you in the eye, and asks, 'Anything from the minibar?'

Hotel Toaster Report

The hand clamp persisted. It must have been an Italian trait. In any case, in our Lerici hotel, I found a Clampa Minora with two basket clamps which did not like to give up their slice of toast. This explained an additional long-handled set of tongs to make the separation. It took some concentration, working all these metal tools in unison, which was why a part-time toast captain was on hand for assistance. Derek Breadchamber pointed out in one of his books that the Clampa Minora baked the bread rather than toasted it and had not won any hotel toaster awards for this reason.

We found a ferry service which chugged along the Cinque Terre coast, calling in at five little towns where most of the commercial buildings huddled down near the water while the houses that were built further up on the impossibly-steep hillsides defied logic. How did they get their groceries up there? There were thousands of steps just to get to a road. Also, how did they make a living? They couldn't all have been retired poets. These little towns seemed to attract tourists and offer beaches for swimming in the deep green waters of the Mediterranean, but by Australian standards, the beaches were disappointing. If there was sand, it was putty-coloured and coarse, but most of them had only stones or rocks to lie on, hence a thriving business in sun beds and umbrellas that cost more to hire than they did to buy.

We went down to the city square to sample the local pizzas. I was pleased with mine, but Michelle hit a low when she ordered a seafood pizza, without cheese. The pizza looked okay on approach but when it was set down, it was revealed as a collection of still-in-the-shell seafood strewn across the crust. The prawns, mussels and clams all sat there defying release from their baked-on, brittle casings. After long and unsuccessful surgery, in which the seafood odour began to hint of decomposition, we sent it back and Michelle chose something else. To the restaurant's credit, a bottle of limoncello was offered as a peace offering – which we accepted.

While waiting to return via the ascending bus to our hillside nest, we witnessed the Lerici ambulance service at work. Somebody had taken ill in the bus shelter. The ambulance arrived with dramatic signage, sirens and blue flashing lights and loaded the stricken person into the back. But before driving away to hospital, the ambulance crew – done up in orange fluoro and hung liberally with lifesaving equipment – proceeded to have arguments with bystanders and then with each other. It grew louder and louder and lasted for about twenty minutes. The patient, who we could see lying inside, was ignored while the opposing teams waved arms and yelled at one another. The fluoro team got into the ambulance, slammed the doors closed, turned on the siren, then all got out again to put the finishing touches to their summing up.

After pondering how we should spend our last day in Lerici before going to Lake Como, we decided to have a splurge and go to a beach club. Eco del Mare was rated the best by our hotel receptionist, and the weather forecast was for a hot day. After Michelle had spent some time negotiating the best Monday rate for the day, we were dropped off at the top of a fearsome cliff. For guests at this self-congratulatory resort hotel, there was a lift, oddly only offering assistance during the middle of the climb. At the bottom was the strangest accommodation I'd seen in a long time.

It was a hotel shouldered into the side of the cliff. It had six guest rooms, all looking out over the beach and limpid water. It hadn't been open long and it came with a romantic history which included the fanciful décor work of its female owner, who scoured the world for all things 'beach'. The public areas were festooned with coils of salty rope, torn nets, pieces of driftwood, and all manner of auld stuff, washed up. The sand comprised grades of coarse grey gravel to pebbles to stones – all doing a more penetrating job on the soles of the feet than Dr Scholl sandals. While the locals walked through this stuff erect and unperturbed, I staggered from one stone pile to the next as though I had two broken legs.

The day rate covered the use of one medium umbrella with two muslin wings, and two pieces of reclining furniture – which could be a flat canvas bed, a bean bag, or a bean-filled ground mattress. A non-lockable storage box completed the suite. I opted for the roly-poly ground mattress but when I tried lying on it, I couldn't escape because wherever I rolled, the sides reared up, trapping me in a live burrow. Michelle and the beach lieutenant had to haul me out. I switched to the bean bag with far greater success. For one day, sitting on the beach and using this spartan equipment, the cost was AUD$180. Drinks, comprising mostly ice cubes, were AUD$22 each. Staying in the hotel, in which you're virtually marooned after sundown, cost around AUD$750 per night.

The day failed to show any sun and the water was too cold

for swimming. It also rained for a while. We'd had a memorable, Italian-style day at the beach.

Since neither of us were weightlifters, European train travel with large, heavy suitcases was a mistake and because it was prepaid, it was too late to change. Our journey from Lerici to Como was looking okay until we reached the La Spezia train station where we had to tackle long, stone, ascending staircases because the lifts were being repaired. Were it not for kind and muscular fellow travellers giving us a haul-up, we'd still be waiting at the bottom of the stairs. There was a certain camaraderie among those who had chosen to lug – and not just in the matter of suitcases. In the lofty and magnificent Milan railway station, we had arrived too early to meet our driver to Como, so we took refuge in a pizza-and-pee-entitlement restaurant – except it lacked the pee entitlement. That obliged a journey downstairs where €1 was required to contribute to the city's urine bank. Back in among the pizzas, we came across a small American woman who'd had a couple of beers and needed relief, but didn't have the necessary euro on hand. She was seriously assessing her options among the rubbish bins when Michelle funded her trip downstairs and was rewarded with a list of good places to eat and buy jewellery in Como.

Our Como hotel, called the Palace (only because its facade resembled one), looked across the road at Lake Como – one of the deepest lakes in the world, at 460 m. We rejected the first room we were offered because it was too small and then accepted it gratefully when offered even smaller alternatives which hotel staff said were normal size. Our first-floor balcony may have been used to wave to the grateful poor below in days gone by. As it was, we could only wave at the rain pelting down. The weather forecast was not encouraging, but because it had proven to be generally inaccurate in Italy, we were hopeful.

Hotel Toaster Report

The Palace Hotel served breakfast beneath massive chandeliers and was overseen by equally massive faux-medieval paintings of near-naked men and women cavorting in cloudy countrysides. I would have expected a toaster of regal style in such grand surroundings, but placed in a corner, almost as an afterthought, I discovered the Como Triple Knobber Cautionhot – a modest machine overpowered by a sign warning of fire if other than sliced bread were inserted. It badly needed a toast captain with a fire extinguishing certificate. Anyway, the CTKC was fairly basic except for its three unnamed knobs which baffled many users into producing no toast at all. I resolved to tell Derek Breadchamber that hotel toaster technology could only advance with good knob signage.

There was an old-style, grinding ferry that travelled right to the end of Lake Como and stopped at thirty-four delightful lake towns on a hop-on-hop-off system. Trouble was, if you hopped off, you could wait hours to hop back on because the ferries were not frequent or reliable. The best solution was to hop-on-and-stay-on until the end – which was Colico. There, you could hop off while the ferry was cleaned and made ready to grind again. That gave about half an hour to explore the town, gulp down a coffee and get back onboard to visit the same towns on the return journey. But by sitting on the same side of the returning ferry, we scored a different view and could convince ourselves that we were on a different lake.

The scenery was spectacular with heavily wooded mountains plunging straight into the lake, and houses built on impossible cliffs. In the lofty distance were the Alps, still wearing a shawl of late snow. We zigged and zagged across the lake for four hours to reach Colico, but the Captain had squandered time and was running twenty minutes late. His crew did a rush cleaning job and told the returning passengers they had to stay on board because the service had to get back on schedule and would be leaving *immediatamente*! Off we growled again, but this time the Captain overcompensated and was soon running ahead of schedule.

Passengers will tolerate a late ferry, but not an early one because it punishes the pious and the punctual. The captain faced enraged ticket-holders waving their fists at the too-early ferry diminishing in the distance. The captain's superior, probably the Admiral of Como Ferries, must have called him about the growing angst because he then tried to slow down by docking at Argegno, doing a big loop around the lake, and docking again. This gave a strange feeling of déjà vu, because we'd already seen the town on the way up and now twice on the way back. However, it seemed to solve the captain's problem.

My career as a fare-evader continued when we took the funicular railway up the side of the mountain to get the aviator's view of Lake Como. We bought tickets at the base camp office and, as Michelle and I stood waiting in the boarding queue, a whole family ducked under the turnstile arms to take the ride for nothing. How disgusting, I thought. I'd never do that.

We eventually got to the top, walked about, marvelled at the view, stopped and paid a handsome price for a drink and lined up to take the trip down again. But I'd lost my ticket. Did I buy another one? Well, no. I got down on my hands and knees and crawled under the turnstile arm — because I had been shown how by the dishonest family on ground level. It was not easy. My body was not suited to such an exercise and it took some time. Just as I was ponderously straightening up, there came a bellow from the open ticket office window which, I discovered, was in full view of the turnstile. I bellowed back that I couldn't be up here in the first place if I hadn't bought a ticket — which I'd now lost. After some high-volume debate, the ticket officer must have decided it was more trouble to arrest me than to let the felony proceed.

That was the second time I had risked jail in Italy for fare evasion. I reminded myself that I must guard against overconfidence. My luck would surely run out.

Hoping to repeat my organ experience in Venice, I visited Como's grand cathedral where, in a whispered conversation with a curate, I was told there was no casual or recital playing of the legendary organ, but it was used during mass. We duly attended mass at 5 pm where the only music was provided by an untalented soprano as part of the service. Not one note escaped from the huge, ornate organ pipes set in two banks either side of the nave. We had to sit through a mass in Italian, stand up and sit down when the crowd did, put some money into the velvet-lined collection bucket — and leave without hearing the organ.

There was a general reluctance among Como locals to identify exactly where George Clooney lived, although it was public knowledge that the town was Laglio and the house was called the Villa Oleandra. He had bought it in 2002, but because it needed renovation, he also bought the one next door to use while the work was being done. Sensible move.

It was such a pity that George was hard to find because I wanted to discuss beards with him. However, I had to consider a law that prevented more than three people from loitering outside his house – in the unlikely event that they found it. Apparently, he moved in during the summer, had a collection of rare motorbikes in his garage, hooned around in a speedboat and went to local restaurants for a feed with Mrs Clooney and their twins.

We followed a rumour that he sometimes frequented one of the most famous five-star hotels in the world, the lakeside Villa d'este at Cernobbio (the average price per night was AUD$2324). We took the ferry there with a plan to spend a fortune having a drink in the lounge and surely bump into George. When we arrived at the gate, looking like typical, daggy tourists – which we were – the security guard pointed us in the opposite direction. Michelle politely thanked him and, from behind a tree, called the hotel on her mobile and requested, in her plumiest accent, a reservation for lunch. They'd heard that one before. Nuh.

Still not having had enough lake, or George, we took a ride plus commentary on a venerated steam boat, hoping we might at least be able to wave to him from the water. The one-hour tour had some shortcomings because the commentator spoke firstly in Italian and then English, which meant we'd steam past the point of interest before we knew what it was — including George's house. Another villa connected to George was the one used for shooting some movies he was in, including *Ocean's Eleven* and *Ocean's Twelve*. George-search aside, the boat we were on was a delight. Built in 1933 and restored just three years previously, the paddle steamer bore the unfortunate name *Concordia* (remember the Costa Concordia sinking?) but this one didn't sink and, as far as I could tell, it had a sober captain. It was unbelievably wide — to accommodate the paddle wheels. It looked pregnant, as though it would soon give birth to six small rowboats. And its steam-driven, deafening horn sounded like God blowing his nose. But the ride was unperturbed and stately — something I couldn't say for the rest of the fumy, shuddering ferries plying Lake Como.

Still more lake; this time by hydrofoil which huddled in the water before it got up and foiled. It followed that we had to descend to sit just above water level, where grubby windows hid most of the view, and we shared shudders with the ferocious diesel engine. Michelle remarked that it felt as though we had been eaten and were now in the belly of the beast.

Our destination, Bellagio, sat right on the point where the legs of the inverted Y of the lake separated. It was virtually compulsory to visit Bellagio if you were in Como. A big, stylish, lakeside town, it was especially steep once we left the wharf-level street. Stone steps led to more stone steps that seemed to have no end. Along the way, there were little shops selling useless but attractive made-in-Italy portable goods designed for heavy-breathing tourists. One enthusiastic retailer sized me up as a car nut and sprayed on my arm the just-released Maserati fragrance. I expected the seductive aroma of warm motor oil, leather, exhaust fumes and burning rubber. Instead, the smell was conventionally attractive and quite sexy, but I preferred my Jo Malone grapefruit. Following Michelle's Google Maps, we were able to locate a recommended restaurant high up in the stone walls that form the Harry Potter-style streets. I was inspired to order perch, because of our bird-territory position and the fact that the fish came out of the very lake we were travelling on. It was served as small fried fillets, along with some sliced roast potato and spinach. This was the best dish I'd tasted on the trip so far. I raved about it to the waiter who, it turned out, used to run a bottle shop in Sydney. I'd actually bought wine from him when I was first trying to convince Michelle's family that I was worth inviting to dinner. He'd travelled all over the world and he'd come back to Italy because that's where he believed he belonged, but he still rated Australia as the number one country in the world in which to live.

There was an irresistible force in Italy to gain weight. This was because the staple food was pasta and even when we were sick to death of it, it was hard to avoid because we adopted the habit of switching from spaghetti to macaroni to penne to pizza to calzone and returning along the same route. Apart from some brief diversions into seafood salad or fine dining, pasta dominated. Actually, it was not quite so fattening as I used to think because when I looked up its GI (glycemic index), it didn't even move the needle past the halfway mark.

One of my favourite dishes was calzone – but it could look daunting when it arrived on the plate. Although it was no more than a small pizza folded in half, it presented as being too much to consume in one sitting. There was a degree of mystery and excitement as I began at the easterly point of the pastry and worked my way towards the middle. After the crust came a quiet dawn of cheese, soon followed by a riot of rampant, runny cheese, ham, tomato and whatever else the chef had thrown in. By the time I'd arrived at the westerly extremity, with most of the calzone having disappeared through my portcullis, a gentle sunset crust was quite welcome.

Before we set out for Rome, we said goodbye to Como with a trip to the beach followed by an alfresco pasta dinner. The dinner was up to expectations, but the beach was a surprise. First, I didn't know Como had a beach. I'd only seen kids jumping off stone walls into the lake on our many ferry voyages, but when we went for a late afternoon walk in thirty-degree heat, there it was: sand, modest waves, people swimming and sunbaking. The only problem was, if more than ten people wanted to have a day at the beach it would have been overcrowded.

Following the miniaturisation principle, whoever designed the Smart Car also designed the beach and the hotel we moved into in Rome. With only five rooms shoehorned into a space that should have yielded no more than two, it was tucked away in a maze of cobbled streets in the delightful, historic part of the city not far from the Trevi Fountain.

The hotel reception was so small that when we opened the front door inwards, it took up most of the foyer. The receptionist, an attractive young woman who seemed to see the funny side of the place, was wedged into a corner behind an encircling wooden desk. The bedrooms were all up a long flight of stairs with a punishing gradient that made us wonder if we really needed what was in our suitcases. To her credit, the receptionist, only slightly built, came to the rescue. She and her colleague, also slightly built, took the risk of heart failure as, in tandem, they groaned their way up the stairs with our cases – based on the principle that dead guests don't pay but you can always get another receptionist.

If our hotel room in Como was small, this one was like looking down the wrong end of a telescope. That is, until we came to the skinny wardrobe that was so tall, I had to jump like a basketballer to hang up my clothes. There were no drawers, only a single shelf that was so high it could only be reached with a step ladder. The tap over the basin remained a mechanical mystery – maybe a masterpiece. It had a single handle and turned on and off a different way each time we used it. Its randomness also applied to the hot and cold function. We'd never get bored with that tap. Maybe to make the room look bigger, the bed was at floor level which also prevented the mattress from sagging. To get up in the morning, we had to get up to get up. This was no bed for people with weak thighs.

I was wrong about our hotel room being the work of the Smart Car designer. I came across the real one, Dr Confineo Shrinkiarie, and the car he designed after he'd finished our room. The Smart was quite large compared to Dr Shrinkiarie's electric two-seater. There were quite a few of them buzzing around Rome – yet another car-choked city that was looking for solutions. This one had room for two passengers side-by-side, with storage provided by a plastic box fixed high up at the rear. The Renault rival, where you had to rent the battery by the month, held two people, but one behind the other, and no storage apart from their laps. Clearly, these cars forced choices upon their owners that were foreign to us.

When Michelle booked our hotel room, the promotional photograph showed a big bank of cupboards, a small table and chairs, and tea and coffee making facilities — all which appeared to be part of our room. It wasn't. This was the shared space where guests assembled for breakfast, provided by the friendly girls who worked for the hotel. They struggled every morning trying to produce something that resembled breakfast — including toast, which was made off-site and arrived so flaccid we could have tied a knot in it.

We went window shopping, determined not to actually enter a shop. However, Michelle was overwhelmed by a spectacle frame shop and emerged considerably richer in frames and poorer in euros. I also unintentionally entered a menswear shop and emerged richer in jackets but only modestly poorer in euros when compared to Michelle's glasses. To recover from these unscheduled setbacks, we lined up at the leading gelato palace on the way to the Spanish Steps. There was a long queue stretching out from the gelato shop, semaphoring top gelato quality. We lined up, but once inside we beheld one of the wonders of the eating disorder world: the liquid chocolate wall. We'd seen chocolate fountains before, but never a whole wall, running at two billion calories per second into a trough and being recirculated. Being a chocoholic, that was a deeply stirring moment for me. However, I couldn't dwell on it for too long because once I was holding a cone-full of chocolate-drizzled gelato, I had to apply myself immediately to the task of eating it. I knew that authentic gelato melted very quickly and wanted to run down over my wrist before my tongue could get a good lick at it. I was reminded of an unspoken rule: never talk to a serious gelato consumer in the act of consumption. Concentration had to be absolute.

As a counter to bodily pleasures, we took a cultural tour of a palace – the 1000 room Palazzo Doria Panphilj – off Rome's via del Corsa. An audio player carried the voice of the current head of the family who owned it – along with massive other property assets. Listening to Prince Johnathan talk us through a huge collection of priceless paintings and sculptures, he sounded like a member of English aristocracy, but he was legally Italian. He had been sent to England for his education and to acquire a plummy accent. The family's history was as intriguing as its wealth. Johnathan was not from the family's bloodline at all, but was adopted as a baby from an English Catholic orphanage, along with a girl (turning her into an instant princess) and they now ran the family between them. Johnathan was single, had a male partner and they had two surrogate children who would no doubt take over the role as custodians of the estates in the future – although the ownership of the properties was now held in a government trust. They all lived within the palace in apartments upstairs, unfortunately not included in the tour.

We left our minuscule room on Sunday morning after another conflict with the staircase, to join thousands of confused, desperate people trying to make the best of gross overcrowding at Rome Airport as they waited in queues to get into other queues – which often turned out to be the wrong queues.

Our Singapore Airlines flight left at 11 am, after which we were served lunch but had to pretend it was dinner so we could then pretend it was night-time and obediently go to bed early in the afternoon. After a long period of pretend darkness, we had a pretend breakfast at about midnight, but it was really 6 o'clock in the morning. And exiting the aircraft didn't restore reality, because the interior of Changi Airport never changed, irrespective of the clock's opinion.

Because we were doing most of this trip on points, we had to take what tickets were available. This obliged an eighteen-hour stopover at Changi where we were able to book a block of hours at the Urgent Lovers' Airport Hotel which claims to be the only airport hotel in the world with a swimming pool. The plan was to sit by the sunny pool, swim and listen to the roar of jet engines. But this was hard to enjoy in the middle of a thunderstorm. Paying to lie in the rain was not good value. We changed plans and booked a free bus tour of Singapore along with a team of other disoriented travellers, most of whom wanted to sit in the bus and go to sleep. But our lively tour guide had other plans. She made us get off the bus to behold the water-spewing Singapore lion, the Bay Sands Hotel and a famous mosque that was unfortunately closed. By this time, the thunderstorm had gone elsewhere, and we would have used the pool, but we were trapped on the bus tour. When we finally made it back to the airport hotel, we were too tired to swim or lie by the pool. Because our body time was the middle of the night, we fell into bed, which we would pay for with insomnia later. I realised, of course, that these types of problems were well known to all overseas travellers, but I noted that they were much worse on the way home after we'd spent our money, seen or failed to see what we'd gone away for and were wearing part of an additional person around our waists.

CHAPTER 8

New York – 2017

Our eyes were bigger than our travel budget's stomach when we booked a trip via Hong Kong, New York, Orlando, Boston, Cuba and back to Sydney. But for me, the main reason for travel was to visit New York. I was actually going there under a court order, as you'll read below.

We were booked for a 10.05 am departure from Sydney aboard Cathay Pacific. The flight arrived late, owing to a suspected loose rear left-hand sprocket pin, and didn't depart until 11.20. However, this delay gave me an opportunity to spend time in the business class lounge where I observed that the 'free' WiFi didn't work, the toaster was inoperative owing to scheduled maintenance (de-crumbing, lubricating bearings, checking belt speed, adjusting angle of delivery), and the coffee machine was making self-determined cups of frothy white liquid because it had a full trunk of spent coffee grounds and was registering a protest.

Eventually, we boarded, not an A380 or a Dreamliner or

nostalgic old Jumbo, but an Airbus A330, a small-medium machine designed to pack 'em in. There was no first class on this aircraft. Business was the best on offer, earning the designation of *Fisness Class*. Across the cabin, there was one seat, an aisle, two seats, an aisle and one seat. In order to turn the solo seats into beds, they were angled at forty-five degrees to the fuselage, which gave the curious sensation of flying around an endless curve when you went to bed. Although I didn't try to convert my seat into a bed for the nine-hour Hong Kong leg, I suspected it would be suited to people with slender, triangular bodies, or perhaps those with one leg – when I took the diminishing little cave at the far end of the space into account.

Now to the story ...

I was at my tennis club a few weeks previously, having a late afternoon drink with other exhausted players, when the subject of travel came up. I had observed that when you have one foot in the grave you are expected to tourist-travel until you run out of money, are unable to walk, or can't escape from the nursing home.

Our after-game discussions solved the problems of the world every week. The tennis club members could run the country if only the country would let them. Into this boisterous, good-natured and noisy conversation I quietly announced that we were planning to travel. Ah, I had introduced a favourite subject. The volume of the babble rose. They all wanted to tell travellers' tales. Through the uproar, somebody asked me where we intended to go.

'New York,' I replied above the din. That spawned nods of approval. 'You see, I've never been to New York,' I added quietly.

The clubhouse immediately fell silent. Everybody was staring at me. The president, who was sitting at the next table, stood up.

'What did you say?' he snarled, ashen-faced.

'I said, I've never been to New York.'

'Lying bastard!' somebody called from the bar. 'Do you expect us to believe that you've never been to New York?'

'It's true,' I said, 'but I had a stopover in Los Angeles once. And I've been to Melbourne many times.'

'That's not New York!' the nimble-footed captain of the club yelled, and ran outside to shout at the players still on the courts. 'Fraser McEwing has never been to New York!'

The president, still standing, picked up a racquet and pointed it at me. 'Pack your bag and get out of here right now,' he warned through gritted teeth, 'before I beat you to death.'

After the tennis club episode, I decided to have a quiet Saturday night at home. I was in my tartan, flannelette pyjamas, fixing myself a Southern Comfort when powerful blows shook the front door. I opened it to find four policemen on my porch, two with pistols drawn.

'Are you Fraser McEwing?' the front one with the headlight-eyes asked.

'I am,' I said.

'Good, then I am arresting you.'

'What for?'

'I am surprised you don't know, sir. You are being charged with never having been to New York.'

'Are you taking me away with you?'

'Yes, sir, to a remand cell, immediately. Hold out your hands so I can cuff you.'

'But I'm in my pyjamas.'

'You should have thought of that before.'

I could feel my wife behind me. 'What's going on?' she cried.

'I'm being arrested.'

'I can see that, but what for?'

'For admitting I've never been to New York.'

She stepped back, her hand to her mouth. 'You idiot,' she hissed between her fingers, 'you *never* tell anybody that. It's a very serious offence.'

The hearing was over pretty quickly. I refused Her Majesty's offer of a barrister and threw myself on the mercy of the court. I thought about claiming that I had once been to New York but I didn't have a passport stamp, or travellers' cheque butts or a Big Apple t-shirt as proof. I could have had perjury added to my crime, so I decided to shut up and take my punishment.

The judge gave me five years, commuted to six months of community service in a travel agency on the proviso that I visited New York within one year and one day of the sentence.

That's why we were at Sydney Airport, about to travel *Fisness* class.

The Langham Hotel in Hong Kong, where we spent a night to recover from the first leg of the trip, was one of our favourite places. As soon as we walked into the foyer, it smelled familiar and right. There was a reason for that. The entire, worldwide Langham Group had a subtle ginger-based perfume that it pumped through the public area air-conditioning systems. The smell was powerfully evocative, able to recreate in the mind the experiences we'd had at previous whiffs. I didn't know whether other hotels used it, or would be even game to, because it could work against them. Recreating the memory of smelly backpacker lodgings would hardly be pleasant. In the Langham's case, it was all good. In fact, we could buy bottles of Langham room perfume and spray it around at home to evoke the Langham.

Returning to the airport the next afternoon, we got a cab driver suffering from multi-ticks. He kept flicking at the tired Toyota controls, placing his hand over his ear and continually counting a bundle of bank notes he had beside him on the seat. He was a haphazard driver as well, but managed to get it all together when it came to us paying the fare. He tried to charge us more than double the total showing on the meter and when I pointed this out, he stared at the meter as though he'd never seen it before. His stash of notes was no doubt proceeds from gullible passengers.

Again, our flight was delayed, this time by about an hour-and-a-half because of another suspected loose grommet pin on our Boeing 777 – a stretched aircraft with two whopper engines and first class at the pointy end. We again settled into business class with the same triangular cave as last time but we now had to inhabit it for fifteen hours. Actually, once I got used to it, helped by some sleep-inducing drugs, the burrow felt like home territory. Cathay food and service on this flight were highly recommendable.

I settled into reading a book about time by Paul Davies. He said that we have created our version of time collectively but, down at the personal level, we bend it again. We left Hong Kong at night in an evening rainstorm, ate dinner, watched a movie, took a sleeping pill, and woke up at the same time in the evening in New York. My watch was still on Hong Kong time, and correct, because it was exactly 12 hours ahead of New York, adding to the illusion that I had simply gone down a wormhole and had woken at the same time somewhere else.

Patrece and Steve, an American couple we'd met in Vietnam three years previously, had flown to New York to show us around. We all booked into the AKA Hotel near Central Park, a triumphant find by Michelle. Unlike the famous hotels that get all the publicity, the AKA was a keenly-priced establishment in the right location. After making friends with our room, which involved firming the bed with a clever device known as a sheet of three-ply under the mattress, we went walking with Patrece and Steve to get some bracing NY air. We walked up Fifth to Nelson Circle and back down 58th. Even at one in the morning, the place was busy. Horn-tooting was a right bestowed by the constitution on every American along with the right to bear arms. Tooting equated to doing something positive. Assault by sound was encouraged because it usually dispelled anger without killing anybody.

Even at night, the sheer scale and bulk of New York bore down on us. Because of wee-small-hour roadworks, the city was jammed with hardly-moving traffic on the few streets that were open. There was a similar situation when the president travelled through the city. The roads on his route were closed and an armada of helicopters scrambled for some showy security. Trump was known for liking this type of flashing-light travel, which allowed him to check out his gold-clad buildings from the safety of his limo.

We stopped along the way to eat a meal at a bar/diner called Red 58. It might have been breakfast or dinner, because it was one-thirty in the morning. By choosing appetiser-sized dishes, we were able to eat most of what was served. We had been warned about monster servings in the US.

I felt like the last carriage of a train being pulled along behind our two striding American friends as we began our first journey into the bowels of New York. Michelle had pre-purchased New York travel passes. All we had to do was go to an address in the city to pick them up, but that was not as easy as it sounded. It involved going to a shop where we had to wait in a huge queue to take delivery of a pass to get into another huge queue for the hop-on-hop-off bus. With no buses forthcoming and the queue growing backwards around the corner, we abandoned the wait for a hop and instead opted for a hoof to Carnegie Hall.

We were just in time for a tour of this famous landmark, now more than 120 years old and host to some of the best musicians the world has produced. With 2804 seats over four tiers, it was simply breathtaking. Our prison-officer-Russian-accented female guide claimed that Carnegie Hall — built by Andrew Carnegie and now owned by the City of New York — had the best acoustics of any building in the world. We planned to go to a concert there to test it, but I didn't doubt her claim. The space was enormous, open and curved — like being inside a giant Fabergé egg. The only sound-absorbing surface was the audience. The prison officer barked that the hall had been saved from demolition in the 1960s by violinist Isaac Stern, who put together a saviour deal the day before a developer had booked the wrecking ball. I imagined that Isaac would be a serious-faced, gaunt fiddler, but a picture of him in the hall museum showed him to be quite stout with jolly, laughing jowls.

The officer's delivery softened when she talked about Andrew Carnegie, a poor, wee Scottish lad who made good in America by getting into steel at the right time. He'd built libraries and public places all over the world, she said. A thoroughly good fellow indeed. I theorised that he may have sailed to Melbourne in the early days and built the suburb of Carnegie, near where I grew up, although upon reflection I doubted it. I think our suburb was named after Dale Carnegie who could win friends and influence people.

A bus in Columbus Circle took us on an uptown tour of this remarkable city – that appeared more like several little countries sharing a huge paddock where lots of people went to do lots of leisurely, lifestyle stuff. From my elevated, moving bus view of Central Park, its main features were its rock formations of schist – a word you must utter only when sober. And you no longer needed a black belt in karate to walk through Harlem.

Our friend, Steve, gave me lessons in tipping. Even though I'd read *Tipping for Dummies*, I still needed further tuition. Twenty per cent was the standard tip and, as Steve said, you tip everybody for everything. You tip every extended hand. You tip the man who hails you a cab, or opens a door, or even glances at you. If a hotel desk clerk coughs, you tip him. If a sales assistant in a department store breaks wind, you tip her.

Dining at The Carlyle invoked a tipping frenzy. I was almost broke before we sat down to a less-than-fine dining experience with entertainment from a gushing, young vocalist and an emotional, misunderstood accompanist. She sang standard talent quest songs – probably in celebration of having won a talent quest and now, almost retired at seventeen, was doing the clubs. Woody Allen played his passable jazz clarinet at this club but it was not his liquorice stick night.

I got into a bit of trouble at The Carlyle and would not be welcomed back – although we wouldn't be returning anyway. At the end of a staggeringly-expensive meal, I was well fuelled with martinis and suffering credit card anxiety. The crowd was either moving out or fawning over the forgettable singer when Michelle told me to sit on the vacant piano stool for a picture. Positioned on the small stage before a wine-stained Yamaha baby grand, she then suggested I play the piano – about the worst taste thing you can do after a show. Decency deserted me. I slipped into a bit of love stuff, whereupon the manager went berserk and pointed me to the door. I suppose I should have tipped him for throwing me out, but instead, I found myself in the street tipping the doorman who opened the cab door for us.

Easter had brought plenty of people into New York, even though Good Friday was not a public holiday and Easter Monday was begrudgingly given as a non-religious day off. We hadn't bargained for the crowds wanting to do everything we wanted to do.

A cruise around Manhattan Island would be nice, we thought, and so did half a million other people who booked out the ferry while we stood in the queue. Okay, we'd book for tomorrow and in the meantime, we'd look over a clapped-out, long-docked aircraft carrier called *Intrepid*, with decaying aircraft on the deck. So did another half million people. We gave that up too, but instead found the beginning of what is called the High Line, where we could walk through Chelsea and the Meatpacking District along an elevated, disused railway that had been converted into public space. It ran for nearly three miles and, notwithstanding crowd dodging, gave a unique view between buildings and down onto city roadways – rather like a dentist looking into somebody's mouth.

The walk finished at the famous Whitney Museum where there was an exhibition of contemporary American art. After another queue, but helped by our passes to cut in, we wandered around five levels of art meant to confront, outrage, insult and stimulate. This it certainly did, but I wouldn't want any of it hanging at home. One 'exhibit' invited viewers to don a virtual reality helmet and witness, with a Hebrew prayer being chanted in the background for some reason, a man in a city street being attacked and having his head bashed in, first with a baseball bat and then finished off with an iron bar. It was totally real and totally ghastly, with running blood and brains. I'll bet some of the viewers would have thrown up during the course of the day. No doubt, the pool of vomit would have been regarded as a piece of art not to be disturbed.

At this point, having walked about four miles, my legs were going numb, but that didn't stop us from marching on to the Chelsea Markets where the people who couldn't fit into other attractions had gathered. In order to rest, we sat at a bar and drank ginger beer – the best I'd ever tasted – and along with it, some bacon and maple popcorn.

A cab ride brought us to Broadway for dinner at Sardi's, where famous actors were supposed to hang out while waiting for casting calls. We looked around expecting to feel warmed and privileged in their presence but none seemed to be there that night. We had to make do with drawings of their familiar faces around the walls. The whole place felt steeped in theatrical history. That also went for my scallops, in this case steeped in green vegetable snippets and aged to suit the café. The joy of the dinner was not improved when I emptied a glass of Pinot Gris into Michelle's lap as I tried to liven up my boring story about Melbourne scallop fishing with a sweeping hand gesture. She took it well, I must say, but I still feared delayed consequences. Another sphincter-clenching, tip-heavy bill behind us and we were in the magical midst of Broadway, where Bette Midler was selling out with *Hello Dolly*, the *Phantom* was into its umpteenth production, and audiences were paying thousands of dollars each to see the latest musical, *Hamilton*.

Our friends had bought tickets for Tennessee Williams' *The Glass Menagerie* at the old Belasco Theatre. The four-person cast comprised Joe Mantello, Maddison Ferris, Finn Wittrock and Sally Field — who was an unexpectedly good live theatre actor. Our seats were in the front row of the upper circle where the stage view was cut in half by a brass railing and my body was suffering rampaging jet lag and leg disconnection. I missed much of the first half through irresistible bouts of sleep, continually interrupted by Michelle's elbow. But I recovered for the engaging second half. The set was quite sparse, with only a table and chairs, plus an open kitchen cabinet. The most spectacular moment came when it started to rain — on stage. Real raindrops pelted down and made puddles on the stage floor. The actors splashed about, probably relishing the disbelief of the audience.

We returned to the wharf on Saturday morning, waving our triumphant tickets for a two-and-a-half-hour cruise around Manhattan Island, joined by a capacity load of other voyagers.

Sitting outside so as not to miss anything, we sweltered in unexpected sunshine while the crowd boarded. But as soon as we pushed out into the Hudson River (more like a khaki-coloured estuary), it became brass monkey cold.

This cruise was the best way to condense a lot of New York viewing into a short time, helped by the best commentator I'd ever heard. The big moment, of course, was seeing the Statue of Liberty, all 150 feet of her plus base – remembering that we were in the US which was still on imperial measurements. She was made of very thin copper, aged with green patina. The statue had been a gift from the French people (not the French Government) in 1886 and arrived in 300 easy pieces which had to be assembled around a steel internal frame. The frame was designed by Gustave Eiffel who also planned a certain tall, temporary tower still waiting to be disassembled in Paris.

I'd seen pictures of the Statue of Liberty on many occasions but they didn't prepare me for the real thing. There was a lump in my throat when the commentator read out part of the sonnet written for the statue by Emma Lazarus: "Give me your tired, your poor, your huddled masses yearning to breathe free." The statue was majestically beautiful, her gold torch held high as a symbol of human ideals.

The tour took us under a great number of bridges, all of them famous for one reason or another, but the one that impressed me the most was Hellgate Bridge because it was an exact, although smaller, replica of our Sydney Harbour Bridge. I thought, the lousy yanks had copied our bridge – probably without asking – until I found out that Hellgate had been built in 1912. Oops. Looks like we did the copying. I hoped they wouldn't sue Sydney.

I discovered that the 1883-built Brooklyn Bridge had far more steel cables holding it up than needed; that finance was the biggest employer in New York; that many buildings in New York had water tanks, made of wood, on their roofs to regulate water pressure, and that New York used to be called New Amsterdam until the Brits conquered it during the War of Independence. We also saw the place where the jet ditched in the Hudson after Canadian geese flew into both its engines. Locals blame the Canadians for the geese. If the pilot — Chesley 'Sully' Sullenberger — had varied his approach pitch by even 4 cm, the plane would have broken up. He kept the undercarriage closed so that after landing, the plane floated for hours and made off on a downstream current because it thought it had turned into a boat. Besides all the passengers being saved, so was their luggage. It was genius flying.

Patrece and Steve had booked a matinee session of a recently arrived musical on Broadway called *Amelie*. Instead of seats up with the gods, this time we were in the stalls, second front row. With no orchestra pit, we looked up the players' nostrils and collected the occasional flying gob of saliva. The show was rompy, novel, surprising and colourful, but had no particular story — that I could uncover, anyway. Odd girl meets odd boy and they both do odd stuff aided by haphazard but vivid characters and a highly-active set that sloped downhill — so that you thought the stage was on an angle. It had no songs that were memorable — or even recallable. But we were at a Broadway show, goddammit.

One thing I'd noticed was that audience members in the stalls of Broadway live shows had an obligation to give every performance a standing ovation and shriek comments like 'Great! Yar! Whoop!' but they had no staying power for curtain calls, having exhausted themselves with all the hysterical spontaneity. In the case of *Amelie*, the star held up her hand for silence and did a sales pitch for an actors' charity before yelling, 'Have a great day!' and sending us forth to be charitable.

Having caught the Broadway bug, we went to the box office hole in the wall where you could shout at a dimly lit man behind bomb-proof glass and plead for last minute tickets to good shows. Michelle took on the task and came away with box tickets for the following afternoon's performance of *The Book of Mormon*.

We dined that night at Tavern on the Green, a famous sprawling restaurant in the middle of Central Park. Trying to avoid being weighed down by another load of meat or fish, I opted for a strange dish in which four modest half-figs sat on goats' cheese and prosciutto hidden beneath a mountain of rocket leaves. Michelle went for lamb and vegetables, a bit of a risk in a country not overrun with sheep. Well-lubricated by cocktails and wine, we set off for a walk through Central Park in the dark. In my head, I could hear Charles Ives' wonderful orchestral piece of the same name. I didn't fear a mugging because big Steve had been a college wrestler and Olympic water polo player, to say nothing of Michelle's ability to cast word spells.

While the title Russian Tea Room might sound lightweight, it wasn't. The story was that the original owner of this exotic Russian-style restaurant found that his eating house needed renovations but lost control of the budget, especially when it came to covering the walls with works of art. He created a US$38 million makeover of Russian nostalgia and went broke in the process. It reopened after four years of darkness. As often happens, the new owner picked it up for a fraction of its worth and now it had become a bucket-list stop.

Breakfast was a specialty. The chef provided me with two soft-boiled eggs that sat up straight in their cups with shells removed and wearing a generous bonnet of salmon roe. Inspired by this performance, I thought a pancake would be nice. For the first time, I experienced a monster serving that New York used to be famous for. Three thick dinner-plate-sized pancakes arrived with embedded chocolate chips and maple syrup on the side. I called in reserve mouths, but the pancake vanquished all of us.

The Book of Mormon was great fun. Grossly politically incorrect, it hilariously offended most principles of decency and would have put its producers in court even twenty years ago. But what a show! Dancing, singing, story, humour, sets: all superb. We left the theatre still laughing. The standout performance – in a cast of high-energy champions – had to be Brian Sears who played Elder Cunningham. He'd come from a two-year stint playing the role in London.

After a recovering long walk from *The Book of Mormon*, we again fitted the nosebags for a late dinner at the much-acclaimed Nobu Japanese restaurant – within a block of our hotel. Extra-large for a Japanese restaurant, the Nobu dishes were correspondingly extra-small, but the flavours were exquisite. So was the sake. In the midst of all this intake, I had a strange experience. At a nearby table, I saw a work colleague who had died thirty years ago. Obviously, it wasn't him, but an exact replica – like the Hellgate and Sydney Harbour bridges. I wanted to go over and ask him how he'd managed to get back above ground, but I would have found myself trying to explain my interest in him to the cops.

More food; this time, a New York food tour by Famous Fat Dave. To quote Dave, 'If you want to start a small, personalised business in this town, *famous* has to be in the title. Only then can you become actually famous.' Appetite build-up involved a 4 km walk to Washington Square Park that Steve estimated would only take twelve minutes. If we'd managed that, we were all headed for the next Olympics.

During our walk, we passed a piano showroom loaded with Steinways and other piano-exotica. In the window sat the most remarkable grand piano I'd ever seen. It was a special order, designed by Fazioli, the most expensive grand piano brand you could buy, costing about 20 % more than a Steinway – and made in Italy. There were arguments as to whether it sounded better, but this Fazioli certainly sounded pretty good when I played a few notes. I noticed it had a price tag, face down, hanging over the side. I turned it over: US$422,000. That would be more than half a million of our money, to which you'd probably have to add taxes - and tip the salesman, of course.

Going on a 4 pm food tour, for which we had been strongly advised to 'come hungry', caused a problem. An early breakfast, followed by fasting, would have been sensible. But we were not sensible. We didn't contemplate breakfast until we'd arrived at a famous deli called Zabars, which had a staggering variety of everything you could put in your mouth plus all the utensils needed to prepare it. Michelle, being an artful cook, ascended to gastronomic heaven. Moreover, looking at all this exotic food drove us crazy hungry. How could we wait for Fat Dave's arrival at 4 pm?

CHAPTER 8 New York – 2017

Zabars had a modest shop-sized restaurant next to the deli. Full of guilt, we slunk in there for a bagel. Eaters shared a long bench on high chairs, while there was a counter along one wall, with food and drinks stored along the back wall. Then, fronted by an anonymous door on the far-left-hand side of the shop, was a tiny room. When the door opened and a lady popped out, I realised it was a toilet. I imagined it was there to satisfy restaurant regulations, but in such close proximity to the food? I couldn't help thinking, 'In one end and out the other, all under one roof,' as people queued for their turn.

Famous Fat Dave turned out to be not famous, not fat, but definitely Dave. With tight rings of brown hair connected to a plush beard, Dave was loud, funny, and knew New York like a cabbie, probably because he had been one. He'd also been employed as a tour guide, pickle seller and bread truck driver. And was still only in his mid-thirties.

Dave swept around the corner to pick us up in a 1982 New York checker cab, no longer officially a cab – although some people still thought it was and climbed in uninvited and told him where they wanted to go. The four of us piled in and I was reminded how these old cars look wonderful, but the ride, rattles, wandering steering and hard seats all sucked. Dave loved this car and often patted it as you might an old family dog.

He explained that his tour was not about fine dining, but about casual, odd places that had extraordinary food. 'Please tell me if you want to eat more at any stop,' he announced, 'or if you want a drink.' With this kind of open invitation, we assumed that Dave's fixed price was comfortably above his costs.

First stop was Fernando's, a strange little restaurant in

Brooklyn where we were served delicious arancini (rice balls) and pasta. Owned by gravel-voiced Italian-Americans, it could have been a movie set in which members of the mob sat at the back and ate spaghetti while they planned their next heist. Closer to reality, Fernando's claimed to be the only place in the world to have a drink called Manhattan Special on tap. It comprised aerated sweet black coffee, 'soived cold', which might sound awful but everybody loved it. Later we found it was also available in bottles, but it lacked the subtlety of the draught version.

Next came another remote deli squeeze-in called Charlie's, in Bay Ridge. Charlie's round, stubbled face sat above a substantial set of chins and he constantly fired great one-liners. He gifted us his home-made mozzarella and Dave paid out for warm rolls with sliced prosciutto, oregano and sun-dried tomatoes. Then on to a Russian deli opposite a huge soviet-style development built by Donald Trump's father. This Brighton Beach neighbourhood comprised mostly unsmiling Russians, except for the one-armed deli proprietor who was chatty and engaging. Dave filled up containers with pickles and took us to Coney Island to munch on them while we sat looking at a cold sea and listened to the shrieks of riders having their insides rearranged by gravity-defying machines. To weigh down the pickles, Dave loaded in hotdogs with ketchup and mustard after which we struggled back to the checker. As a grand finale, we stopped at an odd-looking bar that served big, fat burgers doused in beef broth – rather in the manner of putting out a fire. They looked gruesome but tasted sort-of okay, maybe because we were all well past capacity and only eating to fulfil our contract and please Dave. On the way back to our hotel, Dave gilded the lily with a box of baklava which we could hardly look at, let alone eat.

We had a compulsory list of galleries and museums that failure to see would bring fines and floggings from those we had called upon for travel suggestions. With this in mind, we visited the Museum of Arts and Design on Columbus Circle. It traced, through clothing, the various social movements of the last sixty years. When denim became the rage, Levis ran a competition in 1973 for the most artistic treatments of denim jeans and jackets. It attracted 2000 entries and the results were quite startling. They were captured in a book by photographer Baron Wolman in 1974. The winner was Billy Shire, whose agenda included getting some publicity for his studding business. He liberally coated a denim jacket with his studs and finished it off with a working bicycle bell attached to the front. I thought it was the bell that swayed the judges. The display didn't reveal what first prize was, but a year's supply of LSD would have been appropriate.

We also flashed into the Museum of Natural History and were allowed to touch the biggest captured meteorite to hit the earth. There was also a promising big bang show in a massive sphere where we stood around looking into a dish while the voice of Liam Neeson boomed around the walls and told us how it all started. The whole show lasted four minutes, which didn't seem long enough to cover the history of the universe. Moreover, the pictures were blurry. This big bang was a big fizz.

Along Central Park South, in the Bartoux art gallery, a number of sculptures by Bruno Catalano caught my eye. In various sizes, they were realistic metal figures of people striding along carrying various types of cases, except that half of their bodies were missing – which was the artistic part, because it told us that when we journey, we leave part of ourselves behind. I fell in love with Wade, a black man one metre high. I asked the price. A mere US$38,500, and I'd better snap him up before somebody else did. I fell out of love with Wade.

Our friends, Patrece and Steve, departed for home in California, leaving us now trained to fend for ourselves in the Big Apple. A Central Park walking tour seemed like a good idea. For no reason that I could see, it started in the downtown where a small international gathering of park discoverers began their nature walk along crowded city streets. We lost five Italians to a fast-talking bicycle tour vendor but Maggie, our diminutive tour guide, was not daunted as she delivered her voluminous information, mostly walking backwards.

Central Park was not the biggest open public space in the five boroughs, but probably the most natural because the founding fathers couldn't afford to move the rocks. Nevertheless, it was still well-stocked with man-made pathways, lakes and fundraising features. You could have your name on a park bench. A paving tile would cost US$10,000 up front and US$1000 a year thereafter for upkeep to let people look down on you. In fact, New York was a put-your-name-on-it town. Donald Trump had his name emblazoned on some buildings he didn't own.

Maggie loved pointing out buildings where famous people lived. Jerry Seinfeld, she told us, walked through the park from his house to his office every day. And at one boundary, we stopped to look at the ornate Dakota building where John Lennon had lived and died. 'That foyer over there is where John was shot four times by Mark Chapman,' Maggie shouted above the traffic. Chapman, a serious nutter, then went back to nonchalantly reading *Catcher in the Rye* while they threw the dying Lennon into a car and raced to hospital. Yoko still lived in the forty-room apartment, curtains drawn. In the park, where we were, there was a memorial section called *Strawberry Fields* featuring a paved ceramic circle around the word *Imagine*. Initially, the gardeners put in a plot of strawberries but the park rats, not appreciative of music or John Lennon's place in history, ate all the strawberries the night they were planted.

Central Park was often used in movies or TV series, like *Law and Order SVU*. I was reminded of the comments by the ferry spruiker that there were only three bushes left in Central Park that had not yielded up a crime drama corpse. Sections of the park, along with many other parts of the city, were often closed off in order to shoot movies, the hiring charges being a substantial contributor to the city's income.

If you had enabling legs, lubricated joints and comfortable shoes, New York was a walking town, especially if you were a first-time visitor and didn't mind being buffeted. Subway travel was like trying to escape from a hostile country via an illegal tunnel.

We took a long walk to Lincoln Center where the artistically intelligent went for cultural nourishment in music (New York Philharmonic), dance and opera. We did a tour led by Jim, a tall, thin man with a Luna Park smile and a great knowledge of the performing arts. He took us to a NY Phil rehearsal where they were bumping their way through a recently written piano concerto which did not tempt me to return for the performance. Then a look at the opera theatre and a Wagner's *Flying Dutchman* rehearsal, which looked marvellous. There were many theatres in the center, flanked by the famous Juilliard School for outstanding students of the performing arts. While at the school, the students were housed in a residential tower in an adjacent building, sure to be a hotbed of frowned-upon youthful activities.

We took the stifling, illegal tunnel to the World Trade Center Memorial — something on everybody's must-see list. I was moved by the grand sadness of the place, the two square pools that seem to flow into bottomless pits, forming the ghostly footprint of the buildings that had stood there. I tried to imagine where the two planes came from when they hit the towers.

The vast 9/11 Memorial Museum thoroughly documented and exhibited, almost to the point of absurdity, everything to do with the attack. I was reminded that terrorists had tried to bring down one of the towers in 1993 by bombing the underground carpark. At that stage, a second attack seemed highly improbable. There was also a reference to Philippe Petit, a French tightrope walker whose support team snuck into the towers at dawn just before they were completed in 1974. They strung a wire between the two massive buildings and Petit spent forty-five minutes walking back and forth, at one stage lying on the cable while early morning New Yorkers gazed upwards, pointing in disbelief.

Another have-to-or-you'll-be-ridiculed place to visit was the Empire State Building. But if we'd gone up to its viewing platform, we couldn't have seen the building itself because we would have been in it. Much better to go up to floor sixty-five in the nearby Rockefeller Center, drink a cocktail and, if we wanted to burn some serious cash, eat. This we did, both ordering a seafood salad, which sounded kind of sufficient until it arrived, crouching barely there at the bottom of a dish brought to us by a waitress from Sydney. That grizzle aside, the view from the bar was spectacular and so was the Mama Rose cocktails we downed. Not only was the Empire State Building staring us in the face but on the other side we could see Central Park laid out like a dark green mat surrounded by cubes and spires of buildings.

The evening brought a symphony concert in Carnegie Hall. British conductor, Sir Roger Norrington, not only conducted the orchestra but, seated in a revolving chair, gave a classically educated gentleman's account of the forthcoming Mozart works.

The Radio City Music Hall turned out to be one of the most attractive places we visited in New York. As we were rushing past on a headlong, unspecified shopping expedition, we noticed that a tour was about to start, so we lined up with the peloton and went in. This art deco masterpiece held 6000 people and, because of its balloon-like design, there wasn't a bad seat in the house. Built in 1932, it immediately became the biggest live theatre in the world. It still ranked in the top three. Like Carnegie Hall, all the greats had performed there. It went broke and closed in the 1960s, but was saved from demolition by popular uproar, was totally restored, and is now an untouchable heritage-listed building owned by the city.

What made the Radio City Music Hall so special was its original art deco style — either faithfully restored or carefully preserved. The stage was one of the biggest in the world and it was worked by a powerful hydraulic system that could lift, lower, and rotate almost anything on earth.

The building was designed by architect Edward Durell Stone and the interior by Donald Deskey. Everything about it was huge.

You could almost fly a plane around the foyer, while beneath it, in the patron's lounge, stood a giant female aluminium nude surrounded by deco columns in black glass, and special carpet with a triangular pattern that was designed to encourage people to murmur rather than shout. The men's lounge (you wouldn't dare call it a bathroom) was also an art deco masterpiece; so much so that I felt I'd disrespected a priceless work of art when I used it.

In one of the many casual lounge areas, a glass case held a big, open book where famous visitors had signed their names. In the lower right-hand corner, there was the signature of Liberace, finished off with a little ink drawing of a piano – in case we forgot what instrument he played. After a short historical film, we were joined by a real live Rockette. Radio City Music Hall was the home of this famous dance troupe, known for their leaping about in ultra-unison. I thought an old bird would arrive by wheelchair and cackle about how she used to be a showgirl in 1938. But, no. In walked a twenty-two-year-old dancer, all white teeth and long limbs, done up in a high-kick outfit. After a predictably perfect spiel she recognised me and begged to have our picture taken to hang in her dressing room. 'Aw, okay,' I said. I took a copy just in case she used it for publicity without my permission.

Away from entertainment for the common man, we went off to the ballet at Lincoln Center in the evening. Michelle, who knew far more about ballet than I did, gave it a thumbs up, but remarked that the Australian Ballet ranked well against the New York leapers. We were treated to two short ballets and one major work: *Symphony in C* using music by George Bizet. Without scenery or story, the dancing was exposed and it came off well. The orchestra was supportive rather than assertive with an oboe solo in the second movement that was nothing short of enchanting.

New York sped everything up. People walked fast, talked at chipmunk speed and passed money around as though it was too hot to hold. We were partly to blame, of course, because we were trying to fit it all in before the world blew up or we had to get in line at the heavenly gate.

We had breakfast one morning at Sadelle's, a restaurant with a reputation for fish and more fish. This was also our first attempt at using Uber. We called one, but gave the wrong address. While we were trying to set that right, we accidentally called another one but he was getting lost when three empty taxis came past and we decided to take one of those instead. As we reached for the door handle, we felt guilty about the poor Uber men and let the taxi go. The closest Uber, or maybe the one we may have cancelled, but maybe not, took a wrong turn and did a huge loop of the city before finally picking us up.

Sadelle's was busy dealing with a Saturday morning rush of people desperate for fish. A well-rehearsed waiter brought a menu which could have sent us bankrupt if we'd chosen the most expensive caviar and most expensive vodka. They ran into thousands of dollars. However, we settled for a manageably priced but substantial serving of trout caviar with various bases on which to spread it. We'd never eaten caviar up to pussy's bow before, but we did this time. Although it was delicious, I was cured of caviar for some time to come.

Being fans of *Law & Order SVU*, we wanted to visit the famous courthouse building where the forces for good were lampooned by the media and others for stuffing up. I wanted to stand on those grand steps and pretend myself into an episode. In the flesh, or I should say in the masonry, the place was not all that grand. It was smaller than it should have been, the steps were chipped and stained and the main doorway was shabby. I came away disappointed with this supposed shrine of dignified courtrooms, cranky judges, unbelievably fluent attorneys and conniving crooks.

Macy's department store came next, with a walking tour inside and out. It was absorbing, assisted by an excellent tour guide who could breathe in while talking so as not to interrupt her machine-gun delivery.

Money was flying on every floor. But this was not because of a clearance promotion, nor was it an especially hectic day. Macy's, with 2.2 million square feet of floor space on Fifth Avenue and 34th Street, was the biggest department store in the US and the second biggest in the world. On this un-special day, it was vacuuming in customers at a rate Australian department stores would have killed for.

Granted, there were eight million customers within easy visiting distance of Macy's as against our Australian trickle, but there was more to it than that. For instance, Macy's ran an annual Thanksgiving Day parade that closed off New York streets and attracted four million people to line the route, and millions more who found it compulsive television viewing. Then there was the annual spring flower show that saw half a million flowers brought into the store, giving its customers blooms to see from all over the world in a specular two-week exhibition that attracted 25 million visitors.

The most cherished brand at Macy's was Louis Vuitton — behind it, a remarkable company. It controlled a massive number of leading brands in addition to its own, including Celine, Marc Jacobs, Kenzo, Givenchy, Veuve Clicquot, Nicholas Kirkwood, Fresh Cosmetics, Guerlain, TAG Heuer, Bulgari and Christian Dior perfume. The list went on and on, topping out at about seventy. Between them, they turned over more than US$38 billion a year. The Louis Vuitton brand alone was valued at US$26 billion.

I was shocked to learn that 99 % of goods sold throughout the world under the Louis Vuitton label were counterfeit. The genuine articles were sold only in its own stores or concessions such as those in Macy's. Even then, the company placed a serial number on every item so that it could be proved genuine. Another of its policies was to destroy all raw materials in all of its factories at the end of each production day to prevent illegal overruns.

Down the street from Macy's, was a famous fabric shop called Mood. Many people went there to buy a few exotic yards and to pat the famous dog who went by the name of Swatch. Michelle had the idea that I should buy some fabric to be made into shirts in Hong Kong on the way home. I did not intend to do this, but my love of textiles got hold of me and I emerged with five outrageous patterns that were destined to make me a marked man in Sydney.

Finally, we braved Grand Central Station, a huge art deco cavern that seemed too splendid for a train station. Much of what went on there was not railway business. Several wedding parties were posing for photos and lots of other people, like us, simply stood and stared – without any thought of transportation. The place was also crammed with shops, along with the famous Old Oyster Bar where they might have been selling old oysters that John West had rejected. What was most odd about Grand Central Station was its dull lighting, giving the impression of continual dusk, no matter what time of the day it was.

Russ & Daughters provided breakfast at a café known for variations on the themes of herring, salmon and bagels. But *foist da pickles*. I was told they were prepared with salt rather than vinegar and seemed to find their way into every dish served in New York. After the pickle prelude came the restaurant's signature herring plate in which five different versions of this fish urged us forward. I passed pussy's bow and, like the caviar experience previously, wouldn't be able to look at a herring for some time. Russ and his lovely daughters, who may have been working there but did not identify themselves, then finished me off with my first taste, not to be the last, of halva ice-cream.

We needed to escape herrings and come down to earth, achieved with a tour of the nearby tenement district which became the first place immigrants went when they landed in New York in the late 1880s and early 1900s. These five-storey tenement buildings would each accommodate twenty or more families, living in three-room apartments. The families often had more than four kids. After 1905, the landlord had to provide inside toilets, one toilet per every two families. They washed in water lugged from a communal tap at the rear of the building. The tour took us into a couple of the apartments as they had been more than one hundred years ago – along with the history of the people who had lived there. The area became so popular that, at one stage, it was estimated to be the most densely populated place in the world. This was also the beginning of the garment industry in New York. Not only did families live in these tiny spaces, they ran sewing factories in them as well.

Katz's Deli was famous in New York for pastrami. Although it was born as a deli, it grew into a sizeable restaurant and, on that early Sunday evening, was awash with diners. You more or less had to order pastrami on rye if you wanted to boast that you'd been there. We both did, and were hit will the full force of the famous, gross serving sizes of New York. A quarter-sized serving each would have been plenty but pussy's bow was again violated when we battled to the halfway mark. Like the caviar and herring episodes, I would probably not order pastrami again for a long time – delicious as it was from the kitchen of Mr Katz.

On our way into the deli/restaurant, we encountered a tall, black man holding forth about being hungry and Michelle decided to test him on the way out with half our pastrami which we'd had doggy-bagged. We paid, went outside ready to hand it over, but the man had gone. I schlepped the food down into the subway, to take a train to 57th Street. Michelle spied a homeless man sitting against a rubbish tin and decided he needed to be fed with pastrami. I thought he might tell us to bugger off when we offered the bag, but he took it gratefully and we left him munching into Katz's signature dish.

New York loved metal plates that gave access to an underground network of drains, sewers, steam-making devices, and maybe a whole community of white alligators, to say nothing of Ninja Turtles. The pavements and roadways were alive with these steel plates, many of them open mesh, affording a view into New York's digestive system. Still on the steel theme, all the concrete curbs in New York were finished with a protective steel cap so that if you ground your wheel rims against them with low profile tyres, you'd probably need new wheels.

CHAPTER 9

Orlando, Cuba and Boston – 2017

While we escaped New York without being mugged, intimidated, or seriously ripped off, the parting at La Guardia was not so satisfying. The airport was being rebuilt and had been turned into a massive building site. We'd booked first class tickets to Orlando, thinking we would wait in an elegant lounge and load up on free drinks and food. Not so. First class domestic Delta gave us no access to the first-class lounge unless we had 'joined' for US$80 or were travelling on an international flight. This depressing information was relayed by a laconic check-in girl who couldn't be bothered looking at us but preferred to speak to our luggage.

We found ourselves in a dingy concourse offering greasy food, tipping for no service – it was all electronic ordering – bored staff, and dim lighting. When I ordered a sandwich, I was given a metal fork and spoon, but a plastic knife. Airport security had determined we could kill somebody with a blunt, round-ended metal steak knife but not a metal fork or a spoon. Put into life or death struggle I'd have chosen the fork every time.

The electronic food-ordering system came with a screen sitting in the middle of the table. It offered fast food at close to fine-dining prices. It also enabled us to play gambling games in case we had any money left after the meal. The bill strongly petitioned patrons for an 18 % tip. Fearing an international incident, I paid the tip but Michelle didn't — to protest against the non-existence of service. My chicken arrived promptly but her burger took the scenic route, indicating a silent rebuke from the kitchen.

Delta slipped further down my list of favourite airlines after changing the departure gate without telling us and employing the least-interested cabin crew. One portly steward sat on his seat asleep for much of the two-and-a-half-hour flight.

The young driver who picked us up from Orlando Airport to take us to Cape Canaveral asked if we had alligators in Australia. We told her about our fearsome crocodiles but she trumped that with a story about Mary Thorn, a Florida woman who had a six-foot, fifteen-year-old pet alligator called Rambo. He slept in her bed, went out with her on her motorbike, played with her dog, watched television and was toilet trained. She dressed up Rambo, including sunglasses, to protect him from the elements and slathered sunscreen on him because she feared he might get sunburned. The authorities tried to take the alligator away from Mary, but she fought against them, saying that Rambo could not survive in the wild. They gave her a special permit to keep him, probably on the condition that Rambo didn't eat anybody, but they discouraged other people from keeping alligators as pets. If they wanted to get up close and personal with alligators, there were plenty in the wild in the waterways throughout Florida. We were assured that while they would feast on small children or dogs, they were afraid of adults.

When we opened the door of our room at the Radisson Hotel in Cape Canaveral, Michelle was aghast for having booked it. I didn't think it was so bad, although admittedly it was odd. The fittings were flimsy, the shower was over the bath and behind the ubiquitous cloying curtain. The wardrobe door had gone rusty, but the bed was the saving grace. It was huge and was fitted with a motorised hardener. I didn't know whether that also applied to the male occupants. I hoped so.

The NASA Kennedy Space Center was a remarkable place in that it was a working facility for building rockets and firing them while being an efficient theme park for people to come for a look. Rocket firings were relatively frequent, especially since private enterprise had taken to using the range for commercial space shots. The latest status symbol of extreme wealth was not just to have your own aeroplane, but your own rocket.

I could hardly believe the size of the Apollo rockets that did most of the moon shots. They were built in the biggest single-storey building in the world and emerged on a 'crawler' that took them to a launch pad at a dizzy one mile per hour along a road laid with a special base.

The shuttle program, which finished in 2011, was based on reusing the shuttle plane and the two separate rocket engines that took it into space. The only part discarded was the fuel tank. When the shuttle returned, it had to glide in at a hot 285 mph, the fastest landing speed for a plane ever. Possibly the most exhilarating presentation of the entire center was standing in a theatre showing the designing and building of the space shuttle, and then finding that the screen was transparent as it raised to reveal *Atlantis*, the real thing, suspended in a huge room, its cargo door open, displaying the burn scars on its body from re-entering the earth's atmosphere on its last mission.

Orlando was well known for its shopping, especially direct factory outlet stores. We were keen to unload money to this worthy cause but first we had to check into the Hyatt Hotel. Our Filipina Uber driver had trouble in actually being able to get to the hotel although we could see it from the road. The reason was that this Hyatt, along with some other hotels, was marooned in the middle of massive roadworks so that we had to take tricky detours to make landfall. When we eventually did, I thought about my plans to drive a Mustang to Miami. The turnpike would be fine but I feared we might never get out of the hotel building site. I grew chicken wings, flapped them, and decided on Uber rather than a self-drive Mustang.

Michelle had, by this time, mastered the art of American Uber. The cars were cared for, sanely-driven and the drivers were friendly and chatty. The Filipina lady who drove us from Cape Canaveral to Orlando provided us with a monologue covering her family history, her friends, what she said to her husband, what her husband said to her, what she nearly said to her husband but didn't, and what her husband said to her but shouldn't have. She talked non-stop for an hour. We'd booked her for the four-hour drive to Miami. After that, her autobiography would be complete.

Having unpacked, we hightailed it down to the Premium

Outlet Mall, credit cards quivering with fear. I didn't intend to buy anything, but that all went off the rails. I ended up with shirts I didn't need with shorts to match and shoes that I needed even less. I soon had a needless bagful while Michelle couldn't find anything desirable except a pair of sandals. While we were in Saks Fifth Avenue, I spied a sparkler on 'extra special' and bought it for her. My credit card went into cardiac arrest.

The mall was actually a large number of crisscrossing open walkways with shops lined up like parading soldiers either side. They covered most brands familiar to me plus a whole lot more we didn't have in Australia. About the only items of clothing I really needed were white tennis shorts. When I asked for them in the brand shops, the sales people thought I was crazy.

'You really mean white, sir? You want to play tennis in white? Hey, dis guy wants white tennis shorts! Never hoid of nuttin' like that. The closest we got to white, sir, is black.'

I persevered. The Nike welcoming man said his store definitely didn't have white tennis shorts, but to his astonishment, Michelle found some. They were made from a new, miracle fabric that played most of the game for you and carried you back to the clubhouse.

While we were trawling the designer shops, we came across a kiosk selling tickets to the Universal Studios theme parks (high on our have-to list) at a saving of US$140. There was a condition. We had to pick up the tickets at a resort hotel after sitting through a travel club presentation that would only take an hour. We would be given breakfast as well. Beside the saving, the travel club sounded interesting. We signed up.

Next morning, we turned up at the resort hotel and were

fastened onto by the most aggressive selling team I'd ever experienced. 'Breakfast' comprised a choice of an apple, banana, watery coffee or cereal and we were asked to hurry along because the presentation was about to start. This took place in a little side building where a guy who could double for Usain Bolt went through an alternatively shouting and whispering harangue with the aid of a big screen showing idyllic holiday destinations. If we joined at a cost of US$9900, we would get eight weeks of cheap holidays a year. When we blanched at that, the price dropped to US$7000 if we signed up today, followed by a specially tailored offer — because we were nice Australians — of US$4000. I did not have US$4000 with me, I said, nor is my credit card ready for such an assault, especially after the sparkler. It had to keep us eating for the next three weeks, I added. They were not interested in our possible starvation. 'Okay, okay, tell you what, gimme US$300 to cover the registration paperwork and I'll hold the deal until you get back home and wire us the money.'

We sprinted for the exit, after three hours of verbal defence, and went to pick up our Universal tickets. The previously jovial officials were now icy-faced as they handed them to us.

Universal was a mammoth money vacuum. Not only did it charge over US$200 per person to get in but the minute we were admitted, we were bombarded with other categories of wealth-reduction in the form of food, drinks and merchandise. The rides were free, but even on a moderately busy day, the queues were daunting.

The standouts were the Harry Potter villages. The whole fantasy film set, including crooked buildings, had been recreated as Diagon Alley. If you wanted more Harry Potter you had to take the Hogwarts Express from platform nine-and-three-quarters. The destination, Hogsmeade, was another fantasy in the form of a snow-coated village with the Hogwarts school perched high above on a rock-face and charging another lot of admission.

The train trip was very clever. A realistic steam train arrived at the station, people got in and sat on old-world, hard train seats. The window looked out on to the brick wall of the station, the train blew its whistle and moved off. The trick was that the window was actually a glass movie screen and the passing scenery a projection. We appeared to be going through a magic countryside to Hogwarts School of Witchcraft and Wizardry. Hagrid was out there on his flying motorbike, waving. We passed rivers and forests until the school came into view and we pulled into the station. But in reality, we'd only travelled a few hundred meters.

Another great illusion was the dragon that had landed on top of Gringotts Wizarding Bank. Every so often it roared and breathed out a fireball that drew cries of appreciation from the crowd. Confectionery shops sold all kinds of Harry Potter lollies. I bought a block of Harry's coconut ice and couldn't stop eating it, even though I felt sick halfway through. I washed it down with butter beer and felt even worse.

Michelle went into the wand shop and was confused by the variety. After some help from a serious-faced wand consultant, she selected one for her mother in the hope that she might be able to manifest gold bullion, since we had been unable to achieve it by conventional means.

Hotel Toaster Report

Based on the Hyatt's free breakfast, this was the first time I'd had the opportunity to review a hotel toaster. I was delighted to find a Double Black Mariah, a rare model covered in Derek Breadchamber's famous trilogy on the subject. Derek reminded us that the Double Black Mariah was developed by master Italian hotel toaster designer, Giuseppe Crispintini, who was inspired by two passing hearses in 1998. The DBM was unique in that, in addition to neat front-load and delivery, it had no knobs. The user could not influence heat or belt speed. 'Automatico!' Crispintini had declared as he presented his prototype to loud applause at the company's 1999 marketing conference.

Michelle was keen to visit the Morse Museum which took us to the suburb of Winter Park. Even if there had been no museum, the main street was worth the visit. It was like a movie set, with an idyllic, American tree-lined, brick-paved roadway. I expected to hear 'and . . . action!' whereupon a brass band would come honking around the corner and children would cheer while they ate Shoofly Pie and Apple Pan Dowdy as they watched. The shops were all pristine and quaint. They also had clothing that lit up Michelle's face and she gave her credit card an outing.

The Morse Museum was devoted to the work of Louis Comfort Tiffany (1848–1933) who didn't only design glass lampshades, but was an architect, interior designer, jewellery maker, painter and potter. Although he was best known for his lampshades, his stained-glass windows were spectacular. There was a whole chapel reassembled at the museum after it had been shown at the 1893 World's Columbian Exhibition in Chicago. He produced so many outstanding works of art that I couldn't see how he had time to eat or go to bed. His father was super rich – which gave him a good education and the ability to indulge himself in artistic pursuits. He also designed and built some huge, wonderfully decorated houses.

We arrived at the museum about 11 o'clock in the morning and were advised not to pay the five-dollar entry fee because the museum was free after 4 pm. Instead, we were invited to see a museum-sponsored film about the contribution made by female artists in the eighteenth century. We entered a large, well-appointed room stocked with senior citizens hoeing into free buns and drinks. We joined them, of course, and then settled down to watch the documentary. It was enthusiastically presented by a fraffly, emphatic English woman who outlined the lives of female painters and designers who'd fought the blokes for a go at becoming famous. No doubt riveting viewing for a worthy audience, I kept nodding off, dreaming about overdressed women and being prodded awake by Michelle.

Back in the movie set street, we shopped, ate and returned to the Morse at 4 o'clock. I'm generally not a lover of museums, but this one was a standout. Tiffany was revealed as an extraordinary man, prompting further study.

Going on an enthusiastic recommendation from a friend, we spent a day to Epcot, a Disney theme park supposedly for adults interested in science, technology and the environment. In reality, it was for adults interested in eating, buying Mickey Mouse merchandise, trying to control unruly kids and pretending to be interested in science, technology and the environment. That said, there were some outstanding presentations.

One called *Soarin'* promised a flit around the world from the sky in ten minutes. Michelle read the motion warning sign and feared she would be lifted up in a sling and dropped on her head. Reluctantly, she joined me in our seat on a multi-person chairlift and buckled in. After some dramatic counting down, the chair lifted and propelled us into the middle of a giant dish screen where we flew above, and close to, many of the wonders of the world — all in staggering realism, even down to the smells of the places we passed over. The Taj Mahal smelled of roses — which was not how I remembered India smelling. However, the ocean and the African plain aromas were much more accurate. We were so taken with this ride that we lined up for a second go.

Epcot was not a place that offered gravity-defying rides for their own sake. There had to be conspicuous technology thrown in. *Test Track* promised this, although Michelle was dismayed by the shrieks coming from inside the massive building and sent me in alone. The idea was that you designed your own hot car and then it was assessed on a track test. For stage one, I stood in front of a computer screen and drew my car with a clumsy curser so that it came out looking like a toad on wheels. This meant that it wouldn't take the powerful engine I had intended, nor was it aerodynamically efficient, nor would it handle very well. Its main benefit was that it would be economical to putter around the city. Hardly a racing car. I tried to redesign it but only succeeded in making it uglier and giving it smaller wheels. Time ran out. A toad it would have to remain. It was then entered in a competition with all the other designers — where it came a resounding last, accompanied by some very unkind comments.

Time to get out on the Chevrolet test track in a car that held nine people in three rows, all well buckled-in. It went through various scary manoeuvres in braking, cornering and accident avoidance until the high-speed section, introduced by hurtling in darkness towards double doors that opened just in time. I estimated that we then set off at around 200 km/h on a ridiculous track with turns that could only be negotiated by tilting the car ninety degrees. That had produced all the shrieking – but not from me. I was clinging on, white-knuckled and unable to breathe, let alone shriek.

By contrast, a wholesome boat ride explained how science was working on better ways of producing food to feed Earth's growing population. I think it would have been better to run a boat trip on birth control and forget about having to grow tomatoes vertically or farming fish whose poo fertilised lettuces for the fish to eat.

The Disney & Pixar Short Film Festival was billed as being in 4D. The 3D was achieved with the usual glasses, but the fourth came from the theatre seats which lurched every so often in sync with the stunning animation movies.

Many of the other attractions looked promising, but were inconsequential once we came to terms with them, to say nothing of having to deal with rampaging bullet-headed kids.

Apart from patchy technology, Epcot was an exhibition of the architecture, culture and food styles from ten countries. They were placed around the perimeter of a sizeable lake, dotted by pyrotechnic barges that were being primed for the regular evening show of fireworks. Having walked, ridden and marvelled for most of the day, we decided to stay and eat in one of the simulated countries. Any plans we'd had to try out unusual, but distant fare was dashed when we came upon China and fell exhausted into the first restaurant we found there. We expected a re-heated, prepared-the-day-before meal. How could a Chinese restaurant in the middle of a theme park be any good? When the food arrived, it turned out to be one of the best Chinese meals I'd ever eaten – and washed down by a perfect beer called Buddha Light. I gladly paid the suggested tip of 20 % to the attentive Chinese waiter who, upon seeing it, immediately included us in his family.

Speaking of kids, our hotel had been playing host to a class of final-year high school students on a school break. The boys were accommodated on the second floor and the girls on the third. It was the job of four teachers to keep these hormone-charged, beautiful young people from getting up to immoral and filthy acts during the night. The solution? At 10 pm, the students were told to go to their rooms and a piece of tape was signed and stuck between the closed door and its frame. If the door was opened before seven in the morning, the tape would be broken and an enquiry would follow – and no doubt find its way onto social media.

The Bible says (Acts): "It is hard for thee to kick against the pricks." That's how you feel when you set out to visit Cuba. There are pricks everywhere but if you don't kick against them, you don't get to Cuba.

We encountered the first pricks at Miami Airport where people spoke mostly Spanish and clearly didn't want us to check in for a flight to Cuba. It was compulsory to master an electronic check-in touch screen that asked a dozen questions. If we got one wrong, we had to start again. The prize for getting through that, was a charge of US$30 per bag which, in our case, added up to US$90 because we'd managed to fill a third suitcase with stuff we didn't need and may not even like when we arrived home. We then had to weigh our own bags and if any were over twenty-three kilos, we were fined again. There were many scenes of pathos as couples crawled around the floor with bags open, their possessions on display, as they tried to make the heavy bag lighter and the light bag heavier.

Then there was the compulsory Cuban visa which we had to purchase from a lectern placed strategically in the slow-moving queue. When we reached it, a severe woman with pursed lips seemed to resent us disturbing her day, conveyed with tuts and sighs as she dispensed four forms to fill in. The cost of a visa was US$100, but if we lost one of the pieces of paper, we would be fined another US$100 and would be sent to the naughty corner. I wondered how many people had gone bankrupt trying to check in for Cuba.

There were more pricks at the arrival end, where bored officials clearly wished we wouldn't interrupt them as they bantered between themselves. The airport was straight out of the 1950s, quaint to look at but chaotic in operation. There were not nearly enough luggage trolleys, obliging me to stand by a little Alice in Wonderland magic curtain waiting for one of the pricks to push an abandoned and retrieved one through. There were continual battles as people fought for trolleys.

Outside, a long queue waited to change good money into bad

— in the sense that Cuba's CUC currency was not recognised outside Cuba. That done, we climbed into a beaten-up taxi-van and were driven shudderingly — because the driver insisted on driving slowly in top gear — into town, but became lost trying to find our famous hotel. We ended up meandering up and down very skinny, very old, Spanish-style streets, stopping frequently to ask the way. When we did find the Raquel Hotel, I was required to help unload the cases in the rain because the rear door piston of the taxi-van had failed and I had to hold it up. The grim-faced driver then charged us for the privilege of witnessing him, a seasoned local, get lost and me getting denched.

The hotel, planted on a tight little corner, turned out to be unexpectedly beautiful. Outside, it was very fancy Italianate, complete with statues and other mouldings, while inside was soaring art nouveau. I assumed it has been restored, because the paintwork, stained glass and stonework were all perfect. We fronted the reception desk and came up against the same prickery as at the airport. Can you give us a map of old Havana please? 'No.' Is there internet available? 'No. Try the hotel down the road, but you'll have to pay.' We had booked a room with a double bed and the room we had been given had two singles. 'That's all there is. If you don't like it, find somewhere else to stay.' We stayed, especially because we'd prepaid.

The hotel had been built in 1908 as a warehouse, then later used as commercial offices, then turned into a school and more recently a hotel. Evidently, it was in the middle of the now-defunct Jewish quarter, which explained its display of Jewish symbols and a mezuzah on every doorway.

The internet and WiFi service in Cuba was about where Australia was twenty-five years before. Consequently, we didn't see people, especially young people, staring down at their mobile phones most of the time as they did in Australia. That was refreshing, reminding me of a simpler world and a more innocent time.

Hotel Toaster Report

It seemed as though the Raquel Hotel had sent somebody, who didn't know what a hotel toaster was, into town to buy a hotel toaster. What came back was a large, square, double jaffle iron. Its main function was to heat bread without turning it into toast. Its other trick was to stick the slice of warm bread to the underside of the top lid, creating the illusion that the bread had vanished. This caused great consternation among the largely French guests at breakfast who thought the bread 'as gone!' There was no toast captain on duty to berate, so they went away muttering, haughtily carrying their warm bread. The French were very serious at breakfast time.

Our four-day guide, Israel, and our driver, Edel, arrived at nine in a beautifully restored 1956 Chevrolet Bel Air. When I say restored, the sweet, six-cylinder petrol engine had been replaced by a five-cylinder Mercedes clattering diesel. The suspension, brakes and steering, Israel assured us, had been updated for safety reasons. I doubted this. It felt far from safe. The ride was agricultural and the steering seemed to have a mind of its own. It was not fitted with seat belts either, not that anybody in the city could drive fast; there wasn't enough room.

Havana was a feast for those who loved the grand American cars of the 1950s to 1970s. They were everywhere, in various states of dilapidation, many of them convertibles. They had become a tourist drawcard. In order to keep them going, the government imported and sold very cheap, second-hand diesel engines. But their bodies brought back my boyhood when I could see Plymouth, Dodge, Cadillac, Pontiac, Buick and DeSoto filling the narrow streets.

Think Cuba and you think cigars. We visited a cigar factory where hundreds of cigar makers were hard at work, hand-rolling specially selected tobacco leaves to make the cigars. In the same building was a medical practice, probably specialising in lung cancer. The workers all supported the product, many of them working with a cigar hanging out of their mouths. In addition to what they could smoke their way through at work, they were given a daily ration of five cigars to take home and puff in private. I learned that it took about twenty minutes to smoke a small cigar but an hour and a half to get though a big stinker, depending upon sucking strength.

Havana relied heavily on the memory of Ernest Hemingway as a tourist attraction. Israel took us to Hemingway's house, set on four hectares of gardens and orchards in a suburb called San Francisco de Paula. The house was given to the Cuban Government by his widow and had been turned into a tranquil memorial.

Hemingway's house was large without being pretentious. We could peek into Hemingway's rooms from the outside, seeing where he sat to write in his study, or in his library (he had 3000 books) and finally, up in a tower room where he used a tiny typewriter. We also viewed his bathroom where he sat, but probably not writing, on an elaborate porcelain loo. The man lived quite an active life. He went through four wives, shot a great many deer – whose stuffed heads adorned the walls – went big game fishing and kept fifty-eight cats. They were fed by the output of four cows. On his property was a tennis court and an empty swimming pool that begged a sign: 'No bombing, no diving because no water'.

We visited another Hemingway hangout: an art deco hotel where he lived for ten years before he bought his house. I can imagine the bill when he checked out, especially when the receptionist asked him if he'd had anything from the minibar. Ernest liked a drink, and became an alcoholic before he blew his brains out with a revolver in 1961, at the age of sixty-two. He went on the grog after winning the Nobel and Pulitzer Prizes. We also visited some bars where he famously drank his favourite cocktails, and a fishing village in Cojimar, where he kept his boat and was inspired to write *The Old Man and the Sea*.

One of the highlights of visiting Havana was to witness the firing of the nightly cannon. Originally, it was used as a 9 o'clock signal that the town gates would close in one hour – in case you were getting lucky in an out-of-town haystack with a milkmaid and didn't want to be locked out of the city. This ceremony was full of pomp, with soldiers dressed up in old garb, marching stiffly to a kettledrum beat as they headed for the ancient cannon and went through a routine of barking orders and pounding gunpowder into the breach. Then, at exactly 9 o'clock, the cannon was fired to the enjoyment of the crowd. We got a big bang for our eight bucks.

Interesting and hilarious as the cannon ceremony was, I was brought down to earth by the realisation of how close the world came to catastrophe during the Cuban blockade of 1962. On a headland, not far from the 9 o'clock cannon, a decommissioned Soviet missile stood pointed at America. While Kennedy and Khrushchev argued over the Bay of Pigs, the Soviets had moved thirty-six of these missiles into Cuba, each with a one megaton warhead (seventy-seven times more powerful than the bomb that fell on Hiroshima) and capable of travelling over 1000 km to its target. Just one of these missiles could have wiped out New York. Apparently, there were only minutes to go before firing when the leaders agreed on a deal.

There was a clear delineation between old Havana and new Havana. Old was where the Italianate and art deco Spanish buildings, erected between 1900 and about 1960, stood in narrow streets and were being strictly preserved. That went for magnificent public buildings and churches. 'New' allowed for modern high-rise. For tourist and aesthetic reasons, never the twain would mix.

There were two things you must not do in Cuba. One was, blow your nose in public. It was about as acceptable as urinating on a cathedral. If you wanted to blow your nose, you had to sneak into a secluded place and honk quietly. The other was not to utter the English word for a certain fruit. If you went to a produce market and commented on the female stall holder's nice papaya, you would be talking slang about her vagina.

Although Havana had a magnificent central railway building – in permanent restoration – and several long platforms, there were very few passenger trains running. The reason was that the system had become so obsolete and decayed that it would be cheaper to start all over again – which the government planned to do. A trip between major cities by train could take days because of stops at various towns while carriages and engines were discussed and reorganised. Another problem was that the line was single, meaning that it could only handle one train in one direction – unless regular head-ons didn't worry anybody. Trips between major cities favoured car, bus or horse. In our case the journey was by diesel Chevrolet with clapped-out suspension.

We visited the oldest synagogue in Havana, built in 1924 for a then thriving Jewish population. It was well-fortified with wrought iron and barbed wire but the minders let us in without checking too stringently. I was not looking forward to having to prove my circumcision. We entered a dim office/classroom and asked to see the Rabbi. I expected him to be small, fussy and sad, but he turned out to be just the opposite. I shook hands with the biggest Rabbi I'd ever seen. He must have been at least six-foot-six, with a rampant beard and plenty of ballast around the middle. A black hat would have brought him into contact with the low ceiling of the synagogue. He was also the funniest Rabbi I'd ever met. He laughingly explained that his congregation was nearly all senior and, as such, was literally dying out. Most of the members were poor and attended services for the food that was handed out. These services were timed to fit in with the two other synagogues in Havana so that the faithful could do the rounds and pick up spiritual and physical sustenance from all of them. He was a native Cuban, had a Spanish accent, but had been trained in Israel. He told us that his synagogue's membership was now so small that he had to do everything, which included running the services, being the cantor, performing circumcisions, ritual slaughtering, overseeing kosher food preparation, preparing the dead for burial, and conducting wedding and burial ceremonies – more the latter than the former. He certainly deserved the donation we placed in his *tzedakah* box. We returned three days later with some bathroom products and antibiotics we'd brought for hotel staff to express our appreciation and gratitude, but since we felt neither, the Rabbi got the lot for his flock of impoverished oldies.

I came to understand why so many people in Cuban service industries were generally discourteous and disinterested. It was because the Cuban communist government controlled virtually all employment. The government also fully or partly owned all real estate and businesses, as well as public services like hospitals and schools. Its massive employment department allocated all the jobs. The employer paid the government a substantial monthly rate for employees and, in turn, the government paid the employees – after deducting about 90 % for its own coffers. This resulted in no incentive for good service, or a downside for bad service. Israel told us that a doctor, for instance, after training for seven years to be a GP, earned about US$350 a month. The government paid for his or her training overseas and, in return, demanded two years' service at this miserable monthly rate. After that, the doctor was a free agent – and probably would leave Cuba for better pay elsewhere.

We had dreamed of sitting in the big Havana public square, with live Latin music playing while we ate a meal, drank rum and smoked cigars – which we did on our third night there. Even though the meal was typically tasteless, the world looked decidedly better by the time we were done. We woke the next morning with headaches and mouths like the bottom of a bird cage, but during that night, life could not have been sweeter.

The four-hour road trip to Trinidad, Cuba (as distinct from Trinidad & Tobago) was as bone-shaking as I'd feared. Although we were on the great four-lanes-each-way, central, national highway for much of the time, our driver had to dodge potholes and broken surfaces all the way along, with the Chevy's suspension bottoming out continually – to say nothing of the overpowering presence of diesel fumes.

Thankfully, the Iberostar Grand Hotel in central Trinidad was a rare oasis of calm, good taste and even had a pleasant receptionist. Israel whisked us away to see the local Ancon Beach, a tourist attraction with its white sand and clear water. We'd forgotten to bring our swimmers and had to make do with a paddle. The sea water was astonishingly warm, far warmer, in fact, than the shower at the Raquel Hotel where I'd had a run-in with the bellboy that morning. He'd won a spiteful tug of war over using the hotel trolley. But when I went downstairs later, there he was, doubling as receptionist. I had to grovel my way back into his favour because we wanted to leave some cases at the hotel overnight. I'd also found the staff doubling practice in other hotels. One waiter at Hemingway's hotel was also the security guard. I'd hoped he didn't get the job specifications mixed up and shoot the drinkers.

The Iberostar Grand Hotel tried very hard to be five star, or even four, and I appreciated that, but it still had a way to go. For dinner, the seductive description of a seafood pizza and the high-stepping waiters won me, but the delivery, with a base of uncooked dough, let down the passable topping. The accompanying live music didn't help either as a fumbling pianist and a struggling violinist loudly fought each other for dominance. The trouble was, the well-lubricated diners clapped, making the musicians think they were virtuosos.

Hotel Toaster Report

The Iberostar had as good a breakfast as the Raquel had bad. Furthermore, there were no sparrows helping themselves to the food at the Iberostar – as they did every morning at the Raquel. The Iberostar toaster was a classic. Standing on four legs like a lunar landing module, this toaster was modelled on a theme park ride, which is why it was called the Theme Park Inferno. I strapped the bread in with a metal safety bar and then sent it on a fiery internal trip, while I waited for my toast like an anxious parent picking up his kid after school. For all its engineering wizardry, the toast was pretty ordinary and only gave the Theme Park Inferno seven and a half out of ten.

Apart from its public buildings, Trinidad had quite a different architectural style to Havana. It was more 'Spanish township' than Italianate or Colonial. The narrow roadways were paved with river stones, a continual threat to the ankles. That didn't stop us from walking, climbing towers, looking into museums and the proliferation of art galleries, fending off vendors and stopping to eat what always promised to be enticing food but turned out to be bland. We had grown used to ordering and calling immediately for Tabasco sauce to bring the food into some kind of taste zone. Without doubt, Cuba was the most unappealing place to eat out. But the cocktails worked on the plus side. I walked around partly drunk much of the time because alcoholic drinks were no more expensive than soft drinks were in Australia.

Because we'd prepaid, our last night in Havana was back at the Raquel. This time, the formerly grumpy receptionist was all smiles as she announced that we'd been given a suite. I think she'd set us up because when we opened the door, we found that the suite was the same as a standard room except that it was a little longer and bent around the bathroom. Our big prize was a double bed which comprised a tired mattress suspended between iron railings and propped up by a stout, wooden stool underneath. Unless the mattress was scientifically positioned to sit exactly on the railings, it sank through to the stool and produced a sleep-denying slope.

I noted that the hotel had a well-priced massage service in the basement. I tried it out. I was sealed up in a marble coffin and basted in oil like a Christmas goose — which the masseuse neglected to remove before I left. I shone my way through dinner and then slithered into the double bed in the hope that this may have been the best way not to disturb the critical balance of the mattress on the rails and the waiting stool beneath. Another feature of this room was the unreliability of the room key card which, when placed in its slot, was supposed to keep the power turned on in the room. It lost interest five times during the night, turning off the air-conditioner which effectively heated up the room.

The Raquel had to go down as one of the most beautiful, but worst equipped and staffed hotels in my experience.

Our departure the next morning for Boston gave us the final finger. Because our baggage had now grown to three large suitcases, two carry-ons and two handbags, we called for a big taxi or a van. What arrived was the smallest taxi available in Cuba. Our jumbo case became a front seat passenger as we rattled along, the open windows in the role of air-conditioner and pollution collector.

Boston couldn't have been more of a contrast to Havana. Cool, ordered and scholarly, it had a feeling close to home. After the first Uber driver didn't want to stuff our baggage mountain into his nice car and went away muttering, the second one had an SUV and cheerfully took us to the traditional elegance of the Eliot Hotel on Commonwealth Avenue. The doorman nearly fell over his own feet as he scrambled to take charge of our luggage and, with flourishes and jolly commentary, transported it inside.

The Eliot was built in 1924 as offices for Harvard academics, then turned into a hotel. Not a cheap hotel, I should add, even though our room was minimal for two people and looked down on the hotel rubbish pile rather than the handsome boulevard at the front. All the fawning doorman could say about our room was that it was nice and quiet — as he stood, head bowed, right hand cupped, waiting for the obligatory tip. We appealed to the management for a better room but the hotel was fully booked, so we continued to squeeze past each other and check the state of the rubbish from our window six floors above.

We took a city tour as soon as we arrived in Boston, via the ubiquitous hop-on-hop-off bus. We hopped on, but didn't hop off until we'd done the full loop. It revealed, with the help of a gravel-voiced, wise-cracking driver, that Boston was indeed a beautiful city, proud of its history and distinctive buildings, its sons (like JFK) and its waterways. Apart from designer malls and supermarkets, Boston street shopping was a delight. Near us, there were rows of what used to be brownstone style houses, now turned into shops, restaurants and small businesses.

America had such a huge consumer market that branded products offered more variety than they did in Australia. For instance, the Boston Lindt shop had five levels of cocoa percentages in plain, dark chocolate. I'd never seen 99 % cocoa before, and had to buy a trial block. It contained zero cholesterol, one miserable gram of sugar and hardly any carbs. Furthermore, its military, ration-style, sealed packaging carried tasting advice to the effect that you should work your way up to 99 % via the lesser percentages to prepare your palate for the final assault. This advice came too late, because it was printed inside the wrapping. We had to hit the 99 % cold turkey. This chocolate was the closest I would ever get to eating a ceramic tile. It was bitter, brittle and, although it had almost no taste, it still caused the cheeks to involuntarily retract. The eating advice finished by suggesting that you should let it melt in your mouth. I doubted that could happen in less than an hour, if ever.

The Eliot Hotel had an adjoining Japanese derivative restaurant called Uni. We bumbled in there the next night and ordered from a menu without knowing anything about the dishes. It turned out that the chef, Ken Oringer, was a famous award winner with sixteen restaurants under his control. The flavours of the small-portion dishes we ordered were exceptional, including two bowls of brussels sprouts that were cooked with such imagination as to be almost unrecognisable. The meal, along with a potent cocktail or two, saw us, in a state of delirium, booking in for the tasting menu two nights later.

One of my chief pleasures in visiting Boston was to see my old Murrumbeena and Wesley College school friend, Ross Terrill, who, for eight years, was Professor of Government Studies at Harvard University and then went on to write best-selling books on China – among other subjects. Ross had been a resident of Boston for thirty years and I went to visit him in his apartment. A true academic, he'd bought part of a former carpet factory, turned it into a massive living room, a kitchen and bathroom lined up along the inside wall and one bedroom at the back. His bookshelves could be taken for a school library. He had big, comfortable leather lounges, tables, cabinets and memorabilia scattered around. Downstairs were umpteen filing cabinets holding his written records. His diaries alone ran into hundreds of thousands of words and he was looking for ways to make use of all that material.

Ross had a business partner and together they had invested in a limo service. When they arranged to pick me up in the company limo, I looked for a modest car as I waited in the street, but along came the latest Cadillac SUV – huge, black and utterly luxurious. I'd never been in a quieter car. It had been used the previous day to transport a Saudi princess around Boston. She'd left for the airport with seventeen pieces of luggage.

Harvard is America's most famous university and, in many ways, the most prestigious in the world. It was established by the Great and General Court of the Massachusetts Bay Colony in 1636 under the name 'New College' until John Harvard, a not-so-poor clergyman, tipped in half his estate and all of his vast book collection to dramatically expand the campus. As a thank-you, the name was changed to Harvard University in 1639.

In order to honour John Harvard, a bronze statue bearing his name was created by Daniel Chester French for the Harvard Yard in 1884, but because of a previous engulfing fire in the building that had housed all John Harvard's books and memorabilia, there was no image of him available as reference. This did not deter French, who buttonholed a fellow called Sherman Hoar to sit for the head of the bronze. The result was a fine statue of John Harvard that didn't look anything like John Harvard.

Lining up for a tour on a bracing afternoon, we found the place to be quite magical. We walked through and around many of its old, elegant buildings, all kept in perfect order. The university was so large that some of the departments such as medicine and business were elsewhere in Boston. Harvard's US$34.5 billion financial endowment was the largest of any academic institution. The Harvard library, which is the world's biggest academic and private library system, comprised seventy-nine individual libraries with over 18 million books. Harvard's alumni included eight US presidents, sixty-two living billionaires, 359 Rhodes Scholars, 242 Marshall Scholars and 130 Nobel laureates.

Some of the better-known alumni included Barack Obama, Matt Damon, Bill Gates, John F Kennedy, George W Bush, Theodore Roosevelt, Henry Kissinger and Tommy Lee Jones. When famous people were invited to make speeches at Harvard, they were often presented with an honorary doctorate for their trouble. Mark Zuckerberg, who founded Facebook while at Harvard, was due to give an address to graduates, but there was some controversy over giving him a doctorate because, when a Harvard student, he didn't finish his degree. What a pity, I thought. How financially successful might he have been if he'd graduated in economics or business.

When we saddled up for our second visit to Uni (the Japanese restaurant), we were served eleven courses, all diminutive and all superb. As each plate arrived, sometimes with the food appearing as a few tiny boulders on a vast, white porcelain landscape, the waiter would passionately and minutely describe what we were about to eat. The actual eating took far less time than the commentary. My favourite was 'spicy tuna and foie gras' which was as un-photogenic as it was delicious. Although many of the portions were barely there, eleven of them in total managed to satisfy our appetites and we wafted away convinced that this was one of the best meals we'd ever eaten.

Our last day in Boston, and indeed the US, was spent in cultural pursuits. We visited the Isabella Stewart Gardner Museum, supposedly one of the finest in the US – but not because of size or number of pieces. Isabella (1849–1924) was left US$1.6 million when her father died in 1891 and she commenced putting together a remarkable collection of art, artefacts, tapestries and furniture from all over the world. She then built a Spanish style palace in downtown Boston to house it all. The palace itself sat inside a bland, brick building surrounding a garden courtyard where the sounds of frogs and birds were piped in. The entire project was arresting as we walked from room to room, some of them of meeting hall proportions, to look at groupings of pieces and paintings that went back as far as the first century. Isabella was not only a collector, but a patron of the arts and music. Paderewski played concerts in her music room where you could also see a plaster cast of Liszt's right hand.

The art collection, including thirteen empty frames, covered some of history's great artists. The empty frames marked where paintings had been when, on 18 March 1990, two men dressed as coppers tied up the guards and pinched the pictures. The haul included four Rembrandts (one was the only seascape he'd ever painted), several Vermeers, and others by Degas, Manet and some priceless Chinese vases. Despite the museum offering a reward of US$5 million for information leading to their recovery, they hadn't yet turned up. This meant that they were hanging somewhere in the world, on private walls, and the owners of those walls knew they were hot. I hoped that the descendants of the illegal collectors would hate what grandpa did, package them up, then leave them outside the door of the museum one spring morning.

All too quickly, Hong Kong was outside our Langham Hotel window. Down there was food like no other place, Sam, tailor to the rich and royal, Marks & Spencer whose pants accidentally fitted me without alteration, and shops to bring our near-comatose credit cards out for a final death-defying plunge.

A word about the Langham, that fragrant centre of solace in the final pause before Sydney. Even though we were not Middle Eastern royalty booking out half a floor, we lapped up the false importance we were accorded. This time, we were upgraded to one of the hotel's recently renovated rooms. I had always liked the old rooms. They were not very big but were well designed for overburdened travellers. How much better could the new ones be? The answer was, not better at all. While they'd gone for mausoleum marble in the bathroom, they'd deleted the second basin. In the bedroom, we now had a marble fireplace with real logs sitting in it, but if we lit them, we would be arrested. There was a set of open shelves displaying books and vases and artwork of no particular merit or use. The bed would easily sleep four and the spaces in the wardrobe were largely taken up with its internal organs. There was a laden cabinet housing items that we would have to pay for if we used them and, of course, the dreaded minibar waiting to bring about financial hardship. In the entire, designer dominated room there were only two drawers. The useful desk of yore had been replaced by a round table and two lounge chairs which told me that people who used computers in their rooms were considered downmarket. I still loved the place, but I didn't like to see upgrade money blown on interior design rather than the practical needs of travellers.

 I took my New York sourced shirting fabrics to Sam, the tailor on Nathan Road. His turbaned manager looked down his nose at them and, after waving his ruler about like a magic wand, smugly announced that only one out of the five had enough fabric to make a long-sleeved shirt. Short-sleeved was manageable – just. I was crestfallen. How could New York's Mood Fabrics have been so wrong? Sam shrugged his shoulders in support of his manager – with the non-verbalised message that if you bring your own fabric you deserved to be treated as an ignoramus. I decided to accept the long sleeve plus one short sleeve (in the eye-assaulting print) and took the rest away to try another tailor near the hotel – whose higher price was matched by his optimism because he somehow had enough fabric for long sleeve shirts.

To escape the Saturday rain, which was both depressing and dangerous in downtown Hong Kong because of eye-gouging umbrellas, we allowed ourselves to be prospected by a man with a colourful sign and supporting brochures praising his pedicure and foot massage service. He took us inside a building where he revealed himself as one of the masseuses and his wife, the other. He attended to Michelle while the wife donned a powerful miner's lamp to get a better look at my disgusting feet. She went to work with some kind of scraping instrument, sending down a shower of skin flakes that resembled snow. I feared my feet would be whittled away to stumps when she switched tack with nail-snipping and painful massage. Michelle did somewhat better, only having ordered reflexology. However, we had to admit to feeling more fleet of foot as we again joined the jostling crowd in now heavier rain.

We'd booked at one of our favourite restaurants for Saturday night: The Red Pepper in Causeway Bay. I was not much of a drinker, but I always got drunk at The Red Pepper. The reason is that the Szechuan food was so hot that in order to ward off spontaneous combustion, I had to drink beer. The restaurant could have served its own brand of beer from a fire-hydrant-shaped bottle, but on this occasion, I had to make do with Tsingtao. Chilli beef, chicken and green beans pushed the chilli index near to that of nuclear fission. The beer dousing did the usual job on me. We travelled by train to get there and I travelled home on autopilot, locked on to Michelle's ankles as she led the way, mobile phone in hand, conducting a more meaningful conversation with Siri rather than me.

Hotel Toaster Report

Because the Langham was such an elegant hotel, I expected an elegant toaster, maybe a Fabergé French masterpiece or even the solar crumpetiser used on the International Space Station. But, no. I found two plain, middle-aged, round-shouldered six-slotters. They were, in fact, no better than a long wheelbase domestic model. Each could make one piece of toast or up to six. There was an inspection lever to see how the toast was going but the operator must also inspect everybody else's and, as Derek Breadchamber has so often remarked, some people hate their toast being looked at during toasting. Furthermore, the timer was small and dark and could turn off the toaster by stealth while a disillusioned client ran out of patience and walked away.

On Sunday morning, in the interests of avoiding the consequences of the Langham six-slotter toaster, we took to the subway and went across to Hong Kong Island for breakfast. The underground train system was really an underground walking system in which you covered vast distances on foot between short train rides. Our walk after disembarkation brought us into contact with the Hong Kong equivalent of the Spanish running of the bulls. Here, it is called the meeting of the Filipina girls. They were the employed domestic help for the Hong Kong rich, and Sunday was their day off. They sounded like migratory birds in their thousands at the train stations and parks of Hong Kong Island.

Once through that throng, we joined a queue at Tim Ho Wan, a strange little café in a long, deserted shopping arcade. It had a Michelin star, was famous for yum cha, and it could serve and eject patrons in twenty minutes. Tiny tables and hard chairs deterred lingering anyway. But the reward for such taste-haste was a low price for outstanding flavour – a contrast in this very expensive city.

CHAPTER 10

Myanmar – 2016

The travel company stuffed us in spades when we decided to visit Myanmar. Our so-called cruise kit, with all the vital documentation and travel advice, was delivered to our Sydney home address about a week after we'd left. We had to convince the Myanmar end of the tour that we were genuine, and not imposters trying to score a free holiday.

Our first contact with our travel companions was supposed to be at the Shangri-La Hotel in Yangon. The tour leader, who I immediately dubbed the *commandant*, was supposed to address the platoon in the lobby at six-thirty, according to our original information sheet. We preened and puffed ourselves up and went down at half-past-six. No commandant and no platoon. Enquiries revealed that the meeting had been changed to half an hour earlier in the meeting room on the first floor. Up we went, gingerly opened the door and were confronted by twenty peeved people and a clearly irritated commandant. Sheepishly, we sat down while his lecture continued.

As I looked around, my fear of not being able to physically keep up with the crowd evaporated. Somebody had left the security door open of the old people's home and twenty patients had escaped to Yangon. I didn't feel threatened after I saw florid faces, turkey necks, paunches, walking sticks and a variety of prostheses.

The commandant had drawn a map on the whiteboard showing our schedule. At 6 o'clock the next morning, we would meet in the lobby to be taken to Yangon Airport by bus, then fly to Heho. The commandant had been through the rules for being good platoon members and wasn't going to do it all again just for us. Instead, we were given sheets of instructions to read while we watched him outline our route to Heho and the Aureum Palace Hotel on the shores of Lake Inle. He drew a diagram of the lake the shape of a kidney, and traced our lake-borne adventures to come. When he said that there would be plenty of pee stops along the way, there was murmured approval.

I stole a look at the notes. On the guidelines sheet we were told that we must smile at the locals, wear decent clothes when visiting religious sites; male knees were obscene, as were female shoulders. Feet had to be 'tucked away'. People's heads may not be touched, no kissing in public, don't beckon to somebody with an upturned finger because this is inviting a fight, don't touch the robe of a monk, don't expect any nightlife and do not give sweets to children. Best of all, practise safe sex. It didn't specify how much practise or with whom.

Dinner followed, during which we planned to catch up by asking lots of questions of the platoon members. I was seated next to Don, a retiree from Queensland, who filled the entire meal time recalling his long and exciting medical history, his current medications, his wife's ailments, and his daughter's pharmaceutical career. His wife acted as prompt when he hesitated or dispensed incorrect information. Dinner over, I knew no more about the tour than I had before, but I knew all about what was wrong with Don.

After a pleasant, small prop-plane flight at 9.30 am (we were bugled up at 4.30 am from the Shang), we boarded the bus for a meandering downhill drive to Lake Inle. The commandant provided a knowledgeable commentary about the history of Myanmar and the lake that we glimpsed in the valley that ran between two mountain ranges. He said that Myanmar had a population of 51 million, three quarters of whom were involved in primary production. As so often happened in Asia, once the Brits left, the local warlords moved in and ran the country for their own benefit. Only relatively recently had there been a feeble move towards democratic rule. The trip we were on was nearer the real Myanmar than the opinion we might have formed from the chaos of Yangon, a typical Asian city choked with cars, building hysterically and becoming seduced by Western consumerism. Oddly, the cars were all small, mostly dilapidated and right-hand drive, even though the traffic drove on the right-hand side of the road, meaning that the driver was next to the gutter and couldn't see around the car in front when wanting to pass. And everybody wanted to pass. The reason for the odd driving position was that nearly all the cars came in second-hand and right-hand drive from Japan, where citizens were not allowed to drive old cars.

Along the way to the Aureum, we stopped at a little town to inspect a very old wooden temple where we were asked to remove our shoes and socks. Some of my platoon colleagues declined to go inside because, without their special chairs and long shoehorns, they would be unable to get their footwear back on. I took mine off and paid a local dog to sleep on them.

So many Asian tours seemed to include a ride around town involving horses or three-wheel bicycles. We got the bike (trishaw) treat. The whole platoon formed into a slow, rather mournful procession around the hot, dusty streets. My skinny, older peddler made heavy work of transporting my bulk as I sat on a back-breaking wooden seat behind him. Even a slight upwards incline had him standing up on his pedals and groaning. On the other hand, Michelle scored a strong, young lad whose muscles she much admired. She showered him with praise and money at the end of the ride, even asking me to take chummy pictures of them.

After lunch, we were taken to a local winery for a tasting. This was quite a big enterprise, with new equipment and a building full of steel vats storing gazillions of litres of wine made from grapes grown on the nearby hillsides. The cheery spokesperson, who maintained that he loved wine but hated beer, boasted his wines were now being exported to many wine-discerning countries. He invited us to the tasting centre, a metal shed open to the hillside, and provided us with some bread and cheese to recalibrate our palates after each of the four wines we would be tasting. There were clucks of anticipation as the platoon sat down and the glasses came out. We would be presented with two whites and two reds, along with florid descriptions just in case we ran out of superlatives of our own. One wine was said to have 'a long finish at the end'.

The first white was poured. It had virtually no colour. I sniffed, trying to look professionally cool. The overwhelming bouquet was that of Drano, used to clear blocked pipes. The wine didn't really taste of anything more exciting than diluted mouthwash. And so it was for all four. The Drano bouquet persisted, even with the reds. We then learned that we were booked to come back there for dinner the next night, with generous servings of these awful wines; the platoon went into mutiny. Nobody wanted to see the winery ever again. The dinner was cancelled and replaced with another excellent Aureum evening meal.

Our first full day at the Aureum was spent on and around the lake. It had once been very large and quite deep, but as the accompanying mountains were cleared of their trees, soil erosion and landslides had reduced its size by half. Lake Inle was now only three and a half metres at its deepest. It had so much weed growing in it that it would soon turn into a swamp. During the dry season, the water level dropped to reveal nothing but mud, mud, glorious mud. The commandant explained that the loss of depth had changed the fishing method so that now a much shorter conical frame was used to entice the fish into a net where they could be impaled on a three-pronged spear. If we were lucky, he added, we might see a fisherman doing his stuff. If we did, the driver of our fast, skinny boat (there were hundreds of them whizzing all over the lake) would stop so we could watch. Of course, we were lucky. Just clear of our hotel patch of private waterway, a fisherman just happened to be engaged in his profession. He plunged his conical frame down, pulled some strings and hauled it up to reveal he'd caught a fine fish, which he held aloft for photographs. However, the fish that he held up was limp and had clearly been dead for some time. As we moved away, I saw him set up for the next group of boats. He slipped the dead fish into the net before he pushed the conical frame into the water and proceeded to catch it all over again.

We sped along the shallow waterways to visit a very big, very busy, very retail-oriented Buddhist temple where I ripped myself off by paying twice too much for a faux old clock sitting in a glass ball. After I bought it, I had a severe attack of buyer's remorse when every vendor I passed had the same thing, but much cheaper. One of my platoon colleagues tried to pacify me by suggesting I look upon it as a donation to a poor Myanmar family.

We flew down other water streets, stopping to see fabric weaving, cooking demonstrations, and cigar making. We wandered through a graveyard full of stupas (conical, pointed gold burial towers), to a typical village where everybody had a black pig in a pen and plenty of children — produced by practicing safe sex. In the middle of the trek back from the cemetery, there was a rain shower of huge, desperate drops that drenched us in seconds. When it rained in Myanmar, it came down like a bead curtain.

Hotel Toaster Report

At breakfast, I went to do my usual inspection and found an original Burmese Prometheus with rear tray delivery. Trembling with excitement, I selected two pieces of bread for a test run when none other than the toast captain himself appeared. He insisted that he conduct the toasting. I told him that I'd met very few toast captains in my travels, and never one who actually inserted the bread and manipulated the knobs for the perfect result. I took a picture of him and promised to send it to the editor of the next edition of *The Hotel Toaster Digest*, a fine publication prized by hotel managers around the world.

To Michelle, one of the highlights of the tour was always going to be a visit to a place called Inle Heritage House, a not-for-profit organisation trying to re-establish a pure breed of Burmese cats. The commandant allowed us to take a private day while the rest of the platoon lumbered and limped off either to inspect a cave or meander through more graveyards full of stupas or join cooking classes. These, we'd found, usually resulted in a bowl of tasteless soup with tough chicken pieces bobbing about like abandoned ships – which the students would have to eat because they'd cooked it.

But for us, an elegant skinny boat and an elegant, but more generously proportioned guide arrived at the jetty at 10 am. Forty-five minutes later, we were stroking Burmese cats at a large, well-kept facility on stilts across the lake. In addition to its cat breeding program, Heritage House taught restaurant cooking, had a small hotel (good to recover from a nervous breakdown when you need only to look at water, passing boats and floating weed islands) and taught other hospitality skills, including English. It was clearly a worthy project and relied on donations to keep it going. They charged US$300 for a cat if bought by a foreigner but gave it away for nothing if it went to a local. I couldn't help thinking this was not a good business plan.

The cat breeding program was suffering from not enough

lilac and champagne toms and needed extra breeding queens as well. The few toms we saw looked pretty tired from their heavy workload as they lay around in the boys-own enclosure listening for the next romantic call from the ladies in waiting.

Heritage House should have been on the cruise schedule, especially as the tour passed it on the way to the bedlam of the temple where I'd bought my ridiculous clock. It had a reputation of having the best restaurant in the region. Our light lunch confirmed this.

A cocktail party at the hotel that evening, and dinner afterwards, brightened up the platoon members, most of whom were showing signs of exhaustion from their day and were probably in the habit of going to bed at five in the afternoon. In their weakened condition they offered no defence against Don, who did the rounds, his voice powered up by free cocktails, once again describing his myriad ailments and what he was bravely doing about them.

We were into our third night at the Aureum Hotel and due to leave at six the next morning. It had been a revealing experience staying there. All rooms had water views (or mud views in the dry season), and were very big, entirely built from timber, with a puzzling layout of nooks, places to sit, wardrobes and cupboards, a comfortable bed enclosed in a mosquito net, and a massive, perfectly round toilet bowl that probably served the fancy of a porcelain designer but not human buttocks. The bathroom offered a wooden Jacuzzi sitting up on a platform as if ready for a performance, while the shower resided in a massive, open cubicle. The shower room floor was a pattern of dangerously slippery, black marble tiles with loose white stones between.

Beneath the shower head, the management had placed a rubber mat with painful Dr Scholl's upstanding nipples to minimise slips, trips and falls – and also to discourage extended use of the shower, I suspected.

We boarded another prop-plane which landed shortly after it took off – a bus would have been quicker – and placed us in legendary Mandalay. To quote Rudyard Kipling:

Come you back to Mandalay,
where the flyin' fishes play,
and the dawn comes up like thunder out of China 'cross the bay.

After another bus ride, that stopped to allow the platoon to see how bamboo umbrellas were made from mulberry wood, landed us in the Mandalay Hill Resort Hotel. It looked promisingly grand and colonial but the rooms were tired – not that we had a chance to stay in them for long because we were taken up to Mandalay Hill to witness the sunset from a Buddhist temple. The climb from the carpark to the temple was enabled by a series of single, one-way escalators. They went up for half an hour and then down for half an hour. I wondered what would happen if I nearly got to the bottom and the escalator went into reverse. I'd have to go up again and wait for half an hour before making another attempt to come down.

The commandant told us about the Myanmar health system. Hospitals and doctors were free, but the benevolence finished there. A public clinic doctor could only see a patient for three minutes because of the huge numbers of needy people. If you went to hospital you had to take your own bed, bedding, food and somebody to look after you. After that, you had to pay for all medications and other supplies. An idyllic health system legislation had been passed by parliament, but there was no money to run it. During the military regime, everybody dodged taxes, and all social services were on drip feed until a new tax regime could be cranked up.

One morning, we were bused up at 5.30 am to donate food to the monks. These were mostly boys or young men who relied on charity for their two meals a day. They ate breakfast at 6 am after filing past donors and lifting the lid on their metal bowls to receive a small bag of curry to go with their rice and a modest piece of packaged pastry. They walked by solemnly, making no eye contact with us, and maintaining totally neutral facial expressions. Most of them came from orphanages to join a monastery at an early age. Their eligibility was gauged by whether they could throw a robe over their shoulder and walk without it falling off. They could be as young as six years old. I wondered if any of them grew tired of the monastic life and wanted to get into the secular world with a bit of safe sex. The commandant said no, but I'd heard otherwise. Older men could become monks too, after they'd answered a series of questions, including: Are you human? (dogs had tried to join previously), Does your wife agree? Do you owe money? Are you a public servant?

The rest of the day was filled with more temples, more stupas, more Buddhas, more gold leaf and multitudes of vendors desperate to get their hands on our money and our hands on stuff we mostly didn't want.

Speaking of gold leaf, we visited one of the last hand-made gold leaf factories still operating. Most of this essential item, if you wanted to decorate Buddha, was now machine made, but here, young men simply hammered away at a piece of gold until it was paper thin, and then cut it into small squares to be mounted on bamboo paper, also carried out on the premises by a team of young women sitting on the floor. I asked whether somebody ran a metal detector over them as they left for home each day.

Then on to the world's biggest book, housed in a pagoda built in 1859 by King Mindon. The so-called book comprised 729 marble slabs of Buddhist canon, two pages per slab, making the book 1458 pages long, all carved into stone. When it was completed, the proof-reading monk found three typos, went off his face and made them start again. Each slab sat in a little white temple of its own and could be viewed through bars at the front.

In this same temple was a room with magical brass figures from Cambodia. By rubbing the part of the figure's body that corresponded to the part of the rubber's body that was not performing well, he or she received healing. It was obvious what most men were worried about. The genitalia had been rubbed clean out of existence, leaving a gaping hole.

The platoon was again showing signs of fatigue in the afternoon. The big talking point was about the upcoming river cruise where we could unpack and get into the free drinks. At about 3.30 pm, the bus finished its trundle through dusty Mandalay streets. We arrived at the wharf and had our first look at the *HMS Artist's Impression*. It had another name too, but because it was a brand-new boat, we'd never actually seen photographs of it, only drawings captioned: 'artist's impression'. I'd shortened reference of the *HMS Artist's Impression*, to *AIM*. Still virtually unmarked and unchipped, this was only her fourth voyage along the Ayeyarwady River. The plan was to do seventeen cruises a year. We occupied one of only two luxury suites on the ship. The reason we chose it was that the affordable cabins had sold out when we went to book and we had to move up and pay up if we wanted to see Myanmar before it became overrun with tourists or the army decided to take control again. As soon as word spread through the platoon that we were in a suite, we were labelled as deceptively wealthy, despite my protests that writing had a negative cash flow and Michelle worked for a not-for-profit organisation that paid a barely-there salary.

The *AIM* had twenty-two cabins, sleeping about forty people. The Australian owner, Scenic Cruises, had Australianised it so that it took our power plugs and supplied plenty of free beer. In fact, all the drinks were free unless you wanted get into exotic spirits or champagne. Our cabin had a bedroom, lounge, bathroom and private deck right at the front of the vessel. When we arrived, there was a bottle of Billecart Champagne waiting on ice. Assuming there would be one every day, I opened it and swigged away as I unpacked with decreasing efficiency. Consequently, I arrived drunk at dinner; not a good start, because I was overly friendly and a bit loud.

The *AIM* made quite exotic claims about its facilities, but they turned out to be a little deceptive. For instance, when I peered in through the glass doors of the fitness centre, it looked spacious, with many machines, but when I actually stepped inside, I found infinite machines and infinite Frasers because the three walls were mirrors. There were actually three just-okay machines and one not-okay Fraser.

Speaking of not-okay, Don was offloaded to the Mandalay

Hospital with a blood pressure crisis, accompanied by his wife as prompt. He was expected to re-join the cruise further upriver, but I could imagine him in a grubby bed surrounded by doctors, nurses and medical students all agog as he recounted his medical history, throwing in a brave laugh between chapters. They would soon realise that he was the sickest person ever admitted to the Mandalay General and that most of the occupants of the morgue were in better shape than Don.

The *AIM* was really a cleverly designed ship for river cruising. The food was generally excellent and the drinks almost too enticing. There was a swimming pool on the upper deck which overflowed when more than four hefty platoon members lowered their bodies into the lukewarm water. On the top deck was a synthetic grass walking track and a canvas-roofed sitting area for quiet drinking or a seated smoke for those who indulged.

Our Tardis bathroom defied physics by holding more fittings than it could. What it needed were traffic lights if there were two people trying to move around in it. Because it had an unnecessary bath, the shower door had been hinged so that we couldn't get in and out without impaling ourselves on the soap holder. On the plus side, the shower pressure was far better than I had expected to find on a small ship.

AIM interior designers had paid special attention to lighting in the cabins. The lights were all on sensors — sensibly so to save electricity, but the sensors behaved like naughty children. They turned off the lights when you were in the middle of doing something important and they turned them on when all you wanted to do was scratch your ear in the dark.

Our lounge room had a television (which suffered from being

unable to pick up much in the way of regular signals), a desk, coffee table, couch and a bar fridge that did not cool its contents. We asked how to turn it on but were told that while it might look like a bar fridge, with its glass door and interior shelves, it was, in fact, a cupboard. If we chose to place drinks in there, they still had to first be cooled with ice in a bucket. I discovered a knob that looked like a cooling controller inside this warm cupboard which looked like a fridge. I made myself a nuisance with maintenance to try to morph it back into a fridge. I wanted to experience what it was like to pig out on a minibar without going to debtors' prison.

Because there were no wharves along the river for disembarkation, the *AIM* simply nosed into the sandy bank and ran a rickety companionway onto the shore. It also tied up to the strongest trees the crew could find along the river, fore and aft. As we left each port and headed down the river, I wondered if the captain ever forgot about the aft rope and towed a tree along like a tender.

The cruise planners believed, probably correctly, that tourists wanted to see places or items that had achieved world record status. With this in mind, we were taken on a walking tour in Mingun to see the world's second heaviest bell. Housed near yet another pagoda, this bell weighed ninety tonnes and was made from an amalgam of five metals. The commandant, speaking over his walkie-talkie system, told us that there was a bigger bell in Moscow, but it didn't ring. To reinforce this, visitors were invited to strike the bell with wooden truncheons. It made a wonderful sound. If you didn't mind dragging your stomach across the dusty floor, you could stand up inside the bell to invite hearing loss. I declined, but I saw Don's rump disappearing beneath the bell. That might have contributed to his blood pressure problem.

That same day we visited Amara Pura, once the royal capital of Burma, where we walked halfway along the world's longest (1.2 km) and oldest teak bridge. It came with challenges. Because the water level in the lake was very low, the bridge stood 6 m in the air on skinny, occasionally swaying legs. Looking like a drunk daddy-long-legs spider, it had been poorly maintained and had no handrails. Everybody, therefore, was frightened of falling off and walked in the middle, creating a traffic jam. We descended at the halfway point to pick up a rocking sampan which just managed to hold four people in addition to the paddler. Local bubbly was served and we bobbed about until the sun obligingly set behind the bridge and everybody took award-winning photos with their tablets and phones. I was the only one with an uncool little digital camera, once a stunning piece of technology with its three megapixels but now attaining antique status.

Tourism would eventually become a major money earner for Myanmar; goodness knows the country needed it. The unemployment rate was over 40 % while 36 % of the population lived below the poverty line. It needed a strong department of tourism to plan and control the enormous potential.

As it was, private enterprise, especially retail, was still being run in little, family-owned stalls or walk-and-irritate mobile vendors who could give lessons in persistence. For example, one afternoon we left the mothership for a horse-and-buggy ride through Ava Inwa. Before disembarking, I saw the brightly-clothed vendors gathering like an army on the bank. As we took a grassy track to the assembled horses and buggies, the vendors descended, thrusting beads, bells, statues and bangles in our faces. If we asked the price, that signalled our interest and we then had a fight on our hands to close down the deal. A tactic that worked was that the vendors, mostly women, would let us off an immediate purchase if we mumbled 'maybe later'. But then we became a marked target and the vendor would accompany us on our tour. When we got into the horse-and-buggy, I was relieved that we would shake off a dedicated vendor who had her small son with her. As we jolted violently over rough stone roads, she took to her bicycle, the kid hanging on the back, and tailgated us, with a like-minded peloton behind her. When the boy dropped his thong, she stopped, picked it up, told him off, and powered through the peloton to resume her position. Many tourists simply gave them money to get them out of the way so they could actually see what they'd come to see.

Don was back! He and his wife re-boarded upriver from Mandalay where he had been the week's most exciting case in not just one, but two hospitals. The second hospital called in its leading professor of cardiology and assembled a team of students to see Don go through multiple examinations. It turned out that he had accidentally overdosed on steroids, thus his malady was self-inflicted. While the professor was checking Don's functions, he found evidence of a previous heart attack. This pleased Don no end because it provided him with a new chapter to relate in his battle against bodily malfunction. He should have rubbed everything available at the previous temple with the magic statues from Cambodia. Instead, he did the rounds again at meal times to bring everybody up to date.

The cruise had scheduled a visit to a Yandabo pottery factory – but that did not include a monsoon rain storm. Down it came, while the crew assembled its portable walkway to the muddy bank. Trouble was, we would have to clamber up the bank to begin our walk to the pottery factory. The crew jumped overboard and cut steps into the mud, not the best option for sturdy building construction. The platoon, watching from the disembarkation point near the library, grew increasingly apprehensive. There were mutinous mutterings, resulting in a high percentage of defections. I joined the mutineers, secretly hoping that some of the foolishly brave would come slithering down the slope and land in the river. None did, but the visit got a unanimous thumbs down when many of the foot soldiers, sopping and dirty, returned without seeing the pottery factory.

Hotel Toaster Report

Once again, Myanmar produced a masterpiece in hotel toasters, aboard the *AIM* no less. When set up for breakfast, the dining room staff brought out its Burmaburner, maritime model. While this looked like your average feed-in at the top and delivery at the bottom front tray, it was not. When I put in my three pieces of nice rye bread, one came sliding into the front tray, a second dropped out the back while the third shot beneath the bread box. This was the most entertaining hotel toaster in my experience. The platoon members did not appreciate the novelty of 'hunt the toast'. They became cranky when they put in their bread and no toast was forthcoming. They even blamed the omelette chef for playing games,

> especially when he picked up their toast from the floor like a magician producing an object that everybody thought was somewhere else.

One of the problems, I suspected, was the absence of a toast captain and the toaster being left to its own devices. It fell into the same category as our minibar fridge. Four refrigeration engineers appeared to remove our non-cooling cupboard, replacing it with a bar fridge that looked identical. This took quite a while, with much debate among the engineers before they plugged it in. Now we had a fridge, even though it took a full day to go below room temperature, but at least the free beer was coolish.

I had an inexplicable enthusiasm for palm sugar and was overjoyed when we clambered up the bank to visit a village specialising in the production of palm sugar liquor and palm sugar sweets. They were all made by hand. The palm flowers were boiled down to a caramel-coloured syrup and peanut oil was added to bind it. The ladies of the village earned four dollars a day to produce what looked like caramel lollies. They handed them around to taste. Disappointingly, the peanut oil got the better of the sugar. My plan to buy enough to bring home for a palm sugar party had to be abandoned. Even though the platoon expressed joy at inspecting the village, there was little remarkable about pigs lying in mud, families of chickens, curious children and the occasional white cow. The village had a water purification plant which was never used. The villagers preferred the cloudy water straight from the river. A platoon colleague tried to calculate how long we would survive if we ate and drank like the locals. He thought about a week. I agreed. Having said that, I was sure these people lived far less stressful lives than we did.

Quite a large portion of the platoon had booked for a dawn hot air balloon ride above Bagan. It had become so popular that there were now too many balloons and the government threatened to shut it down. It would probably have taken an accident to make that happen. Luckily, we didn't partake. The brave balloonists assembled at 5 am in pelting rain, were taken by a rusty bus to the flight field and promptly brought back again, un-ascended. They each paid the balloon company AUD$330 in cash to go aloft and were trying unsuccessfully to get their money back.

Still in the rain, we visited Bagan's biggest market — or was it a fly farm? Chicken, fish and meat were all in the open on the ground. The vegetables went black very quickly. Added to the soggy occasion was the fact that the market was half closed. In any case, we'd already visited a similar local market in Ava Inwa and seen the produce, including buckets of green cow shit, sold by the kilo, sitting between the carrots and cauliflowers.

With the weather clearing up, the platoon became cheerful, especially because the commandant had been temporarily replaced by a local tourist girl with better English and a plethora of interesting facts. However, as she stood up at the end of the bus using an old PA system, her words came out very distorted. For instance, she was talking to us about peanuts, but what we heard was, 'There are three sizes of penis in Myanmar. Penis oil is good for cooking.' She also told us that Buddha had forty teeth as opposed to her own excellent set of thirty-two. While at a beautiful temple, she pointed to the trees in the overgrown garden where there were several tear-drop shaped nets hanging from the branches. These had been made by male tailor birds. Once the boys had finished their work, the girls decided which nest they liked the most and its builder was rewarded with safe sex, eggs and family life.

She hosted us through several temples, all old, falling apart and beautiful. Bagan was in an earthquake-prone region and many of the pagodas, temples and stupas had been destroyed or damaged by severe tremors. In the gardens where the tailor birds built their nests, two of the stupas were tipping over because of shifting foundations. The locals had capitalised on this by putting up a sign claiming an affinity with the leaning tower of Pisa. I suggested to Robert, a Queensland solicitor travelling with us, that he could represent Italy in an action for misrepresentation against Myanmar. 'We'd have a good case,' he said, 'but who would I send the bill to?'

Although Robert and I had not played chess for thirty years, we organised a challenge during one of the rainy afternoons. I was going well until I didn't notice that he had a bishop sitting on my queen and while I was busy saving a pawn, her majesty was marched off the board to a dungeon. Consequently, he won, but not until I'd given him a fright by nearly trapping his king with a knight and rook combination.

The platoon was made up of endearing people. They were mostly retired, overweight, unfit and friendly. Vern, for instance, was a long-retired aircraft re-fueller from the NSW Central Coast. He had a megaphone voice that you could identify in the crowd. He seemed to attract vendors, and I often heard him sounding off: 'No, I don't want it! The price has nothing to do with it. I just don't want it! I don't like it! I can't tell you why I don't like it and even if I did, I wouldn't pay the price you're asking. No, I don't want it at a cheaper price. Look, go away. I don't want the fucking stuff!'

What I couldn't work out was how these people managed to pay for cruising. This was our first cruise but most of the platoon members were cruise junkies. They loved sitting down to compare cruise companies, destinations they'd been to and where they were going next. I realised just how big the retiree cruising market must have been. Yet, with few exceptions, they were not wealthy. In Don's case, he took up collections from his kids, telling them, no doubt, that his next trip would probably be his second last – followed by his final journey in a hearse. Others were spending their superannuation before their kids could get their claws into it.

One of the blights of exploring developing countries was the endless teams of vendors thrusting clothing and handicrafts under our noses when that was not our reason for making the trip. But every now and again, someone stood out from the vendor crowd – without trying to. Someone like Layla. We didn't want her bangles but we were taken with her vivid personality, awareness and command of English. I was curious to know more about her. We passed her as we were preparing for another horse-and-buggy ride, this time around the township of Salay. I told Layla that we would be back and that I wanted to speak with her. She replied, with a huge white smile, that she would be waiting. Peter Dawson sang *The Road to Mandalay* in my head.

On our return, with the *AIM* ready to sail, we sat down with

Layla on a rough wooden bench and found out that she was eleven years old, had left school, but was obviously a good student because that's where she had learned her fluent English. She was now a full-time bangle vendor to help support her family. She had three sisters and one brother. Her father was a boat driver on the river and her mother looked after the family at home. They lived in a village not far from where we had docked. I asked her what she wanted to do with her life. Most eleven-year-olds just shrug their shoulders, but Layla immediately replied that she wanted to be a tour director. Time had run out and the *AIM* captain was eager to cast off. We had to leave Layla with so many questions unasked. We gave her some money and wanted to find a way to help her to pursue her dream. She asked our names and, as our ship pulled out from the bank, called out, with perfect articulation, 'Goodbye Michelle and Fraser.' Layla was going to make it.

Between our two meetings with Layla, the program provided a highlight of our cruise. After a short bus ride, we came to a waiting line of horses and buggies. Having done something similar recently, I dreaded the experience of hard wheels hitting potholes that changed the location of ribs and backbones. We walked along the line, trying to select a horse that looked big enough and strong enough to pull along our combined weight plus that of the driver and the buggy. Because we were last to arrive at the line, we had no choice but to clamber into the last buggy, with a small horse – which we calculated was about to make its last trip. The driver, however, was reassuring. 'Small horse, yes, but strong horse. No problem with this horse. Guarantee good horse.'

If this were England, we would have been trotting down country lanes, with waving grassy fields and magic trees taken from children's story books. The only difference was that dotted throughout this idyllic landscape were stupas, temples and monasteries – in their thousands. Nowhere else in the world would you see this. Once finished with a coating of plaster, these variously-sized buildings now stood denuded in their brickwork – adding to their uniqueness in a world where religious buildings and monuments were invariably built of stone.

The captain of the *AIM* who, even with his official cap on, looked as though he'd been plucked out of high school, invited the platoon-curious for a wheelhouse tour. There was no wheel to be found in the wheelhouse, only two rotating handles that controlled the dual 600-horsepower diesel engines. Top speed was twelve knots when going with the current or four knots against. There was no rudder because the thrusters directed steering. The ship and its engines were made relatively recently in China – although one of my more cynical platoon colleagues thought the *AIM* might be a refit because he found a grasshopper in his bathroom. Refits, he said knowingly, always left gaps for bugs to get in.

The *AIM* was well-equipped with radar, sonar and satellite navigation. Even then, it took onboard a local pilot who knew the river sandbars and currents that may not have shown up on the electronics. There may have been an element of superstition in this, too.

Still in Salay, the commandant took the puffing platoon on a walking tour of the village. It seemed peaceful and orderly, with muddy streets and bamboo houses, schools and a fire station.

The fire engine stood ready to charge out from its shed, bell clanging. It had no ladders visible, but instead, a water cannon was mounted on the roof for more distant assaults on a fire, with a possible secondary function in crowd control. It was backed up onto a ramp so that, if the battery couldn't get the engine going, a clutch start might.

There was something mysterious about this town. Its grandest brick and plaster houses, built early in the twentieth century by the British, were mostly abandoned. Everybody I spoke to about this had a different opinion as to why. Some said the houses had been holiday retreats for wealthy Brits from the big Burmese cities, while the commandant suggested that they had been owned by well-off locals who'd moved away looking for better business opportunities. What they agreed upon was that they were now worthless. They sat there, these fine examples of grand, British city houses, being devoured by tropical rot, with nobody wanting to live in them. This was no village for real estate agents.

Because the number one attraction in Myanmar was looking at pagodas, temples and monasteries, the visitor quickly became overwhelmed by them. Even as we glided down the Ayeyarwady River, stupas arrived and faded along the banks, or sat like random gold jewellery cast into the low, green hills. When the schedule announced that the platoon would visit the Mya Tha Lun Pagoda, the general reaction was, 'So what?' An added disincentive was trishaw transport, where the seats would be too small for the average platoon member's buttocks and the peddlers might expire trying to reach even walking speed. Moreover, if we did arrive at the base of this pagoda, there were more than one hundred steps plus intermittent slopes to be traversed in bare feet. The platoon, however, had toughened up. There was not one defector as we mounted our trishaws and the peddlers gritted their teeth.

Once at the temple compound, we de-shod and commenced the long climb, with the commandant stopping every so often to get his own breath while explaining something about the endless array of myths and merchandise we were passing, including local cures for superficial complaints, and a fortune teller for more serious life problems.

At the top we found a massive, tiled terrace which looked out over the Ayeyarwady River where the *AIM* was moored. I realised that this was not a river in the accepted sense, but a series of elongated, connected lakes. While the view was impressive enough, behind me stood the most magnificent, commanding *stupa* I had ever seen or imagined. Immensely tall, beautifully proportioned and perfectly maintained, it was covered in gold leaf, blazing defiantly back at the sun in the diminishing afternoon light.

On the way back, we stopped to look at *chinlone*, a game played in Myanmar and nearby Asian countries. Using a hollow cane ball, two teams must keep the ball from touching the ground while using only their feet to keep it moving. A variation was to put up a volleyball net and kick the cane ball over it into the opposing court. Before dinner that evening, a famous cane ball foot exponent entertained the platoon on the pool deck with some remarkable acts of balance, foot and ball skills.

A talk was given by the commandant's tour director colleague, Gareth. He outlined the process whereby a boy became a monk. Most remained novices until they turned at least sixteen, when they could be confirmed as monks. At that point, they were expected to obey 227 rules which denied every pleasure I could think of, plus some I wasn't even aware of, such as acknowledging flavour in food; it existed for nutrition only. No saying yum-yum. At meal times the monks didn't talk or look at each other. They were not allowed to sit in comfortable chairs or sleep in reasonable beds, but instead retired to a mat on the floor. They renounced all worldly possessions. Upon acceptance into the brotherhood, they were issued with three dark-red robes and a bowl for alms and food. While they may be given an umbrella and thongs, they were not supposed to use them. Rough ground and rain were considered good for spiritual wellbeing. If there was a choice of sun or shade, they must stand in the burning sun. They must avoid peeing in long grass in case they drowned an ant. They were not allowed to be in a room alone with a woman, or sit next to a woman on a bus. Even ordinary people trying to faithfully follow Buddhism were denied many pleasures we took for granted in the West.

Gareth said there were over 400 million Buddhist monks currently in the world. Then there were many other religious orders that had monks as part of their systems. Although some orders taught and did community work, the principal occupation of monks was studying texts and praying – for which they were supported by their communities. In Myanmar, they relied upon donations of food for their two meals a day. It was similar in Thailand. Monks were undoubtedly good people, but I questioned the validity of denouncing worldly goods and then relying on support from those who were working to attain the same worldly goods.

Since, by default, we occupied one of the two *AIM* suites with large front balconies and had other privileges such as free laundry and my one bottle of Billecart, we decided to exercise our right to hold one private dinner party for four people. We gave our two guests – a fun couple from Wollongong – a choice of anything on the exotic menu, to which I added a bottle of champagne. What we all wanted, it turned out, was a change from exotica – which manifested itself in four hamburgers. Adding to the down-to-earth evening was the place along the river chosen by the captain for an overnight stop. Of all the quaint villages and tree-shaded sandy banks where we could have tied up, we found ourselves tethered to a rubbish tip, with white plastic bags fluttering in the humid breeze. At a certain point in the drinking of champagne, rubbish tips, along with everything else, seemed of little importance. We raised our glasses to our fortunate lives, the country where we lived and the era into which our births landed us.

It seemed that the cruise was suffering from not enough places of interest to visit. Away from the few big cities, Myanmar was still a primitive country and there were limits to how much stimulation the platoon could expect from seeing more bamboo-and-thatch houses and more stupas, temples and monasteries. Mud also had a repetitive quality about it. On the last day, I forsook a buggy ride to a nine-hole golf course with a tin shed clubhouse of claimed historical importance, in favour of another game of chess with Robert. This time, I hung on to my queen and was doing quite well when Robert's wife whisked him away on the golf course shed excursion. I sat staring at my promising position on the board when one of the crew, a dull-looking lad who had been watching us from a respecful distance, offered to take Robert's place and let me finish him off. Of course, I accepted, my ego bristling. 'I have played before,' the boy murmured as he made what looked like a mistake with a rook. Ten minutes later, he'd checkmated me. My king glared up at me as I was putting him back in the box. 'You should never play chess with the crew,' his majesty said.

Early in the morning we were brought back to earth with a seven-hour bus trip to Yangon. Another platoon would replace ours, the commandant would stand tall and begin his introductions, the new platoon would ask silly questions and *AIM* would blow its horn and edge out into the river. We had two more days back in Yangon at the Shang where we'd no doubt look at more pagodas and markets and temples – plus plenty of carbon monoxide and exciting traffic.

Since travelling from Melbourne to Sydney during a plane strike about forty years ago, I had never been a fan of the long-distance bus trip. Leaving *AIM* did nothing to change my opinion. The platoon was in a jubilant mood as it tackled the taxing cardio climb up the mud bank with hand-cut steps and climbed into what was a far superior bus to those that had come before. The driver had to blow into a breathalyser before he could start the engine and pull out into a narrow road that ran alongside the river.

'We'll soon be going onto Highway One,' the commandant announced. Ah, that would be so much better, I thought. We'll belt along without motorbikes, dogs, chickens, other buses, trucks and monks to dodge. We continued thus for an hour. I asked the commandant when we would enter Highway One.

'We are already on Highway One,' he replied, somewhat tersely. For the next six hours we dodged motorbikes, dogs, chickens, other buses, trucks and monks. We made a comfort stop and then stopped for lunch, accompanied by a team of friendly flies. The cruise organisers provided plastic boxes of fillings for bread rolls, but there were no bread rolls. I ate my fillings after which somebody on staff remembered the rolls. We then tucked into bread rolls with no filling except butter which we had to spread with a fork. This didn't rate as the company's best lunch. However, the local beer was very acceptable and considerably safer to drink than the water.

Our last stop before hitting the suburbs of Yangon was at the British war memorial cemetery. What a bore, I thought. Who needs this? I was in for a surprise. A superbly designed open building sat in the middle of lawns in which the graves of the fallen from the Second World War were marked with plates bearing their names and a message from their loved ones. There were soldiers from Burma, Britain, Australia, Pakistan and India, 27 000 of them, who died in the campaign to hold back the Japanese advance. Nearly all of them were in their twenties. Walking past their graves was a moving experience. I was glad we'd stopped.

The Shang gave us a better welcome than last time, a couple of weeks before, when we were allocated, in hindsight, a modest room. Nothing depressed Michelle more than a stingy hotel room. After that, she wrote the Shang management a polite but pointed email about the dubious benefits of being a member of its 'Golden Circle' club, which we had joined. It had not even acknowledged her birthday. And an answer came directed, in a writing unexpected, and I think the same was written by a manager dipped in guilt. When we returned, the letter said, the Shang would make it all up to us. The Shangri-La Golden Circle Club then lavished upon us a suite of apartment proportions with a wonderful view, two televisions, plus lounge and dining spaces. Furthermore, we were a marked couple in the dining room when, in turn, two attractive ladies from upper management fawned, grovelled, bowed, scraped, praised and thanked, blessed the day we were born, and expressed how they would be forever grateful that we had chosen their humble hotel about which to grizzle.

The cruise company wanted to stamp a final impression on the platoon by finishing on a high. Just when we thought we couldn't stomach another pagoda, we were taken to two more in Yangon. The first sat in the middle of town and was only worthy of a bus stop and a short battle with vendors until we moved off to view a giant reclining Buddha. It was housed in a special building and, being Sunday, was well patronised by tourists and worshippers. Built from brick and then plastered and painted, the figure was 66 m long. We were told that monks were responsible for cleaning it. If that were the case, I'd have fired the monks. It was very dusty and had been used for bombing practise by pigeons. At a certain time in the afternoon, a gong sounded which set off a loud chorus of dog-wailing. I suppose that after one dog had taught itself to wail on hearing the gong, the rest caught on.

The biggest reclining Buddha in Myanmar was at Monywa, quite a way from Yangon, and was 91 m long. It was so big you could go inside (no internal organs), entering through the ear or up the nose. For the record, the world's biggest reclining Buddha was in China. It was over 400 m long. There was probably a hotel in there somewhere. The significance of a reclining Buddha was based on Buddha's lifestyle. The story went that he worked twenty-two hours a day and then spent the other two hours reclining while talking to his followers.

Then off to the jewel in the crown: The Shwedagon Pagoda which sat on the highest hill in Yangon. The *stupa* went up for 100 m on top of that. Consequently, when it was lit up at night, it was like a Buddhism-beckoning beacon, visible from all over the city.

If the reclining Buddha was busy, this was bedlam. Thousands of people were trying to catch the lifts up to the tiled terrace around the *stupa* and other thousands were trying to do the opposite. However, once we arrived on the terrace, we were exposed to the most unbelievably exotic and decorative side of Buddhism. For a belief system based on detachment from worldly goods this was difficult to reconcile. Surrounding the *stupa* were the most lavish temples with hundreds of Buddha images and gold decorations gleaming everywhere. The *stupa* itself had half a ton of gold on it, and right at the top, under an umbrella, there was said to be a seventy-two carat diamond among a massive collection of gemstones.

Buddha images on public display took advantage of lighting technology, with moving, coloured lights around the head to imitate auras. I thought that the lights cheapened the beauty of the images, but the commandant told us that the locals liked it that way because it stimulated their imaginations. 'Some of them think it is real,' he had added behind his hand.

The farewell dinner was held at a hotel called the Governor's Residence – which it may once have been. An excellent meal put the platoon in a mellow mood. Robert, my lawyer chess friend, who was used to addressing groups of people, dinged his glass and made an impromptu speech flattering the tour company. The commandant responded in a similar vein. I didn't think either was totally accurate. Don called out something silly, but didn't mention his health. While the commandant spoke briefly and diplomatically, his colleague, Gareth, turned in a command performance. Gareth had been guzzling the free wine, in spite of being a practicing Buddhist. He rose uncertainly to his feet and then couldn't shut up as he waved his arms in massive, all-encompassing embraces. I could only catch a word of English here and there. 'Hub gribba wunnerful people,' he thundered. 'Gob bonna wakwak blessing!' He seemed on the verge of tears as he told us we were all family. It looked as though we were in for a filibuster when another brave soul from our platoon leapt to her feet and loudly toasted the children we'd met. That closed Gareth down.

The Governor's Residence, incidentally, looked to be a great place to stay, with its beautifully preserved timber joinery and fine British club architecture. It could have been used as a set for a PD James murder mystery. Room rates started at a sobering one thousand dollars a night.

Our last day was spent in Singapore. Michelle had joined us to the Conrad Hilton Honours Exclusive Society of Special Guests, giving us a better room and free refreshments on the club floor as long as we adhered to the timetable.

On this trip, especially, I had observed the common practice of hotel room temperatures. Because it was hot outside, a bedroom had to be like an ice-chest. Being so cold, you were then forced to sleep under a quilt to get warm enough to survive the night. Nobody did this at home, so why did hotels change the pattern? After the quilt was lowered to half-mast to achieve an average bodily temperature, the bed at the Conrad was very comfortable, once we got onto it, but being so high off the ground that short people, unless equipped with steps, would have considered sleeping on the floor.

Hotel Toaster Report

At a lavishly laid out breakfast offering, I encountered one of the worst hotel toasters in my long career of reviewing them. I would write to Derek Breadchamber about it. Dented and spooky-looking inside, the toaster was a miserable four-holer-double-delivery model with quite a few clicks on the clock. We were late to breakfast so it was not under pressure, but it would be unable to cope with a peak rush. It could cause violence among the guests. Incidentally, breakfast finished at 10.30 am and by 10.20 am, the toey hotel staff was already clearing up. The toaster was marched out at exactly 10.31 am. I would have advised them not to bring it back.

Singapore presented itself as so clean, ordered and thoughtfully designed that I got the feeling I'd slipped through a wormhole into the future. It showed what could be achieved with discipline and leadership, to say nothing of stiff penalties for tax evasion. We visited Gardens by the Bay, something I would normally find of little interest, yet I was enchanted by its beauty and inventiveness. We paid to go up in a lift and take the walkway suspended between huge man-made trees. Although we could wander around the gardens for nothing, if we wanted to experience anything involving height or service, there was a substantial charge. As a whole, Singapore was not cheap. For the most part, it was dearer than Sydney, but there was no argument when it came to value for money.

On our last night, we ate at *Spago* in the Marina Bay Sands, the three-tower iconic building topped by a swimming pool and restaurant in the shape of a ship's hull. Over dinner and a powerful cocktail called 'Gin and bear it', we watched the sun set from the fifty-seventh floor, while the swimming pool crowd luxuriated by peering over the horizon edge into oblivion.

CHAPTER 11

Khao Lak, Thailand – 2016

Our travel plan was Sydney, Singapore, Phuket and Khao Lak, where we would be received into the Thai arms of the JW Marriott Hotel. Obstacles awaited us. The 7 pm Singapore Airlines flight was in a soon-to-be-retired 777 which took off in what seemed annoyance at being disturbed. It roared and rattled for seven-and-a-half hours while we attempted to work the 'sleeper' seat, a far cry from the lay-flat variety that had become the business class norm. These tired warriors of the sky laid the attempting sleeper on a slope, so that the body compacted towards the feet and had to be stretched back into former shape on arrival.

Arriving in Singapore at 2 am, shorter than when we'd left Sydney, we found the Ambassador Transit Hotel in which to stretch out. It didn't look like a hotel at all; more like a cosmetic store with one crooning sales assistant in front of a blindingly bright wall. We were allocated a room, with a wake-up call booked for 6.30 am in case we overslept.

This was my first time in a transit hotel. The room had no windows and was totally silent. Instead of a wardrobe there were three hooks on the wall. Obviously, the transients didn't need drawers either. Two severely single beds greeted us. I assumed that these were to discourage sexual encounters being realised between people who had made promises during a flight.

Another oddity: the bathroom was vast. It was clearly designed to cover the needs of the disabled, with chrome railings and a shower seat. When Michelle took the first shower, she suspected that the builder had left his spirit level at home the day he'd laid the floor. The water ignored the drain beneath the shower and ran in a torrent under the shower door until it filled the floor of the bathroom to cover her toes.

Once dressed, we hastened outside to have our allocated US$10 coupon breakfast at Burger King. It comprised faux scrambled eggs, faux meat patty, half an exhausted tomato and very fried potato testicles – but not before I had a noisy argument with the elderly, diminutive Chinese manager. She announced that I'd exceeded my US$10 breakfast allocation by forty-five cents and therefore I had to have powdered milk instead of real milk.

I renamed the JW Marriott Hotel the 'JW Merriment', such was the variety of ways for guests to spend their time as they emerged from the 300 rooms over three levels. The design of the hotel was clearly inspired by water. First, a tiled river system with lakes had been built, remembering that the sea was out the front – and there was quite a lot of water there already. Then the rooms were pressed into the banks of the manufactured river, meaning that everybody had a water view, while people like us on the lower floors could open their double doors, walk out onto their terraces and drop into the drink.

It quickly became apparent that the hotel was overrun with children. The dining room was like a schoolyard at lunchtime, to say nothing of a large flock of sparrows that perched in the elaborate ceiling and swooped down to clean up the tables. This was an environmentally friendly hotel, we were told, so the sparrows had to be tolerated. The one saving grace was that they'd learned to shit outside. I'd have hated a dot of lookalike sago added to my muesli at breakfast.

The hotel activities centre was a small city in itself. It boasted a well-equipped gym, bicycles, table tennis, library, tennis, exercise room, water sports, volleyball, golf, yoga, Pilates, Thai boxing, language classes, and the artistic skill of fruit carving. There was also an extensive children's entertainment department full of games, both educational and frivolous. The greatest nostalgic attraction for me was the squash court, where I would surely die of heart failure if I played, but I'd hit the wooden floor with a smile on my face. I so much wanted to again feel the exhilaration of slamming that small black ball along the wall.

The further we were away from Bangkok, the less English was understood. Many people who tried to convey information to somebody who didn't speak their language believed they would be better understood if they shouted. Not in anger, of course, but controlled yelling, along with exaggerated lip, jaw and tongue movements. In this mode, Michelle and a phone shop lady went at it for some time at increasing volume when Michelle needed a new SIM card for her mobile phone. The lady called another shop to clarify what Michelle wanted and the proprietor of that shop suggested Michelle went and bought the SIM card from him instead. Hearing this, phone shop lady had a spirited row with him and negotiations with Michelle began afresh.

There was no dress code at the Merriment, but unofficially, men could wear shorts into dinner as long as their knees were covered. I'd only brought mid-thigh shorts. With the phone shop negotiation still raging, I walked along the street past a sign that said 'Tsunami Tailors' (rather poor taste at that tragic time, I thought) to a dismal clothing shop where most pairs of shorts were cut for an undernourished boy of ten. I found two baggy-at-the-front pairs that nobody else wanted, but at least they were my size, and covered my seductive and suggestive knees. I bought them for AUD$12 each.

Now flushed with retail success, I decided to buy some sparkling mineral water because the Merriment only served Perrier at the price of cognac. The shop assistant didn't understand any English, even when I shouted at him. In exasperation, I pointed at a stack of still water and said loudly, 'I don't want this water. I want mineral water. Mineral water different. Mineral water have many bubble!' That didn't work either. I needed some theatre. I pointed again at the stack of still water bottles and made bubbling noises while demonstrating effervescence with my fingers. After several simulated boil-overs, he understood. He beckoned to me. I followed him around the back where he showed me an electric jug at a special price.

Hotel Toaster Report

The JW Merriment had a fine matching pair of large Brownaway toasters which occupied their own booth at breakfast time. Some of my PhD research had revealed that the Brownaway toaster was invented by Herbert Brown in London in 1923. He was trying to build a tanning machine to relieve the pallor of European women who didn't get enough sunlight, especially in winter. His early experiments were such a flop and so costly that he finished up in Wormwood Scrubs debtors' prison, surviving on bread and water. He thought often about his now-abandoned machine and how nice it would be to toast the bread he was living on. While making left-handed lawnmowers in the prison machine shop, Brown saved up enough scrap metal to build his first toaster, the Brown One. He was caught testing it, but because the prison superintendent saw such great value in the machine, he let Brown out on the condition that they go into partnership.

The model at the Merriment was the Brownaway Protect-the-Child variant. Its in-tray slide was set at a carefully calibrated height so that no normal child under the age of eight could reach it. Very young, or very short children, were encouraged to pitch the bread in, like scoring a goal at netball. Grandparents were told to applaud and hand out lollies when a piece went in. The Brownaway was a fine machine, but thick slices could get into trouble around the Devil's Elbow at the back — which called for a fully qualified toast captain to be on hand with firefighting equipment. When I loaded in two pieces of bread they only turned into toast after three passes. This was because the speed knob was poorly set. I dared not change it since there was a Thai criminal charge for creating a fire hazard by unlawfully interfering with a hotel toaster knob.

A tropical holiday in the sun? No, a tropical holiday in the rain, and lots of it, at the JW Merriment, in spite of this not being the wet season. Owing to the confinement indoors, we were preparing for a children's revolt. They would not tolerate rain. These children had to be given what they wanted, otherwise their parents would be charged with neglect, cruelty, and causing pain and suffering to minors. The children would be removed to more caring government facilities.

The children quickly infiltrated the gym where they dropped weights, ran backwards on the treadmill and changed the settings on the rowing machine. I escaped by hiding out in the squash court where, with borrowed racquet and ball, I tried to recall my competition days when an hour-and-a-half of high cardiac stress was not nearly enough. I gripped the now strangely-shaped racquet and hit the ball against the front wall. It didn't come back the way it was supposed to. Did I have a dud ball? No, I had a dud body. I applied some ferocity to striking the ball and it sulkily returned. I found that I could hit it all right, but chasing down where it landed ran me out of energy in ten minutes. I could hear my cardiologist telling me to stop unless I wanted to return to Australia coffin-class. I therefore stopped. That would be my last game of squash. Tragic to finish like that, on my own, buggered, in foreign lands.

JW Merriment could have qualified as the wateriest hotel in the world. There were many choices of granite-lined lakes of the type designed by city planners and architects, or we could jump into the tiled river and go for a kilometre wade, sometimes chest deep and sometimes waist deep as we passed the terraces of people with similar rooms to ours, who may be sitting or reading or, more interestingly, undressing.

There were other sights along the way, like a water monitor (a very junior version of the one I'd seen in Malaysia) haul itself out of the tiled river, its long, blue tongue darting from its lizard-like head.

The JW Merriment had a cat. We discovered it complaining in the corridor one night on our way back from an excellent Thai dinner. We estimated this cat to be a teenager, with a smudged tortoiseshell coat. It offered friendship and face-rubs when it worked out that we were cat people. The following morning, after having survived the breakfast riot, we asked our room service girl about the cat. Was it being properly fed? The distance between our Thai and her English produced our following declaration: we didn't want to eat in our room, we didn't want to eat the cat in our room or elsewhere, we didn't want the cat to live in our room, we liked the cat and didn't want it taken away, we were not afraid of the cat, we already had two cats at home and could not fit in a third.

One night we dined at the upmarket Waterfront restaurant, offering European cuisine.

Feeling especially mellow, I ordered a beer to go with my penne pasta. While the beer was standard Singha, we fell in love with the glass it came in and wanted to buy some for home. We enquired of the waitress. This was always a trap in Thai establishments. It created an instant crowd of helpers. The waitress was soon joined by other waitresses, then the floor manager and his assistant. The assistant had the best English. According to her badge, her name was Poo. 'This is Poo,' the manger confirmed with a radiant smile.

I admit to being childish and I don't allow for different languages giving words different English meanings, but Poo? Many lines came to mind. Poo in restaurant. Poo has gone out the back. There was Poo on the bed. Poo was charming and helpful, with a beautiful, animated face, but I couldn't get through the conversation without a silly grin on my face. I had to stop looking at her name badge. Upon hearing about this, my cousin, Mark, sent me a picture of a book cover with a smiling Thai girl preparing food. Its title: *Cooking with Poo*.

We were in the habit of prepaying as much of a trip as possible – which reduces, but doesn't eliminate, nasty fiscal surprises. But by doing this, we entered voucher land. At the JW Merriment, we had to take our voucher ration book to be stamped and signed for each meal. There were different vouchers for the spa and massage. Although vouchers made perfect sense, they ran counter to human nature. When we stepped up to do business, there was no haggling and no cash – just the voucher. The vendor's face falls because, at a primary, subconscious level, we're about to steal the goods. Previously we paid for the voucher but that was a different transaction at a different time. We'd handed over money and got a voucher in return. Done and dusted. But now we were seizing goods in return for a lousy piece of paper, making everybody feel disappointed without knowing why.

The tiled river produced a passing flotilla of people, some

of whom greeted us, while others pushed forward, faces set in default mode, looking neither left nor right. The children were different. They didn't talk, but puffed and gurgled past on all manner of blow-up water craft. There was a kerfuffle when a giant pink flamingo went missing, presumed stolen. Where it could be hidden was a greater problem than stealing it. There were many other sea creatures, including a shark, a green crocodile and a blue turtle, but the best was a huge white unicorn which took up most of the tiled river when it went on a voyage. It could hold up to five kids, plus the propellant father with his hand under its rainbow tail. When it passed, I asked the Dutch dad how he'd blown it up. 'Ve haf der pomp,' he replied. I wanted to know if he intended to take the beast home. Even deflated, it would have filled a large suitcase. I could see them arriving back in Holland and having to declare a deflated Thai unicorn and later appearing on a border protection television program.

Thailand was the home of massage. On most massage menus was a body scrub, achieved by rubbing rough stuff all over the body to remove dead skin, inevitably along with plenty of live skin. An essential of the body scrub is an immediate shower to get rid of the grit and grime. The Merriment Spa body scrub would call for arrangements to be made with my Bank Manager but, on the other hand, the cheapie down the road had no shower. I therefore took a taxi into town to a reasonably priced establishment that the driver assured me offered both body scrub and shower.

When I arrived, I was confronted by the usual floor-mattress booths divided by flimsy curtains, but as the mamasan directed me to a cell-like concrete room secreted at the rear, she promised

I would get my shower. The scrub was really quite good, even if a bit severe. Then I requested the shower. Naked, I crept across the slippery passageway into a tiny room with a barrel of very cold water and a dipper in the corner. Treating me like her grandchild, the senior scrubber scooped up dippers of water and poured them over me, taking great delight in my yelping. I emerged shivering, with the intention of enlightening the taxi driver about the western definition of a shower.

Our last day at the Merriment was not without some excitement. For a start, it was Michelle's birthday and the Merriment sent a 15 000-calorie chocolate cake to our room. The delivery boy sang Happy Birthday as he brought it in, to which I added my wavering baritone voice. If we ate it, we would be unable to leave because of stomach failure. Maybe this was their way of extending our stay.

Still on ailments, I found that I hadn't brought enough of an important medication to see me through the trip. Where to go for help but the hotel medical centre – looking like a B-grade movie set of a medical centre. It had a bed on wheels, a small metal bucket with some instruments sticking out of the top, a petri dish and a glass cabinet full of popular headache and cough cures. The diminutive, whispering nurse, done up in a pale blue uniform festooned with a 'I recently passed the course' badge awaiting the arrival of the sick. I got the feeling that her specialities were sunburn and diarrhoea so that when I presented her with a seriously needed blood thinner, she was out of her depth.

She stared at the packet, looked it up on the internet, photographed it with her phone and telephoned two people to talk about it. Her carefully considered solution? Ask a taxi driver to take you to a pharmacy and show them the packet. Which is what I did. We visited six Khao Lak pharmacies and the pharmacists all did the same thing: looked at the packet at zero distance from their noses, took out the pills and held them up to the light, gave me a blank stare and said, 'No hab.' I took to the telephone and found they were available in the pharmacy at Changi Airport at ten times the Australian price. But, I thought, at least they *hab*.

CHAPTER 12

Malaysia – 2015

Some health resort destinations not only offer an interesting journey to get there, but the promise of bodily transformation – if you can put up with starvation, being made to hate your current body and embrace fat-vanishing machines you didn't know existed. We were overweight and looked for a health resort that would return us to Australia as prime examples of how humans should look. Our search finished at The Orchard Wellness & Health Resort, one of a few such establishments in Malaysia.

We'd already notched up a short stay at Chiva-Som in Thailand, undoubtedly one of the world's leading health resorts, but a budget crusher as well. Malaysian health resorts were a fraction of the cost and, if you believed their website claims, just as good. Four weeks at The Orchard would cost little more than four days at Chiva-Som.

The Orchard seemed to be our answer to our search for the

Land of Thin, that magical place where one goes to gain health and lose weight. Communicating with The Orchard became a little unnerving when it got our stay dates wrong, asked for no money, then suddenly asked for all the money without a secure credit card portal. When we offered a deposit only, it grew sulky and went back to no money now, pay later. What we didn't realise was how recently The Orchard had opened and that it was still trying to get the bugs out of its booking system.

We mused on the possibility that the place did not exist, that somebody had cut and pasted images of swimming pools, bedrooms, trees and smiling, uniformed people behind reception desks and combined them as an imagined health retreat. Serious but smiling Asian doctors holding qualifications from unknown universities would complete the picture. But since we'd not even been asked for a deposit, the financial risk was minimal. Even if the address delivered us to nothing more than a swamp, it would be an adventure.

A two-day stopover in Kuala Lumpur prepared us by building up more fat tissue, which the retreat would then triumphantly remove. We wanted the staff there to feel a sense of achievement as they measured our circumferences and attributed the upcoming reductions to their program.

Hotel Toaster Report

My first toaster report came from Sydney Airport, Singapore Airlines business class lounge, where we went for a pre-flight breakfast. The management hadn't gone to much toaster trouble, providing a rather domestic, vertical four-holer that was browned-off from a few bread flare-ups. My score: three out of ten. Then we had a second breakfast on board, our first lunch before arriving in Singapore and another lunch on Silk Air on our way to KL. We were pleased to be doing all this for the benefit of The Orchard Resort.

Silk Air wasn't very silky. It specialised in bug-like A320 aeroplanes still with Austin A40 brown vinyl seats (lavished only on business class) for short hops around South East Asia. On our flight, the English captain had given first officer, Tong, a go at the controls. Tong liked working the throttle up and down to dodge clouds and landed with a jolt that tested the suspension of the A320.

We trained it into town at KL and found the Shangri-La. Michelle hypnotised the hotel manager and, when he woke up, he'd upgraded us from an ordinary room to a suite: excellent bed, two toilets, bidet, generous-rose shower and a lounge room that we immediately made homely by emptying the contents of our cases all over it.

Hotel Toaster Report

The joy of the next morning's breakfast, held in a football-field-sized dining room, was to write my first proper hotel toaster report from KL — which provided a landmark in the definitive history I was compiling about these machines. Here was a genuine toaster family. The large mother toaster was the belt-driven variety where bread disappeared into the hot-slot and returned via an aircraft-style escape slide to a tray underneath. The toaster came with impressive buttons and switches on the front and a dial to increase intensity. A young lady of most pleasing appearance put her cold bread in and was quickly rewarded with a piece of warm bread. 'My goodness,' she exclaimed, 'it needs more heat.' She bravely turned the dial from beige to red, and returned the bread to the machine. Being a hotel toaster veteran, I knew that the dial didn't increase the heat but slowed down the belt. Her bread now proceeded at slo-mo speed on the moving rack while she peered in as it turned black and started to smoulder. Just short of ignition, it slid into the tray. She prodded the thin layer of charcoal and declared it inedible as she reached for another slice of bread and wound back the dial.

Next to the mother toaster was its offspring, an identical but smaller machine. One day, the kid would be a big toaster like his mother, but for now he was training on single slices. I gave him a small slice of sourdough, set his little dial and he performed beautifully. He had a bright future.

On the way back to our table, the devil spoke to me as I passed a chocolate fountain. I went weak at the knees. A chocolate fountain at breakfast? How ridiculous. 'You may not pass this way again,' the devil whispered as I stopped to marvel at the erupting chocolate cascading down the domed mountain. I cried out, 'Lord, help me to be strong,' but the devil had won and I returned to the table with a glass half-full of liquid chocolate – which I drank in a trance and then felt sick for the rest of the day.

Since I didn't dare test my abstinence resolve in the presence of the chocolate fountain in the main dining room, I retreated to the club lounge for breakfast the next morning. And what did I discover? The dining room's mother toaster had a twin sister living upstairs in the club lounge. As far as I could see, she was a spinster, and a hot one at that. I discovered this after feeding in four pieces of sourdough and retrieving them from the escape slide, beautifully browned.

We had booked tickets online to see the Petronas Twin Towers, but all that did was put us into the queue to exchange those tickets for real tickets, which we immediately exchanged for other tickets, swung from the neck on a lanyard.

While there were not many 'have to see' places in KL, the Petronas towers were high on the list. I remembered the brand on Formula One racing cars and I recalled Harry Potter yelling out, 'Petronas!' as he waved his wand to summon murky, magnetic cyclones to thwart his enemies. Maybe he was also sponsored by Petronas, the oil company.

When the towers were built in 1996, they were the world's tallest buildings. Now they had fallen to number three, but still held number one position for the tallest twin towers at 452 m.

The owners paid US$1.6 billion to have them built and were now recovering the money, one ringgit at a time, from tourists who wanted to go up and come down in a series of elevators. Taking the tour was based on cattle-yard good management: herded in here, sent over there and channelled through the souvenir shop where we could buy all manner of Petronas inspired items, including some ugly clocks that straddled the towers.

Commercial matters aside, the ascent offered a sensational view from the walkway that joined the towers at about their waist level, and then even better from the top, eighty-eight floors up where, if I stood on tip-toe, I could see Bondi Beach in Sydney.

One man had base-jumped from the building, while, in September 2009, a French urban climber called Alain 'Spiderman' Robert, using only his bare hands and feet, and with no safety devices, scaled to the top of Tower Two in just under two hours after his previous efforts had ended in arrest before he reached the summit.

One strange sensation at the top was the continual, minuscule movement of the towers. They had to be flexible structures, otherwise they would have snapped off and made a terrible mess. Some of it, in fact, might have landed on Bondi Beach.

Even though it was raining in KL like a spasmodic water cannon, we went to a highly recommended Chinese restaurant whose serving staff treated us as though we weren't there. The management clearly preferred locals. But the food made their indifference worthwhile. Towards the end of one of the best Chinese meals we'd ever eaten, there was a typical downpour. Could they kindly call a taxi to take us to our hotel? Ah, not possible. No taxi. You wait long time. Better you walk to look for taxi.

Outside, in the hammering rain, we dodged along, mostly under small shop verandas, until we came to the Park Royal Hotel where a huddle had gathered outside the foyer waiting for taxis that normally streamed up the ramp. Demand had soaked up the taxi supply, which exasperated the shuffling crowd. Heading one large group was a tall, fancy-shirted Dutchman attempting to establish his credentials by demanding two taxis ahead of everybody else. He did this by towering over the young bellboy who was trying to sort out the queue, and ordered him to produce taxis. The bellboy couldn't oblige, but instead explained to the Dutchman that his party had to wait their turn if, perchance, a taxi did appear. The Dutchman then turned on a tantrum, telling his followers, all small Asians, that bellboys were always trying to pull this old stunt – whatever that was – and that he'd report this particular one to the hotel management. Still, no taxis arrived. The Dutchman went into another tirade. Then, miraculously, the rain stopped. 'We don't need your antics or your taxis, you arsehole,' the Dutchman spat at the bellboy. 'We'll walk instead.' With that, Pied-Piper-like, he led his troupe of ten obedient people down the ramp and into the street. 'Not my fault,' the bellboy lamented, clearly upset. 'No taxis.'

We didn't have long to wait before a taxi arrived. As we got in, there was as clap of thunder and it began teeming with rain again. I imagined the Dutchman and his followers in the steamy street, running for their sodden lives, having left behind one bellboy believing in karma.

As a city, KL was haphazardly laid out. It had huge buildings, many quite beautiful, and more on the way, but it seemed as though they were simply set down where there was a space. Roads? Their function was to train people in cars in the art of patience, inner calm and bladder control by not moving for long periods of time. But there was something missing in KL. Maybe a soul? That may have been because there were three distinct cultures vying for supremacy. But in many respects, the way Malaysia handled its racial confluence stood as a guide for the rest of the world.

I had become so obsessed with the toaster intrigue at the

Shangri-La that I was compelled to engage the toast captain in conversation at breakfast in the main dining room on our last day. 'Mother and child?' I said, pointing to the duo standing there with their innards aglow. The captain, a young lady done up in a white sailor-type uniform, took a step back from her counter, thinking I was crazy. I explained that I was joking because that's what the pair of toasters looked like. She smiled and stepped forward again. 'The management order first the big one,' she said, 'then find it not enough, so they place second order, but out of stock. Only small one available. They buy that. Maybe not a good decision.' I was, of course, devastated. My idea of a toaster family was dashed. I should never have asked her.

When we boarded a mini-bus with *Orchard*, the name of our destination, painted on the side, the likelihood of the health resort being real got a boost. But I had some other matters to deal with. It was not until we were halfway to Malacca that I felt fully recovered from the chocolate fountain experience. We whizzed along an admirable expressway that ran down the spine of Malaysia, all the way to Singapore. This was where to test your Ferrari, or kill yourself on a motorbike. The 110 km/h speed signs were ignored by plenty of hot cars and bikes howling past us. We later discovered that Malaysian speed cameras could not register a vehicle travelling at more than 180 km/h, which explained much of the speeding. We passed little villages set in dense foliage until we entered the gates of The Orchard Wellness & Health Resort, capital of the Land of Thin.

The lobby we walked into was huge, its floor covered by leagues of club-type carpet whose writhing pattern wanted to devour us. The interior designer had placed some reception desks at one end and then looked around to see how to fill the rest of the quarter-acre. The answer was to visit very old French palaces and copy the furniture. The result was overwhelming. We sat in the biggest chairs and lounges I'd ever seen or imagined. The whole place was in the same style. The owner later told us that she wanted to give guests an environmental experience they wouldn't have at home. She had succeeded.

Our room, actually a villa looking like granny's quaint timber cottage, was set in a dense tropical garden. The cottage was outfitted with more colossal rococo furniture, carved, gilded, buttoned, bejewelled and pumped up to near bursting. The bed could have had Napoleon sleeping in it. There were chandeliers, wood mouldings, burgundy curtains looking as though they had come from a 1920s theatre, huge urns with paper flowers rioting to get out, and a faux timber floor that bounced like a trampoline when we walked across it. All this was virtually new, because the resort had only been open for a few months and hadn't yet been mistreated by careless guests.

We were the only people in the dining room on our first night. We sipped soup (consommé of can't-get-fat) and ate grilled chicken, vegetables and fruit from the hundred-acre orchard that was a feature of the resort. There was another couple staying there, but they had made off into town in search of entertainment. We realised that this whole complex was currently being run for four guests, resulting in an intensity of care you'd expect for royalty or the dying. The dining room staff held their breath every time we opened our mouths. As we chewed, they continually asked how we liked it — in between exchanging geographical anecdotes about where they were from and what they knew about where we were from.

Prior to dinner, we had been taken to the health assessment department. In the first room, a handsome, young Chinese man sat me in a padded chair, asked me to put headphones on – no reason given and no sound therefrom – then opened a computer program, which showed up on a big screen behind him. Next, he positioned opposite me on the desk a little silver cylinder with a blinking red light in it. A flash on the screen and we were away, taking a reading of the condition of my entire body, one organ and joint at a time. For instance, a pancreas would flash up, dots would appear all over it and they would go different colours. Then my pancreas score would be posted at the side of the screen. The scores mostly showed that my body was hardly worth selling for scrap. I was quite suspicious of this machine. How could the little red light see past the desk and down to my legs?

The second room had a beautiful Indian girl done up in a white dust-coat to make her look like a regular doctor. She was actually the official Nutritionist. She weighed me, measured my body fat – which she said was worryingly excessive – and informed me that, for my height, my ideal weight would be 66 kg. I was that weight when I was about twelve – with no fat. Again, I queried the findings.

She also instructed the kitchen on how to cook tasteless, boring, bland food. Michelle resolved to tackle her about it, but ran the risk of being appointed assistant cook.

The charming Chinese manager showed us over the rest of the resort. There were treatment rooms for a great many mysterious ailments. Lying naked in the salt room, not accompanied by the manager — she hastened to point out — was supposed to cure complaints we didn't know we had. There were exercise programs, orchard walks, a lake-sized swimming pool, saunas and steam rooms.

On our first morning, I met my gym trainer. I called him Mr Muscles because he was a fine example of body-building. He had a languid Indian female assistant. Her main claim to exercise instruction was that she used to be a good hockey player. These two took us on a 3 km walk through the orchard and jungle. It was a hilly path, obliging me to go up slowly in first gear and stop often to point out interesting views as an excuse for catching my breath.

We passed the poultry farm where our tasteless chicken came from. It was very free range, with chooks and ducks wandering through the thickets. A white rooster, enacting ancient fertility rites, chased two hens at a breakneck speed around the yard. I don't know which one he caught but it was obvious that neither was in the mood for love. Some crowing from behind a shed semaphored that he'd done the job. I realised, for the first time in my life, that God had created roosters to run faster than hens, otherwise there'd be no chickens.

One wall of windows in the cavernous, empty dining room we visited three times a day looked into a large aviary. It could have been a great drawcard, offering diners a variety of birds to watch while they consumed slim dollops of good health. Disappointingly, the whole aviary was given over to budgerigars. I soon knew everything a budgerigar could possibly do. It was not very much. Okay, they were cute enough and some of them might talk in isolation, but what about a substantial parrot or two, maybe a randy breeding pair of macaws, or a few scrub turkeys? The aviary was screaming out for watchable birds. Even Indian mynas would have been more interesting because they continually fought one another. I really wanted them to bring the white rooster and a few speedy hens into the aviary for some great chase scenes.

By day four, Michelle was feeling confined and suggested we go AWOL for a couple of days into Malacca township, which was about an hour's drive away. She had good reason, because a full day of activity at the resort was like a week of workouts elsewhere.

One great disappointment was that there was no hotel toaster and never would be. There was no role for toast in the Land of Thin.

By day four, we were the only guests in the entire resort, giving us a staff-to-guest ratio of about forty to one. We prayed for some arrivals so we could move about without being continually pampered and helped.

A typical day began at 7 o'clock with Mr Muscles and the Languid One waiting in the misty dawn for a trail walk – after taking our blood pressure and encouraging us to drink a glass of dark green 'good-for-you'. The walk took us through a mixture of orchards, animal enclosures, jungle and staff accommodation comprising randomly placed buildings among the trees.

When we arrived back at home base, we were ushered into the gym where Mr Muscles worked me over on the latest torturous, high-tech machines. He told me he'd trained some famous tennis players, including Steffi Graf, who had given him the racquet she used when she won Wimbledon. As a mark of respect, he had it restrung every year, even though he didn't play tennis.

CHAPTER 12 Malaysia – 2015

The Languid One tried to train Michelle – who knew more about the exercises than she did. Motivation was therefore very low but Michelle still battled through, glaring jealously at me. She wanted Mr Muscles as her trainer.

We'd tumble out of the gym with only enough energy to make it to breakfast, which initially comprised fruit, fruit, and more bloody fruit, until Michelle terrorised the chef with the news that fruit had high quantities of sugar – which we were supposedly trying to cut out. The meals improved. She also had to convince him that we liked Asian cuisine.

After breakfast, we'd lie naked in the heated salt room, a modest two-person space whose walls were made of thick salt tiles heated from behind. It was evidently good for respiration and most other ailments that might come to mind. We'd lurch out of there, sweating lightly, to enter the sauna to sweat heavily.

The sauna comprised two little wooden dolls' houses, each holding one seated person. The heat they generated fell just short of cremating the occupant. Loud, meditative piano music helped pass the time. After twenty minutes, as our skin was about to peel, they would let us out.

One day, I had a lymphatic drainage treatment scheduled. I was wrapped in a hard-plastic shroud, which acted like a blood pressure machine cuff – but for the whole body. It squeezed and let go of various sections of the torso, sending all the retained fluid rushing in a frenzy out of my fat cells, seeking refuge in my bladder.

After a can't-put-on-weight lunch, the yoga lady awaited. I hated yoga and told her so. She smiled benignly out of a perfectly square face and reassured me that she would give us very gentle exercises. She stood with her back to us but facing a wall mirror in which I had to confront my substantial stomach and turkey neck. And if that wasn't bad enough, she instructed me to place my left foot behind my right foot as she was doing. I become confused because I could see her image in the mirror more clearly than I could see her, and her right foot in the mirror was where her left foot really was. When I followed the mirror and placed my feet in the wrong position, she became cross and turned around to show which foot was which, but now the backs of her feet were showing in the mirror and I started thinking that she had four feet, none of which corresponded to either of mine. We sat down, she and Michelle cross-legged, but I couldn't cross my legs. Even sitting on the floor always made me roll over backwards. She assumed I was clowning around and became cross again. After the session was over, I think she complained to the management about me. Needless to say, we cancelled yoga for the remainder of our stay.

In another fat-fighting treatment, I was laid on a bench, face up, while two diminutive Indian girls went to work on my stomach with what looked like a cattle prod on the end of an electrical cable. It made a sound like a machine gun and was drawn over my stomach as though the operator was writing a letter. This machine was supposed to break up the fat cells that thought they were safe there. After seven thousand shots, I was released into the steam room for the usual twenty minutes of slow cooking.

The Languid One met us regularly in the thermal swimming pool building and put us through an aqua aerobics exercise routine. It was really quite good, except that the pool was shallow, and at bath temperature, so that if I was low enough in the water to obey the Languid One's instructions, I capsized and looked as though I was making fun of her efforts.

After the fourth shower of the day, we'd go into the vast dining room and eat dinner on our own, apart from visits from the manager, the chef, the nutritionist, the waiter and the magical machine-operator who all wanted to see if we were okay.

After dinner, we'd visit the salt room again and then hobble to our springy-floored granny's cottage. We'd brought fifty DVDs to watch and we settled on the huge two-seater and selected one. It wouldn't play because the Asian DVD system was different to ours – and the rest of the US and Europe, it seemed. In a desperate bid to please its only two guests, the management ran around Malacca trying to source a 'foreign' DVD player. We couldn't have sat up using it for long anyway. By 9 o'clock, we were seriously exhausted and had to ready ourselves for Mr Muscles and the Languid One at seven the next morning for another workout.

After a week, it was hard to believe that we'd been in transformation camp for only that length of time. Since we'd told the chef we really, really, liked Asian food, the meals had improved. Our nutritionist kept an eye on the chef to make sure he didn't give us normal restaurant-sized portions. Partial starvation was important in weight loss.

Even though our intake was way down on our usual eating, we didn't feel hungry between meals. We put this down to a total absence of processed sugar which, the Nutritionist told us, made the victim feel hungry. Feeling hungry can lead to eating which leads to girth expansion, which would lead to staff depression at The Orchard.

The therapies were almost all about heat. There was the cremo-sauna, the steam room simmer, the outside air, the hydro pool, the Jacuzzi, chilli in the food, and then our first two treatments by a machine called Vanquish. It was the hottest of the lot. The treating doctor told me that we were born with a set number of fat cells and they never increased. The buggers just got bigger. Their weakness was heat. They were supposed to collapse at forty-two degrees Celsius – never to return. That was hard to believe. The difficulty was in targeting them and not other body tissue that we didn't want to collapse and never to return. Enter Vanquish, which supposedly attacked fat cells via microwave. Each treatment – we needed four – took forty-five minutes. A three-section plate was positioned over my stomach 1.5 cm from the skin and the machine was turned on, producing a menacing hum. I began to feel pleasantly warm, then very warm, then definitely too warm, then so hot I'd swear my skin was on fire. The passive-faced nurse, who seemed to have been selected for her poor command of English, couldn't tell me how many minutes to go to switch-off. It was more a case of 'let pain be your friend.' I could, of course, have screamed and told them to cease and desist, but I would have lost the prospect of ever seeing my six-pack again.

The doctor said that I would get the full benefit of Vanquish over the two months after I arrived home, when my trousers would fall down and my belt would run out of tightening holes. She added that because I'd annihilated a number of fat cells, and they don't reproduce themselves, the 'cure' would be permanent. Did I believe her? I wanted to, but another voice in my head raised serious doubts. Magic machines had failed me before.

After a brief flurry of arrivals and departures by people we never got to meet, we were back to being the only guests — and again being overindulged by the staff. They couldn't have been more charming, helpful and attentive; we appreciated that. But a few companions to spread the intensity would have been welcome.

The manager invited us to dinner and a 'show' in Malacca, about an hour's drive away. This was the major tourist town in Malaysia, having been attacked and occupied by at least five countries in the last 600 years, leaving a mixture of cultures that attracted foreign and local visitors. We arrived at night, making it hard to see the sights but the crowd was certainly there. Jonker Street, boasting a famous night market, was like boarding a Japanese train in rush hour. The offerings were the same as you find in night markets all over the world: plastic novelties, dodgy sunglasses, watches, clothing, animated toys and local food.

But the real purpose of our invitation was to visit a new hotel, the three-star, down-market sister of the health resort in which we were staying. With 340 rooms, it loomed up into the hot, night sky, its attractive, black wrought-iron balconies standing out from the white painted concrete of the walls. However, these balconies could not be used because they provided an ideal place — probably an afterthought — for the individual room air-conditioners.

The third-floor conference room had been converted into an odd-shaped theatre, not deep, but very wide, with a small stage in the middle, against the wall. The show was supposed to attract a paying audience, some from the hotel and some from tourists who might like to know something of Malacca's history and culture. The show originally was a serious didactic documentary, but attracted too few patrons. To enhance the show, they'd thrown in a funny-man singer who did impersonations, unfortunately always in his own voice, along with barely referential costuming. But his energy, Asian-type humour and passable singing voice got him over the line. He was supported by a bland, middle-aged woman done up in a traditional Chinese outfit who did a bit of forgettable singing and also tried to explain what was going on. She didn't really succeed, because they'd combined a traditional Chinese wedding ceremony with unrelated appearances by Mr Funny. There was also a dance troupe of four girls who twirled here and there without much purpose. The show would have been infinitely more popular if they'd taken their clothes off.

Because the production was still being market tested, the stage lighting was restricted to two severe overhead burners that lit the top of everybody's head but left the faces and bodies in shadow and looking a little sinister. As VIPs, we were seated in the front row, right in the middle, within touching distance of the stage. This was not a good place to sit when there was a funny man on the rampage and a very small audience to work with. The minute he came out as Charlie Chaplin, I knew I was a sitting duck. He pointed at me, sang to me, made me sing to him, and then forced Michelle and me into the drama where we had to play the roles of elderly relatives in a typically Chinese wedding ceremony. Thankfully, we didn't have to say anything.

Back at The Orchard, we quickly became familiar with our personal trainers, since we met them at dawn every day for scientific body beautification and later for aqua aerobics. I had to upgrade Mr Muscles to Dr Muscles. He was an exceptional personal trainer as well as holding me spellbound with stories of famous people he had trained and the qualifications he claimed to hold. The stories expanded to the point where I wondered how he could have fitted all that into his forty-three years. More to the point, why, with such vast experience, was he working in an elaborate, out-of-the-way start-up health retreat with currently one guest to train?

He claimed to have trained many world-famous sportspeople, including Tiger Woods (before being clobbered by Mrs Woods), a world champion Chinese table tennis player and a world champion female badminton player which resulted in another racquet being presented to Dr Muscles. Maria Sharapova had also been a trainee. During her preparation for Wimbledon, she drew a tennis ball out of her knickers, signed it, and gave it to Dr Muscles. I searched for his name on the internet but came up with no references. That seemed strange, since he'd claimed to have occupied so many important positions in the areas of sports training and medicine. He told me his qualifications included five university degrees, senior lecturer, professor, faculty dean and doctor of philosophy. Along the way, he had been an Asian Latin dancing champion (and leading instructor), a champion body-builder, boxer and wrestler. He also had many successful bouts in mixed martial arts, better known as cage fighting.

He told some wonderful tales about combat in the cage. He went to Thailand to a championship (which, of course, he won) and came up against a Thai fighter who was carrying on about how tough he was, snarling and pulling aggressive faces at Dr Muscles during the introduction. 'Usually, I take fighting as a sport and respect my opponent,' Dr Muscles said, 'but for this man, I took it personal! I decided to knock him out and then throw him out of the ring.' And, of course, that's just what happened. I don't know how he got the snarling opponent over the top of the cage, but over he went, landing on his head. That put him into a coma for a month. It paid not to snarl at Dr Muscles. But then the Thai police were called and they handcuffed Dr Muscles and charged him with assault. After five hours in the lock-up, he was able to convince the sergeant that this was a sport and not a street brawl, whereupon Dr Muscles was released on a wave of apologies and admiration.

Dr Muscles had only been knocked out once, he claimed. He was beating the tripe out of a Chinese opponent when the bell went for the end of the round. Dr Muscles released his opponent from a deadly grip and turned around to go to his corner when the Chinaman belted him in the ear, producing thirty seconds of incomprehension. 'This was a gift,' said Dr Muscles nonchalantly. 'I'd never been knocked out before and I needed to know how it felt.'

Later, when training a Saudi prince in mixed martial arts, he passed on the gift by knocking him out three times a week. Not good for the prince? On the contrary, the prince became a champion fighter and always acknowledged the contribution of Dr Muscles in his victory speeches.

In the end, it didn't matter how many of his tales were true — if any. He certainly knew all about personal training and how to fill in the gaps while I was recovering from each set of exercises.

Our other trainer, the Languid One, turned out to be less languid and told a far more believable backstory than Dr

CHAPTER 12 Malaysia – 2015

Muscles. She had a sports training degree and became highly valued as our aqua aerobics' instructor. Being Muslim, she felt compelled to cover up with layers of Lycra to nullify the female form, but that didn't stop her from jumping into the pool with us to demonstrate how to do some of the exercises. I imagined the struggle she would have had later, pulling off her wet gear. It would have been like peeling an onion. Although not a potential beauty contest winner, she was intelligent, with an intense, quiet sense of humour.

Along with heat treatments, another high frequency experience was peeing. When the doomed fat cells collapsed, the water they used to hold went rushing off to the bladder where it joined the litres of water, herbal tea, fruit juice and detox drinks I was obliged to take by mouth. The result was a maximum bladder tolerance of about half-an-hour or less during the day. I made at least four visits to the toilet during the night, often dreaming dangerously about peeing – but thankfully, it didn't result in the dream crossing over to reality.

Going anywhere out of toilet range was asking for trouble. However, serendipity brought rewards when I did get caught short. We went to a small town about fifteen minutes' drive away one Sunday, to visit a coin operated laundry. All over the world, hotel laundry was an outrageous rip-off. You could generally buy a new shirt for less than having your existing one hotel-laundered. We went to Majid Tana to beat the system.

A bank of coin-operated laundry machines sat in an open shop. It took about thirty minutes for a wash and twenty-five more for a dry. The facilities comprised washing and drying machines, sorting tables but, unsurprisingly, no urinal.

The dusty street, with its closed shops — being Sunday — offered no obvious solution. During the drying cycle, I was becoming very interested in the small park opposite with some strategically placed foliage that looked more and more attractive as time passed. Finally, I picked my way through the traffic and went bush. As I was standing there looking down with a benign smile on my face, I found I was above a creek fed by a council drain. Swimming towards me, down the drain, was what I identified as a Komodo dragon — in this case, the smaller Malaysian version of the Indonesian dragon that chases people in order to bite them. This dragon was the size and shape of a medium crocodile with a lizard's head, including a darting blue tongue. It flopped out of the drain and into the creek, swam unhurriedly past me and vanished into the reeds.

The fact that the resort remained in the state of seventy staff looking after two guests weighed heavily upon us. The dining room was serviced by two chefs, two waiters, and a receptionist who assisted us in choosing a table from an empty range of about forty. The chef generally came out to discuss his handiwork at length.

One night, the head chef offered to slaughter a goat and make a dish out of it — but how could we eat it? We'd visited the goats and liked them. Michelle suggested that she would prefer they milk the nanny and make cheese. The chef wrote that down for discussion at the next management meeting.

When Dr Muscles took me walking every morning, he picked the steepest hills, but I'd become fitter because I could manage them without stopping or calling for oxygen. I was also distracted from my fatigue by his ongoing revelations of qualifications and sporting highlights. To his already prestigious list, he also claimed to be an expert rock climber and a qualified scuba-diving instructor. For his PhD, he didn't write the usual book-length thesis covering a hitherto unexplored subject. Not our Dr Muscles. Confounding his supervising professor, he wrote a remarkable manual for personal training, which had now become important reference material for sports medicine institutions — certainly throughout Asia. It was, of course, a bestseller.

There was more. He modestly claimed to be a mixed martial arts Asian champion, undefeated in the light heavyweight division. I asked him if there was a heavy lightweight division as well, but he didn't see anything funny in that. He intended to defend his belt early the following year when a worthy contender rose from the ranks. Tragically, Google had missed all of this too, and had failed to list him.

Dr Muscles liked fighting tall men because they had longer legs upon which to land debilitating kicks. He revelled in turning their legs purple with bruises, which was a bit unlikely, since it took more than ten minutes for bruises to turn purple. He could also surprise tall opponents by leaping high enough to grab their heads and slam them into his iron thighs before he landed back on the mat.

On his last title defence, Dr Muscles was going toe-to-toe with a tall fighter who had been skilful enough to open a cut above the doctor's eye. Blood clouded Dr Muscles' vision, so he switched to the very-difficult-to-master 'fight by sound' method, since his ears were still in good working order. He looked out of the cage to see his wife in tears nursing their recently arrived baby. This was a terrific spur to Dr Muscles and he immediately used his hearing to knock out the tall fighter. On that occasion he didn't throw his opponent out of the cage.

One probably genuine, gruesome account was about his seven months working for a prince in Saudi Arabia. Weekends in the capital, Riyadh, comprised Thursday and Friday, with Friday being execution day. The city square attracted a big crowd to see criminals, found guilty of a variety of crimes (some unproven) have their heads cut off with a meat cleaver.

We had reached our halfway mark and celebrated by going into Majid Tana to visit our favourite Malaysian coin laundry and, hopefully, see my Komodo dragon in the creek. We even contemplated buying a shaving of dark chocolate just to remind ourselves of the evil that still existed in the culinary world.

If we'd gone home right then, nobody would have seen much change after two weeks of deprivation and intense therapies. It was over the next two weeks that we expected some results, but even then, it wouldn't be spectacular. The point of difference about this program was that, if we were to believe the hype, improvement would build for months after we arrived home. This was a handy philosophy for the resort too, because it was a long way for us to come back to exhibit our stubborn blubber if we wanted a refund.

My Komodo dragon turned out not to be that at all. What I'd seen swimming down the creek in Majid Tana was an Asian Water Monitor. I had been misinformed by the locals — as often happened in this part of the world. This lizard grew up to 3 m long and was found in many parts of South East Asia. It ate fish, frogs, rodents, birds, crabs, and snakes. One of its specialities was knowing where people fed their cats and pinching the food. According to my research, the Asian Water Monitor was the most intelligent reptile on earth. It could count snails, among other feats of brainpower, although I couldn't imagine why snail counting was important.

Still on reptiles, Dr Muscles took me on a privileged detour during one of our punishing walks to see the resort's crocodiles. I thought they lived in the man-made lake and were free to hunt anything in the huge orchard, including people. But, not so. They lived in an enclosure surrounded by a high concrete wall. The two of them were not much bigger than my Asian Water Monitor. Dr Muscles told me they were quite old and religiously fed one chicken a day each. I imagined a cartoon where one was saying to the other, as dinner arrived, 'Not another bloody chicken!'

On our next visit to the coin laundry in Majid Tana, we found watching clothes going around in a washing machine was not as engaging as walking around the night market next door. It was just setting up for its Sunday sell. The shops were foldable canvas tents with open fronts to take a counter. The butcher, a star attraction, had his sides of meat and various cuts on display on a bench at the front of his canvas shop or hanging from hooks attached to the tent frame. He didn't bother with refrigeration, or even a half-hearted piece of ice to keep the meat from going off or the flies from going on.

Walking along the roadway between the stands, we came across a pet vendor. He had several rabbits and a cage holding three kittens. We fell in love with the one in the middle who gave us the 'take me home' look that kittens do so well. The price raised our eyebrows. They were asking more than AUD$200 for each of these moggies. The Languid One later told us that was cheap because cats were highly prized in Malaysia. Purebreds would cost huge dollars.

I hit upon a great potential business: importing abandoned and stray cats from Australia. Our council pounds were full of them. I was sure we wouldn't have to worry about vaccination or de-sexing. *Auspuss Corporation* was born.

Since I didn't die of heart failure on the first orchard trail walk, Dr Muscles decided to see if he could induce one. He designed a route especially for me. We began by following an up-sloping, wide road, which turned into a narrow, paved road that went past a helipad and then mercilessly climbed and twisted into the orchard and jungle hills. When I thought I was about to reach the summit, it would take another turn, revealing another hill. When I finally reached what I thought was a turnaround small plateau, I was actually at an intersection with the choice of a gentle down-slope or a horrible, bitumen road climb that got closer to vertical the further it went. Using his thumb as an indicator, Dr Muscles chose the climb for me.

Two middle-aged Chinese women joined us one day and assured Dr Muscles they'd be able to handle the cardio challenge. They did pretty well until we reached the intersection and got the thumb. When we reached the top, one of them threw up into the jungle while the other looked for a toilet.

Dr Muscles believed that had shaken them off, because we were back on our own again the next day and he made me go up the dreaded climb twice. When I didn't fall down with exhaustion, he announced that I would have to go up and down four times without a break before he'd be satisfied that I had worked hard enough.

Little knots of people drifted in and out of The Orchard for short stays, but for most of the time, a staff of nearly seventy was still deployed looking after just the two of us. Intensity aside, I think we lucked out. This was a new, very well-equipped health retreat at a very competitive rate. Its main problem was that of organisation. Rather than laying down a schedule for the various daily exercises and treatments, the manager tried to please everybody by moving the service time slots around. The system clogged immediately when the two Hong Kong ladies wanted their orchard trail walk at the same time we had arranged for our gym workout, because it required the same two staff members.

The Chinese lady manager, of whom we became very fond, frothed at the mouth trying to solve the jigsaw. I couldn't imagine how the place could function with, say, even twenty people out of its potential eighty. It could lapse into chaos. Design problems would also surface. For instance, the male and female spa changing rooms had twenty lockers each but could only fit about four people to use them. The three beautifully tiled circular shower recesses in each offered a hand-held shower head or an overhead rose which I couldn't stand under because there was a marble-and-tile stool built just where the water landed. This meant that I had to shower sitting down – not the best posture for washing the undercarriage. The water pressure and temperature had a will of its own, too.

The swimming pool was vast and looked wonderful in the brochure, as long as we didn't mind a constant depth of 1.2 m. Up one end was a roofed section where water pressure therapy was offered by arranging the body in front of various jet streams for massage. It would have cost plenty to build but, in truth, few people would return after experiencing forced water entry into all of their bodily orifices.

The gym was equipped with Technogym machines, which were the best in the business and a delight to use. While walking, pushing or pulling, I had the choice of watching a screen with Facebook, internet, Twitter, and YouTube. If I were a tycoon, I could have jogged my way through a major business deal.

We were massaged every day. A team of three massage girls squabbled over who would massage whom. Michelle got a Filipina girl and I chose Wina as my regular. Wina by name and weenie by stature. She had the hands and feet of a six-year-old girl, but enough strength to crush a coconut. Javanese, she had huge, engaging brown eyes and continually smiled. But she spoke in a whisper and then only uttered necessary sentences like, 'Are you comfortable, sir?' and, 'Is the pressure satisfactory, sir?'

In all the massages I had from Wina, I never felt totally comfortable. She told me she was Muslim, which meant she was not allowed to come into physical contact with any man other than family members. Since she was still single, that placed me in the position of representing the devil. The daily massage lasted for fifty minutes, conducted in nicely appointed treatment rooms, but I had to wear long, baggy, dark blue disposable shorts, lest an accidental flash of my genitals turned poor Wina into a pillar of salt.

While scanning my body in the mirror, desperately trying to detect some signs of blubber-deflation, I arrived at my head and couldn't help noticing that my hair had suffered from the tropical sun, steam, too many showers and the salty swimming pool water. Instead of the usual rampant russet, it had become very pale, not quite white, but hovering around beige. That prompted me to buy a box of *Bigen Speedy Hair Color Conditioner with Natural Herbs* from a Malaccan pharmacy.

Not being familiar with hair dye, I pulled out the instructions that were written in ten languages, to which English seemed to have been reluctantly added. I put my faith in following the diagrams, which told me to squeeze from each of two tubes enough goop to fill the two channels in the plastic 'comb through' applicator. It was like an Araldite system, in this case one being the colour and the other the developer. They needed to marry at the critical moment. Leave for ten minutes and wash off, it said. I squeezed, combed through and repeated the process until my head looked like a neatly ploughed hillside. The man in the mirror remained disbelieving and beige until the eighth minute when the chemical reaction struck like lightning. I rushed for the shower, but too late. Instead of the autumnal hue showing on the packet, I had been rendered dark brown, bordering on black. I desperately shampooed but to no avail.

I hoped it might lighten when it dried, but it didn't. I looked like a Choc-top on legs. My massage girl did a double-take when she saw me, thinking that I was a new client. She managed to mutter that it made me look 'more young', but I knew what she and her colleagues were saying between laughter: 'mutton dressed like the lamb'.

The owner of The Orchard and her rich husband were determined to become hoteliers – among many other things. Earlier in the year, they had built and opened a 340-room hotel in the tourist heart of Malacca to which we had been invited to see not-the-greatest-show-on-earth two weeks previously. This time, their generosity extended to providing a car and driver to take us back to the hotel for a one or two-night stay as part of our resort package.

We thought a short break of one night with a day either side would be a real-world contrast to the strictures of controlled food and hard exercise. The Imperial Heritage was one of the most peculiar hotels I'd ever stayed in. It stood on a skinny piece of land that had probably been sold at a very low price because nobody thought they could build anything commercially viable on it. The resulting building resembled a huge wafer in that it was very tall and wide but only one room deep. The guest rooms were accessed by an open walkway, which meant that, in a rainstorm, guests would get wet going to their rooms.

There were eighteen floors – but really there weren't, because floors four, thirteen and fourteen had been deleted so as not to offend superstitious Chinese guests who could not abide the number four. Each room, plus the walkway, took up the entire width of the building. Our room seemed okay at first look but then some design shortcomings surfaced. The bathroom had the narrowest shower cubical I'd ever seen. It was a like a crack in the tiled wall, with either a hand-held shower head, which was about to fall out of the wall, or another shower head, higher up, that fired water at forty-five degrees and missed the occupant. At the end was a shower curtain that received most of the water. The toilet was positioned right next to the door on the door-opening side, meaning that you'd know your partner pretty well if you blundered in at the wrong moment. And to finish it off, the ceiling was leaking and provided water and bits of plaster to decorate the vanity bench.

Michelle and I had a restless night and discovered why in the morning. The room had been fitted with a short bed. The mattress was of good quality, but when we lay down flat, our feet hung over the end. It reminded me of Laurel and Hardy comic strips where the two, wearing their hats, shared a double bed that was also too short and showed their boots hanging over the end. I think the hotel was trying to attract diminutive Asian guests, where anybody under five feet would have found the bed to their liking.

Hotel Toaster Report

Ah breakfast, and a chance to do a toaster report. This was quite a bright spot in the hotel, but only after I had spooned out some baked beans onto my plate and found they were stone cold. The baked bean captain had forgotten to turn on the heater. The other hot dishes were also cold for the same reason.

Back to the toaster. This unusual model stood on four spindly legs that made it look as though it was expecting to survive a flood. It presented itself side-on because you put the toast in one end and it came out the other in the manner of a digestive system. Two passes and you had good brown toast. However, there was a mystery tray that ran underneath. I asked the toast captain about its purpose. He bent down condescendingly and, when he straightened up, he announced that it was part of the machine. Yes, I knew that. It could hardly have been part of some other machine. I asked again, and again he pursed his lips and bent theatrically from the waist for a prolonged

> examination. It was there to collect crumbs, he sniffed, and walked away to avoid this annoying Australian asking any more questions. Nevertheless, I gave this toaster seven and a half out of ten.

Malacca was a mixed-up city, a potpourri of the architecture left behind by five conquerors, three races (Malay, Chinese and Indian), a number of religions (which Islam dominated) and a largely corrupt government. It suffered worse air pollution than Beijing because it was choked with cars and overlaid by ash clouds that drifted across from its close neighbour, Indonesia, burning off crop stubble and forest residue.

The city boasted an eighty-meter-high tower called Taming Sari that took sightseers up and down in a revolving glass doughnut to look over the city and out to sea. Fancying such challenges, I bought a ticket (Michelle pleaded heat distress and retired to the car) and ascended in the company of fifty squealing school kids. At the top, the pollution was so bad, even at that height, I could only see a few kilometres, and certainly not out to sea or anywhere else worthwhile.

Malacca had a few historical places we wanted to visit. One was the Baba & Nyonya Heritage Museum that occupied three adjoining houses in a very narrow street in the old part of town where many Chinese had lived nearly two centuries ago. These houses had been preserved more or less in their original state since the Chan family bought them in 1861 and had owned them ever since. Now into their fourth generation, the multiple Chans didn't live there anymore but visited en masse on special occasions like Chinese New Year.

CHAPTER 12 Malaysia – 2015

The carved furniture and some staircases beggared belief, they were so ornate and intricate. All joinery was achieved without the use of nails, since they believed that nails should only be used to seal coffins. Their crockery, glassware and utensils were still there, along with a 170-year-old bottle of Hennessy brandy that had gone almost black with age. But in spite of the wonderful furnishings, it was how the family had lived that fascinated me the most.

Marriages were strictly arranged by the family elders. The newlyweds usually only saw each other properly for the first time on their wedding night in the nuptial chamber. That really worried me. How would it have been watching the bride struggling out of her layers of official clobber and finding that she had huge buttocks when the groom had always been turned off by huge buttocks. Or he may have stepped down from his built-up wedding slippers and only come up to her chin – when she couldn't stand short men. Once women reached the age of twenty, they were considered unmarriageable because they were too old. The guide commented sourly that brides under twenty these days bordered on being considered victims of molestation.

The house had a low-cost, never-fail, non-electric surveillance system to see who was knocking at the front door. A tiny, square peephole cut into the upstairs front room floor gave a view down onto the street where the knocker would be standing. Reading my mind, our guide assured us that the man of the house might be tempted to pee through the hole but didn't, because there was an ornate chamber pot for that. Since the toilets were downstairs, this chamber pot was the only designated receptacle upstairs.

After candles out, the staircase was locked until morning against thieves or late returning husbands.

These three houses were very long and narrow. The reason was that the government levied taxes according to the width of the frontage and even the wealthy Chans didn't mind a bit of tax avoidance. Each house had two internal courtyards open to the sky, bringing light and fresh air into the house, plus a bit of rain water, which was cleverly drained away and stored. Wedding nasty surprises aside, they must have been good houses to live in.

Another drawcard in Malacca was the Floating Mosque. Of course, in keeping with such fanciful claims, it didn't float. Rather, it sat out in shallow, cloudy seawater on pylons. It was quite sizeable, with the usual open field of carpet under the central dome where the faithful knelt to pray and listen to the imam instruct them how to avoid sin.

As we approached the mosque, we had to pass the dress code barrier. A frowning inspector determined that I was not required to augment my clothing since my long shorts covered my knees, which, if they had been visible, might have driven women crazy with lust. Michelle was not so lucky. Although she was wearing a black floating two-piece cotton outfit, her neck and elbows were discernible, which was a no-no. She was obliged to go into the costume department and then emerged in a pale blue almost-burka with only her grim face framed by the headpiece. For some reason I was reminded of *The Sound of Music*, but Michelle was in no mood for singing. Through clenched teeth, she told me that she was choking and that the outfit had a distinctive worn-often-by-other-people smell. I persuaded her to persevere while we walked around the mosque and looked out across the thick haze at nothing discernible. That done, she disrobed and donned her sinful outfit.

We visited the famous, old red church in the middle of town that was the number one landmark of Malacca. It began as Catholic, but the Dutch took out the statues and glittery stuff and made it Anglican. A punishing up-steps walk from the church brought us to a museum but it was closed because a Thai princess was taking a look around and should not be disturbed by raucous commoners. More punishing steps brought us up to a ruined, very old cathedral. The Japanese did the ruining during their WW2 occupation. It was patched with concrete and steel supports and was a sorry sight. The best part of the visit had been the cardio workout provided by the steps.

One of the food specialties of Malacca was supposed to be *nyonya*, a blend of Chinese and Malay cooking that had been designated a separate taste genre. Since Nancy's Kitchen had the reputation of being a leading exponent of nyonya, we took some trouble to search it out. It had moved from Jonker Street to a new suburb in which the shop numbering system was a guessing game. It took us many attempts to find it, during which we drove past it several times. Finally, we made landfall and settled at a table to study the menu – which made no sense to us. We relied on an impatient waiter to make our choice of chicken tamarind curry and another meat dish, which turned out to be more chicken, this time cut into discs that imitated leather buttons. Fried rice made up the trio. This restaurant did not respect the dissection of chickens. Somebody had attacked the carcass with a chopper and threw the pieces into any dish that went past. The curry had a minefield of bones throughout.

Bones appeared in the fried rice as well. This was turning into a memorable meal for all the wrong reasons.

The saving grace was Nancy's famous dessert: *cendol*, in which shaved ice was lightly doused in palm sugar syrup and sat on a lake of coconut milk, red beans, and *pandan* jelly noodles. This unlikely combination was delicious. But as for the rest of the fare, either Nancy was an overrated cook or we had ordered the wrong dishes.

If Malacca had more to offer, we didn't want to know about it. We asked the driver to take us back to our sanatorium where the staff members had hopefully taken things easy while their two guests had been away. They were in relaxed moods when we returned, maybe because we'd become part of the backdrop. For instance, they let us run out of toilet paper and then, to mend the rift, brought us a pack of twenty-four rolls and later came and took them back again. They turned off the air-conditioning in the passageways and half the lights as well. And we had to ask one of the three waiters to turn on the air-conditioning in the dining room. Because we only had three days until checkout, we were becoming yesterday's newspaper.

Having said that, we loved these people. There was not a nasty one among them. They were victims of human nature when seventy people are trying to look after two.

On our last day at the resort, Dr Muscles took me on a new walking route outside the property. We strode along a deserted road just after dawn. In the total stillness, mist lay still sleeping in the jungle valleys. The only sound was the occasional call of a triumphant rooster. I thought Dr Muscles had taken pity on me and was going to let me off with a flat final journey. Not so.

We passed a steep side road and he gave me the dreaded thumb. He'd been saving another Pike's Peak for my send-off. It was just as close to vertical as the one on the orchard trail, but longer. We did it four times, the reward of each summit offering a view that was a metaphor for tranquillity.

The owner/doctor visited around noon to give us a final health report. She relied on a before-and-after comparison produced by the weird, sci-fi machine. It went by the name of a Bio Resonance Scanner and claimed to rapidly measure the energy level in every bodily organ and pinpoint those that were weak and needed rectification. By way of credentials, the man who developed it was also responsible for the often ridiculed Scientology E-Meter. How it worked, or whether it did anything worthwhile at all, was anybody's guess.

I was told that my bladder was now working at 100% efficiency after a shaky start. All other organs had shown vast improvements except my heart, which had only managed an 11 % gain. This all meant that I should be suffering random hand tremors and memory loss, the operator said. I denied the hand tremors but said I couldn't remember having lost my memory. That didn't humour the handsome, young Chinese technician who was in charge of calibrating.

During Michelle's scan, she observed him pressing an 'improve energy' button and suspected this was to beef up our final readings.

The doctor wanted to treat us both with 'cold sculpting' (attacking the fat cells again but by freezing them this time) but we'd done a bit of reading on that. The patient would be very sore for up to two weeks after a session. Twenty-four hours of travel was painful enough without the addition of inflamed love handles. We swapped it for some more Vanquish, the treatment that was supposed to collapse fat cells by heating them up to forty-two degrees Celsius.

Our departure from the resort was quite sad. The place was mismanaged and misdirected by its owners who didn't know how to run a complex health retreat. I failed to see how it would ever break even, let alone turn a profit, but the staff had become our temporary family and did their best to help our cause. I had imagined that we'd meet plenty of interesting people as waves of health-seeking guests came and went. But for most of the time we were the only guests, meaning that we'd turned inward to personally interact with the staff.

The owners primarily wanted rooms occupied. They'd assumed that would happen through offering a unique, high-quality Asian health resort. Since that hadn't yet eventuated, they gave the manager the impossible task of marketing on the dual fronts of 'health and weight loss' or 'drop in for a good time'. This shattered the focus. The drop-ins would be disappointed to find no bar, entertainment or gourmet food. The health crowd had yet to endorse the place. Many would be disappointed to find the kitchen had not mastered offering spa food. Unfortunately, we lived in an era where so much of holiday enjoyment was food-driven.

The manager was at her wits' end trying to attract and satisfy both types of guests and was succeeding with neither. What she didn't want was the budget crowd. One point in her favour of keeping them out was the resort's pricing that only foreigners could afford. She told us of a local Malay couple who booked a double room and then announced that they intended to put six people into it. To them, the logic was plain: We're paying for the room and we do what we like with it. Another Chinese family with an out-of-control kid came for a fun stay whereupon the kid ran down the decoratively papered passageways, crayons in hand, practicing his graffiti skills. Budget travellers were also notorious for pinching hotel property. Towels and sheets departed with guests at checkout, along with more serious items like bedside lamps and small pieces of furniture.

Did we succeed in our endeavour to lose weight, get fitter and become healthier? Weight loss, well, um, a little, with much more expected to come at home. Fitter, definitely. We both worked out in the gym every day and did an aqua aerobics class and swam every afternoon. In addition, Dr Muscles had taken me walking up long, exhausting hills at 7 o'clock every morning. The day I arrived, I found it hard to reach our villa up a short slope without stopping for a breather. By the end, I could go up the winding hills to Pike's Peak and do five climbs before breakfast. Healthier? Yes again. I hadn't tasted coffee or alcohol for nearly five weeks. Of course, I'd indulge again, but under Michelle's renewed zest for healthy food, we'd rebuild our eating base. We also needed to keep up the exercise levels. That wouldn't be easy because we didn't have the exotic gym equipment or a Languid One or a Dr Muscles.

CHAPTER 13

North Vietnam and Cambodia – 2014

When you take a trip on points, you can't be too choosy about departure times, types of aircraft or the length of stopovers. The aeroplane waiting for us at Sydney Airport at seven-thirty in the morning was like a large, old, trustworthy dog, grey around the muzzle, with a preference for staying in its kennel. It had not heard about business class lie-flat seats. Fortunately, this was a day flight.

We had a two-hour stopover in Singapore. Two hours was just long enough to power walk between gate lounges to deliver us into the arms of Singapore Airline's plain daughter, Silk Air. It hopped about Asia in short bursts. Some of the planes, I suspected, were in God's waiting room. Ours was anyway – an A319 that they would probably keep for spares. We were ticketed to sit in rows 3A and 3B, but were told that row three didn't exist. Should we therefore sit on the wing? Not necessary, sir.

Row two specially selected for you. Business class had two rows only, upholstered in 1958 Austin A40 brown leatherette (vinyl).

For our three-and-a-half-hour flight, entertainment comprised a screen the size of a small paperback which dropped down over the unoccupied row in front of us. Sound was not included. The solution was to show silent movies, Buster Keaton no less, probably made at the same time as the plane. But nevertheless, it was an enjoyable choice to help me recall my boyhood.

And then the meal. Warning, warning, Will Robinson, do not choose the meatballs. We chose the meatballs. They resembled old rubber bands that nervous people collect and turn into bouncy balls. They offered about the same texture and flavour. Accompanying it on the plate was a dash of purple mash and some tomato-flavoured dribble, all reposing on a bed of spaghetti which had bonded to the point where it could not be separated and therefore escaped being eaten at all. We abandoned the main course and moved on.

Dessert was a block of something yellow, also totally without flavour. All this was served by the three attractive female flight attendants, chosen for their diminutive size, but still unable to fit into the galley together. One often fell out through the curtain when they tried to turn around.

Vietnam had a population of 91 million people and accelerating. They rode around on 37 million motor scooters. Cars were ridiculously expensive. A Toyota Camry cost about AUD$150 000. Hanoi, the second largest city, had a population of 7.4 million plus unofficial workers who shouldn't have been there. That made it closer to 10 million, also accelerating.

The traffic in Hanoi made Bangkok look like a quiet Sunday drive in the country. If you could imagine a swarm of bees which are angry because they've lost sight of the queen, that's Hanoi. The unofficial rule: If there is a space, it must be filled by a scooter. After a while, we learned to cope with it, especially as pedestrians. To cross a busy road, we had to pretend we were blind – and just walk. Stopping was fatal.

Our guide and driver picked us up at Hanoi Airport in the dark, which largely hid the smog and the rioting bees until the next morning. I realised, as we drove along, that the art of being a tour guide was to become two people, the asker and the replier. As in: 'Ho Chi Minh then take himself into the country. Why? Because the French were after him. Did he come back? Yes, of course, and he live here in this house. This is really his house? Of course, but fix up a bit because it got bomb in the war.'

Hotel Toaster Report

At the InterContinental, where we were staying, I found a Vietwarm, an erect, locally-made six-slotter where the toast captain produced hot toast sitting up like a shooting gallery, ready to eat. A big tick to the hotel staff, but it gave no potential for those, like myself, who like to engage with a hotel toaster and try out its knobs.

In the morning, we were driven to Tam Coc for a voyage up the Ngo Dong River in a *sampan* – the ancient forerunner of the bedpan. I thought a bedpan might have been a more stable shape for a vessel when I saw our sampan. It was like a traditional tinny after it had been run over by a light steamroller. With Michelle and I aboard, it left 3 cm between the water and us. Forward motion came from the oarsman who rowed with his feet. Mechanical principle in Vietnamese speak: the leg stronger than the arm. All sampan boatmen rowed with their feet. Getting in and out of the sampan required an act of faith. The trip took about an hour and a half, all at bridal speed, but it was spectacular, with its phallic limestone mini-mountains standing in olive green water.

We had the first of many set menu lunches lurking within the tour package. The guide cleared his throat and announced the courses, which sounded far better than they tasted. Chickens in this part of the world were tough critters, having escaped an early death on the roads by quick reflexes. When they came to the table, they were still muscular, with the meat clinging resolutely to the bone. Beef was leathery, while vegetables were hard and aggressive. Pork seemed to be the most successful meat dish.

Halong Bay was about three and a half hours drive among various configurations of swarming scooters. It was a relief to board a luxury, old-world timber boat that had tried to grow into a junk but couldn't get its back end high enough out of the water. Welcome aboard, me hearties! Here's your cabin. Yes, but where's the rest of it? The designer of the A319 had been at work here as well. He'd designed a nice boat but had forgotten to allow for cabins. We should not have brought any luggage. We had one small drawer each, a minute wardrobe mostly taken up with a safe and other internal-necessities, and an almost double bed in which a huge sleeper had flattened the mattress on my side to make a slope finishing on the floor.

We couldn't unpack, because there was nowhere to put anything and nowhere to put the suitcases if we emptied them. We did, however, have a front deck with two wicker lounges that offered some relief from the afterthought cabin.

The boat took about twenty people. A fine dining dinner was advertised as included in the fare, but we had to pay for water, tea and coffee as extras. The waitress kept our personal bottle of water in the refrigerator so we could finish it the next night.

Halong Bay offered more phallic limestone mini-mountains but they now rose out of jade-green salt water. There was an armada of white, painted boats like ours that cruised the bay. We were then transferred to a smaller boat for a journey to a more secluded part of the bay where I leaped off the side into the extremely salty water to find that the current wanted to take me on a private, one-person journey towards the horizon. I fought my way back to the ladder that had been hung over the side but the bottom rung was set too high for my foot to reach. I finally managed to hoist myself up using only my arms. I crawled back on board, dribbling and panting, having lost the macho image that I'd worked so hard to establish by jumping in.

Another long car trip brought us back to Hanoi, this time to the Metropole, one the best hotels we'd ever stayed in. 'Many famous people stay here,' the guide to the historic bomb shelter told us. 'Bill Clinton, Roger Moore, Charlie Chaplin, John F Kennedy, Joan Baez, Fraser McEwing.' I took a bow.

Hotel Toaster Report

This was the only let-down in otherwise outstanding accommodation. It was an old, cubic model fashioned from heavy steel, showing signs of rust, with a slow-boat-to-Vietnam rack that required three passes to change the bread into beige toast. Toast was obviously not held in high regard at the Metropole.

Before exploring Hanoi, our printed itinerary warned: 'You should not wear shorts, tank tops or indecent clothing to mausoleum and pagoda.' I would have liked a debate on the meaning of 'indecent' but didn't get the chance. We visited the required cultural sites like the Museum of Ethnography, One Pillar Pagoda, Ho Chi Minh's Stilt House and the Hoan Kiem Lake in which was supposed to live a 500-year-old giant turtle with magical powers and a liking for grabbing items from passers-by. It had apparently once snatched a sword from the King.

The day finished with a ride in a 'cyclo', a bicycle-powered rickshaw where the passenger, sitting in front, was the first object to be struck in a head-on collision. Thankfully, we only had one minor collision – with a girl on a motor scooter who was busy talking to her friend as we wobbled past. At the end of the journey, our guide advised us that a tip of US$2 was expected. Being generous, we gave each pedal-pusher US$5, whereupon we were abused for being stingy. I had never been to a more tip-hungry place than Vietnam – although the US was yet to come. After paying for the goods or the service (including service charge) you then paid another tip, probably for some relative's bone marrow transplant, somebody's needy baby, or granny's new teeth. It never stopped, and was never enough.

Arriving at the Indochine Palace Hotel in Hue (pronounced 'whay'), I thought we'd been taken to the local houses of parliament. It was white and huge. The foyer was huge. Our room was huge. Everywhere there was space to spare. And it was sparsely occupied because this was the off-season – further enhancing its hugeness. In our room, we ate a beef burger that only a crocodile could bite. The next morning, breakfast was served in a three-storey high restaurant.

Hotel Toaster Report

I found another middle-aged, mesh-conveyor-belt model that needed three passes to improve on warm bread. This toaster had an interesting fault; the collection tray at the bottom had become detached, meaning that my toast went in but didn't reappear because it dropped mysteriously beneath the toaster. A cockney Englishman, waiting patiently for his toast, said to me, 'Wot's goin' on 'ere? I've put three lots in and none's fuggin' come back out.' Underneath, we discovered a graveyard of undelivered toast.

During the day we trailed through the citadel where the emperor once lived. It was fortified with twenty-foot-thick walls and watchtowers. It could hold back any invading army but the emperor hadn't taken into account flying machines with bombs. It took a terrible pounding from the Americans during the war.

The next day, we boarded a dragon boat for a trip down the Perfume River. Our dragon boat was so frighteningly skinny that if Michelle, myself, and our guide all stood on one side of the cabin, it would have capsized. The dragon boat was, in fact, shaped like an underfed dragon with its raised head blocking the driver's view of where he was supposed to be going. The boat was owned and run by dad, mum and cute baby. They lived on the boat, conceived on the boat, and slept on the floor when not running passengers.

Travelling down the river, we passed a police launch moored near the bank. Our guide told us that every boat that passed the cops had to stop and pay a bribe, otherwise they would be inspected and found un-river worthy. Getting a job as a cop meant bribing somebody higher up, but once in, you began collecting serious money. Police generally became rich. The politicians were also part of the game. Although elections were held, there was only one communist candidate for high offices.

Our dragon boat deposited us at King Minh Mang's (second dynasty) tomb which, incidentally, was not constructed to accommodate the deceased. A beautiful, tranquil place, the king started building the memorial for himself and then died before it was finished. His son, the next king, finished it off and his dad was traditionally buried in an undisclosed grave on a wooded hillside behind a series of breathtaking pagodas. The tomb builders, who also knew where the king was buried, had to die because nobody was allowed to know exactly where the corpse lay. Tomb building was therefore a dead-end job. The upside was that their surviving families received a generous pension. Tomb builders had a choice of death: hanging, beheading or poisoning. Most chose poison. They had a few nasty surprise parties and one of the dishes did the trick, but the victim never knew which party or which dish when he arrived for the festivities.

King Minh Mang had 500 wives. They produced 124 children as the result of very occasionally getting lucky. The king relied on the forerunner of Viagra to reload. He was reputed to take on five women at a time and make an average of four of them pregnant. Another king got a dose of the mumps when he was twelve — which turned him sterile. But just to be sure, he accumulated and tested 105 wives before he acknowledged he was firing blanks.

I bought a small, bronze, four-faced Buddha head from a street stall outside the mausoleum, took it back to the dragon boat and put it on an empty chair. 'No, no!' our guide cried, grabbing it. 'Never put Buddha on a chair. Why? Because that's where somebody's arse has been.'

After surviving the dragon boat, we took a car along the main highway and stopped for lunch at a seafood restaurant where the locals ate. It was a bony, wood-and-steel structure sitting on poles out in the water. We watched in amazement as a table of six neatly dressed Vietnamese diners brought a full case of beer in with them and set about drinking the lot while they ate from hot pots bubbling away in the middle of the table. They threw the empty beer cans on the floor, along with any other rubbish from the table, including rejected bits of food, bones and scraps of paper. The restaurant staff were expected to clean it up — and did so without comment. A further understanding was, if any of the diners got drunk during the meal, they were permitted to sleep it off lying on the table or sitting slumped on a toilet bowl. 'The customer is king,' our guide said with resignation.

Our next destination was the Pullman Beach Resort in Danang. It was newish, big, and trying very hard to please ever-increasing tourist numbers. English was in short supply. I ordered a gin and tonic, which convened a meeting of four conferencing waitresses who worked diligently on the project. Eventually, I was given the ingredients separately in elaborate glassware, after which I was carefully observed by the four amigos to see if I would kill myself with a chemical explosion.

Eventually, this strip of beachfront would become crowded with wealthy locals and flashy foreigners staying in a string of international hotels, but for now the numbers were at a pleasant, low level.

Hotels, especially in Asia, didn't mind taking a dive on the room rate and handing out generous vouchers, as long as you availed yourself of the laundry service. This was where the profits were made. It cost substantially more to launder a shirt than to buy a new one. I talked to our guide about this and he said, 'No problem, sir. Take to the laundry across the road. They charge by the kilo.'

Thus fortified, I filled a plastic shopping bag with our stale and smelly gear and headed out of the hotel and across the road – a feat in itself. My appearance on the other side started a footrace of substantially-built women with arms outstretched to grab not me, but my bag. The winner snatched it away and said, 'Lornry, very goo pri for you. Two hunred thousand.' (AUD$10). This had already beaten the hotel's price by 900 %. But you'd be seen as a fool if you accepted the first price in Vietnam. 'Too dear,' I replied. 'I am a poor Australian; not a rich American. One hundred and fifty thousand.'

CHAPTER 13   North Vietnam and Cambodia – 2014

'I do for one hundred fipty,' bleated the woman who'd come second in the race. 'Okay, okay, one hundred and fipty,' the winner responded. 'Iron very good, too. Now you like buy beer, hire motorbike, give you massage with beautiful girl?' – probably her. She had what you might call a mixed business. The massage could have tempted me for a laugh, but the hotel package already included six hours of free spa treatments, which we had to use up first. When our guide, helping to book us in, saw the wad of vouchers we were given, he warned, 'You could have six one-hour massages but if you spent all vouchers on one six-hour massage, they carry you out looking like a snake. Not much left.'

We motored into Hoi An, a well-baited tourist trap, but still offering relatively good quality products. The streets were only for walking or riding pushbikes after 2 pm. Before 2 pm, the bees were busy. We set out determined, as usual, not to buy anything – but then we did. That obliged the purchase of another suitcase to bring it all home where it could be thrown out in private.

Our first walking tour was just a warm-up. During this orientation trek, it rained heavily. The tourists, taken by surprise, rushed to buy garish protective plastic coverings. Many of them had also hired bikes. The combination was surreal: powerful European legs attached to bright burka tops in a slow but determined bicycle procession. One family rounded a corner during the worst of the downpour, all done up in matching fairy-floss pink, with dad at the back bellowing instructions to the two kids at front who were managing their bicycles far better than he was.

The food offering at the Pullman bordered on infinite. There must have been at least 50 m of counters offering a huge international variety — and all very nicely prepared. There was also a chocolate fountain. I went weak at the knees when I saw it. I whispered to myself, 'My name is Fraser Beath McEwing and I am a chocoholic.'

Hotel Toaster Report

Here was another discoloured chunk of heavy metal. Probably the slowest belt speed I'd come across. A Japanese lady waiting by the delivery tray, which was bent up so you'd have to burn your fingers in order to retrieve your toast, muttered as she peered into the glowing interior: 'Maybe not inside. Maybe gone already.' When it finally appeared, she said, 'Oo, still bread.'

The following morning, I caused a fire. Since the toasting bread was cut into paving stone thickness, I cut three pieces of my own from an oval-shaped loaf and sent them down the red tunnel longways. Number one was delivered to the tray, number two followed after a suspenseful delay, but number three failed on the U-turn, where it wedged itself until it ignited. The female toast captain attacked the problem not with a fire extinguisher but with a long knife, which Derek Breadchamber says should be a hanging offence if trying to dislodge trapped toast. In this case it worked. The fire died away and she was not electrocuted.

Our room was smaller than the town hall we'd had previously, but it offered a comfortable bed, generous shower and plenty of bathroom bench space. Unfortunately, being new, this hotel had fallen for an up-to-the-minute design of double doors opening from the bedroom into the bathroom to reveal your partner bathing, showering or sitting on the bowl.

We'd been told that Danang offered great value spectacles. We went into town searching. The first place was very swept up with a critical lack of English – or we of Vietnamese. There was much pointing at eyes and squinting until we found the prices were higher than in Sydney. The second place was what we wanted. Michelle had her prescription to give the man behind the counter and she found some keenly priced, very attractive frames, but the man's son had to be called down from the loft to speak to us in English. He was a calm, intelligent young man who had two thumbs on his left hand. One was a normal thumb and the other, only slightly smaller, was fully operational and sported its own manicured nail. If he played the piano there would be many new chord possibilities. Marilyn Monroe was rumoured to have six toes on one foot but this man was for real with his thumbs.

I did buy several shirts. Off the hook was okay but the tailor-made ones would have fitted me in the third trimester. They had to be sent back for frontal reduction. The lady tailor tried to talk me out of alterations. 'Better stay big size because your tummy not show so much,' she told me. 'You got Buddha tummy,' which she rubbed for good luck and bent over laughing.

I developed a liking for Vietnamese coffee – the hot version. It began its life as seepage through fine-ground coffee beans sitting in a metal container above my cup. The result was a muddy, Lebanese-style black coffee to which was then added condensed milk. Rapid stirring was necessary as the condensed milk and coffee were joined in an arranged marriage. The result would make anybody without a sweet tooth gag, but since I was a paid-up member of Chocoholics Anonymous, I could admit: 'I love this coffee but I will desist from consumption once I arrive back home.'

In Hanoi, retailers were selling Vietnamese weasel coffee, a great delicacy. I thought weasel referred to the brand, but no. The weasel was an animal that loved coffee, and to make it happy was fed coffee beans. Its poo was then reverently collected, ground up and packaged as genuine weasel coffee. The taste was, apparently, excellent, but I could not bring myself to confirm this. American travellers who we met along the way took some home, but didn't know whether to declare it as coffee or poo. Anyway, they believed that US Customs would allow it through. Civets were also used for this type of coffee. Australian Customs wouldn't allow any of it in. No like poo.

Part of every great hotel is the spa. Once the hotel architecture is finalised, a separate spa designer is engaged, because the general ambience of the hotel has nothing to do with that of the spa, which must be a world apart. If I died and found my afterlife had deposited me in a hotel spa, uniformed angels would be looking after me, floating a couple of centimetres above the ground, and directing me with outstretched palms to chairs and doorways that I may not have noticed. They would speak in whispers, always smiling, but never laughing. Nothing funny went on in a hotel spa.

Not yet being dead, I decided to book a tea-leaf-and-salt scrub in the Pullman Beach Resort spa. As I walked across the dimly lit bridge over heavenly water leading to the spa door, I met a skeleton coming out. 'I had a salt scrub,' the skull said as it rattled past. 'They went too far. Be careful.'

I was assigned an angel inside, taken to a celestial chamber and asked to change into a pair of camp brown satin shorts. Face down on the scented bench, I waited for the first heavy handful of salt, mixed with powdered tea, to land on my back. But this angel was not up to the task. She weighed about as much as one of my legs and was unable to exert pressure without lifting herself off the floor. Her hands felt more like a cat licking me. I suppose I shed a few flakes of dead skin, but I obviously had not been allocated the same angel as the skeleton.

There were quite a few Australians staying at the Pullman. One especially nice family of five from Broome told us that friends took them to a typical local Vietnamese restaurant. They were not prepared for the practice of throwing food, paper, empty drink containers and any other rubbish, onto the floor. The parents said they took a little time to accept the hurling, but the three kids embraced it immediately. 'They loved chucking rubbish all over the place,' the father said. 'All their lives they've been told to be tidy but at that dinner, their primitive instincts were allowed to take over. They had the best time.'

What would happen, I wondered, a traditional Vietnamese family, who had never previously travelled, came to Australia for their first trip, and dined at Sydney's upmarket Rockpool restaurant? I could see the news coverage. 'They behaved like wild animals,' the Manager said. 'The floor under their table will have to be re-laid. One of our waiters fell over a gnawed T-bone. An empty wine bottle rolled from under their table down the whole length of the entry passage and ended up in the street.

The police arrived just in time to save them from being assaulted by nearby diners.'

At Silk Village we were shown silk worms munching into mulberry leaves and cocoons being unwound and processed. The final act in all this was a selection of silk fabrics and a tailor to sew them into clothes. But when we came to try on the clothes we'd had made, the system failed. My shirts were so big that it took two subsequent attempts to reduce them. Conversely, the incorrectly named tailor made Michelle's loose jacket too small – by a huge margin. Michelle had given the tailor a very expensive silk print she'd been saving from a China trip nearly two years previously. The tailor tried to convince us that it was Michelle's fault for not fitting into the jacket. That didn't work. The tailor then offered to enlarge it as long as Michelle could supply some more fabric – if she didn't mind a quick trip to Beijing. That didn't work either. Then the tailor said, 'Let me 'splain what happen. I cut the jacket in the right size but then when I iron, it shrink. Could not believe it. I iron it again and it shrink some more.' If she'd kept ironing, we'd have had a tiny fragment of silk that defied the principles of physics. A long silence cast me in the role of referee. I cleared my throat. 'You keep Michelle's jacket and sell it to a dwarf while she selects another fabric and you make again, no charge.' Another long silence. Downcast eyes. 'Okay, we do for you.'

Our room at the Pullman had a splendid view of the South China Sea, enhanced by a net fence, which gave the impression that the water was a brilliant turquoise until we realised that the fence had coloured in the ocean. No matter, it invited us to swim. We lunged into body-temperature water without so much as an ooh or an ahh, but when we stood up, we fell down again as if drunk. The reason was that the sand (hidden in the opaque water) had formed into a series of invisible peaks and troughs that we could not negotiate - sight unseen. These undulations also produced nasty little rips so that when we decided to return to the beach, the forces of nature were against us. After a struggle that reminded me of armed troops trying to come ashore in a war movie, we reached the beach, only to find that the heat in the sand would boil a saucepan of water.

The Pullman had claimed its section of the long and attractive-looking beach. Many other international hotels would have staked out their territory, too. Future brochures would show miles of sunny sand and a beckoning sea, but this would be no costal paradise as we know it in Australia. The sand was scorching and the swimming hazardous.

We were sad to pull out of the Pullman and be driven in a lashing downpour to Danang Airport where we were again delivered into the unadorned arms of Silk Air. The business class lounge, along with Hanoi, was hardly worth the trouble. Neither had a dedicated bathroom and the Danang food offering at four in the afternoon was still stuck on breakfast. I thought of getting partially drunk on local beer to deal with the Silk Air flight. However, when we boarded, we found the same sized aircraft as before, but this one was almost new. It took less than an hour of smooth flight to change countries and land in Cambodia.

Siem Reap presented an international airport in chaos. We clumped down the mobile metal stairs to board a bus that travelled 5 m to deposit us into an arrival queue where we found that our six sheets of filled-in forms were not enough.

We had to fill in another blue one and were given, in exchange, a yellow one. Then a move to queue number two, immigration, which thoughtfully led us past an ATM machine so we could extract cash for our visa fee. The visa officials looked like highly decorated officers of the Cambodian Air Force, with formal blue uniforms bedecked in braid, epaulets, and some decorations awarded for looking fierce and diligent rubber stamping.

There was a delay while the takeaway dinner for the staff arrived in individual plastic bags. Arguments arose over which bag was whose. One of the officials returned to her knitting and began eating dinner at the same time. Finally, the blue printing machine started up again and we were given our visas. At the currency exchange counter, we tried to decide whether we should use US dollars in Cambodia or the local currency, the riel. Nobody was quite sure, so we bought both. One US dollar equalled about four thousand riel. And one Australian dollar was worth about eighty-six US cents. Buying anything required complex calculations before we knew whether we were being diddled or not.

Raffles Hotel immediately engaged my interest. It was originally opened in 1932 as the Grand Hotel d'Angkor and went through some good times and some bad times. By 1996, it had been refurbished, extended, and taken over by the Raffles Group to become the Raffles Grand Hotel d'Angkor. It had retained the art deco style of Raffles in Singapore and tried to be fraffly English, with lots of old-style tiles, paned windows, timber floors and a fumbling pianist trying to entertain in the lounge.

Our room was right out of the 1930s, with dark wood, toggle light switches, standard lamps and wall rails. The bathroom showed more work by the designer who did the cabins in the Halong Bay cruiser. It was tiny. The shower was can't-turn-around triangular and the toilet had been built for a very small child.

Breakfast had also retained the 1930s flavour, with a huge range of cooked and cold food, including as much champagne as we could drink. As soon as we stood up to go to the buffet, a waiter dashed over, refolded our napkins, adjusted the positioning of our utensils and, upon our return, helped us back into our chairs. The only thing he didn't do was eat the food for us — which might have been an advantage in my case because of my indulgent selections.

We had a day of temples. They were mossy, enchanting, full of steps and tricky paving, and crowded with people all wishing the others weren't there spoiling their photo opportunities. One of the more overgrown temples had been used in an Indiana Jones movie — which gave a significant boost to Siem Reap tourism.

The final stop in our temple tour was Angkor Wat, a huge Hindu (later Buddhist) temple built in the twelfth century. It was the main attraction in Siem Reap — a city based on tourism and producing little else. But Angkor Wat was undoubtedly worth journeying to see. It was made from mammoth blocks of stone, endlessly carved, with chunky, beautifully proportioned towers showing architecture and engineering that would have led the world at the time. I couldn't see how the builders had lifted these huge stone pillars and beams 100 m in the air without cranes. I later discovered that they hadn't. First, they dug a massive moat and used the soil to form a hill where they wanted to build the temple. They were able to haul the stone components up the soil slopes by elephant and human power and began by forming the tops of the temple, then digging out the soil beneath to put in supports. With those in place, they dug some more and put in more stone supports. Ultimately, they reached ground level, having built Angkor Wat from the top down. They carted the soil away and set about exquisitely carving every exposed surface of the temple, along with painting, much of it in bright colours – now faded.

I'd seen plenty of impressive temples in two weeks, but Angkor Wat was a standout. It took more than forty years to build but was now so overrun by tourists that it would be destroyed in a similar timeframe unless there were restrictions placed upon where the tourists could walk and what they were allowed to touch.

One night, we took advantage of the hotel's offering of a barbecue feast plus a display of cultural dancing. A covered auditorium had been set up with a stage at one end. As we finished a tasty dinner, the show began with the band sauntering it. It comprised drums, xylophone, bells, flute, and a couple of other instruments that I could hear but not see. The members of the band sounded as though they had never played together before and were making the music up as they went along. I have no doubt that this was because of my ignorance of the musical genre, but is sounded like a mess. I could have done a better job on the drums – and I don't play the drums.

The dancers were a little better, although some of them were learners and had to follow the more experienced dancers about half a bar behind. In extravagant, Lurex-enhanced dresses, they depicted various unlikely stories of princesses in trouble, young women resisting unwanted advances, young men fighting, monkeys falling down and bridges being built. Only on a couple of occasions did I become engaged in the beauty of the movements. The lead female dancer was a genuine star and another of the girl dancers had seductive neck movements.

Saturday was our final full day of tropical Cambodia. I had two glasses of Mumm Champagne and orange juice at breakfast and the world looked decidedly nicer afterwards. We had to beg our guide and driver to let us relax for just one day. Please, no more temples. A thousand Angkor Wat stairs the previous day had just about crippled us. Feeling like escapees, we crept down to the swimming pool and set up camp under an umbrella. This pool looked like the utterly calm lake you'd find on the cover of a CD of meditation music. As I was contemplating its tranquillity, the pool captain hurried over to us carrying a laden tray.

'Good morning, sir and madam. I have here for you two towels, two straw hats and some fruit on a skewer. Now, can I get you a drink?' We nominated water. He returned quickly with two icy glasses and set them down. 'Is there anything else I can do for you?' I was waiting for him to say he could swim two laps of the pool to save me having to; he could jump in – bombing and diving not permitted, of course – and call out how nice it was in the water. He could then come out and dry himself. All this would be so I could participate in water sports without having to rise from my lounge.

Hotel Toaster Report

Things were looking up in the hotel toaster department, although it may have been the effect of the breakfast champagne. Raffles had an Angkor Superwatt with a moving mesh conveyor belt model controlled by numerous knobs and dials in which the toast captain had been trained and licensed. It took only two relatively rapid passes to produce excellent toast. I decided to award this toaster the Derek Breadchamber Asian Division Medal after he'd tasked me with choosing the best hotel toaster during my trip.

The Correct Asian Traveller

Reviewing my notes, I saw that I had been guilty of looking at Asian travel only from my point of view. I'd never bothered to consider what the travel providers, such as hotel and airline staff, wanted of me. Money was only part of it. It was time I put together a comprehensive guide to proper behaviour by travellers. I called this guide *The Correct Asian Traveller,* and I commend it to all those contemplating travel in Asia. It could also be applied to other parts of the world. I may even publish an outward-bound brochure to be available at Australian airports. For brevity, I've abbreviated *The Correct Asian Traveller,* to CAT. This is how CAT should behave.

Whenever hotel staff members knock on his door, CAT grabs the handle and opens it immediately. No groaning, cursing, getting out of bed or being caught in the shower. Even a short delay in opening the door angers the hotel staff and they may start shouting and shoulder-charging the door. On the other hand, they may rush away, never to return. CAT should position a chair near the door and spend as much time as possible sitting in it when occupying the room.

When arriving at a hotel, CAT leaps from the car or bus and begins to distribute money, preferably in US dollars. Everybody in hotel uniform is included in the handout. When checking in,

CHAPTER 13   North Vietnam and Cambodia — 2014

CAT cheerfully accepts a room downgrade, knows his passport number off by heart and hands over his credit card in case of excessive minibar activity. And, speaking of the minibar, he eats and drinks from it continually so that, when checking out, he can answer the cashier's question, 'Anything from the minibar?' in the affirmative and then happily pay for items inflated by 500 %. Peanuts, he calculates with a smile, cost about a dollar each.

When CAT's bags arrive in his room, he pays absolute attention to the explanation given by the baggage deliverer of how the room works. He cherishes the surprising announcement of where the bathroom is, how to open the curtains, how to identify the television screen as distinct from other framed pictures on the wall and how to find a drawer and slide it open using a device known as a knob. As the hotel staff member is withdrawing, CAT discretely hands over a wad of banknotes in gratitude for this masterclass.

CAT often eats in the hotel restaurant and rises to the challenge of selecting a bottle of vintage champagne which has been placed at the top of the drinks menu either as a joke or in case a rich person is celebrating their one-hundredth birthday.

CAT prefers to buy from the hotel gift shop rather than paying a quarter of the price outside. But when he does buy from street vendors, he goes into every small shop where there is a spruiker outside calling, 'Take a look, sir!' and he comes out laden with the goods they suggest, having paid the first asking price. He also buys fruit, drinks and local, unidentified, fried food from trolleys and temporary kiosks. The luggage shop, seeing CAT hardly able to walk under his load, sells him the bright green, large suitcase that's been in the shop for some time. Eyeing a prospect, the pedal rickshaw driver then insists on taking CAT on a dangerous ride through the traffic via the driver's sister's clothing and jewellery shop where CAT is measured for four suits and fifteen shirts. As he staggers out, a passing taxi invites CAT aboard and takes him back to the hotel via his brother's arts and crafts emporium where CAT snaps up three original, Oriental, idyllic scenes and a pendant finishing in a guaranteed perfect ruby at a remarkably low price.

On those occasions when CAT requires a massage, he selects the establishment with the biggest fluorescent sign. If, during treatment, he is offered a happy ending, he expresses outrage, threatens to call the police, reports the girl's inappropriate behaviour to the manager and, after it is settled, immediately calls his wife to explain the entire sequence of events. Before leaving, CAT extracts a statutory declaration from the manager to support his verbal account.

When flying, CAT happily pays for excess baggage, confesses to deceptively heavy carry-on cases and is willing to get on the baggage scales himself if there is concern about overloading the aircraft. Once aboard, he never unfastens his seat belt, diligently practices the brace position as demonstrated before take-off, stows his tray table well before the captain tells him to, opens the overhead locker carefully in case the items inside have shifted during flight, doesn't stand up until the cabin doors have been opened, doesn't use any electronic devices at any time during the flight, and doesn't object to the back of his seat being kicked by a bored, out-of-control boy in the row behind.

Needless to say, CAT doesn't travel very often. He simply can't afford it.

CHAPTER 14

Thailand and Hong Kong – 2013

The destination was worth the shaky, two-hour road trip from Bangkok Airport. We arrived at Chiva-Som, a world-famous beach health resort overlooking the Gulf of Thailand. Chiva-Som was not trying to be a luxury resort hotel amid five acres of swimming pools with endless piña coladas and seductive food. Rather, it was a cross between resort, health retreat, hospital and boot camp, with plenty of combinations to suit differing expectations.

Chiva-Som's food was remarkable in that, although it was delicious, we couldn't eat ourselves fat. The chef wouldn't have anything to do with oil or butter or sugar. Neither was there an opportunity to report on Chiva-Som's hotel breakfast toaster. It didn't have one. Bread was barely tolerated and mostly appeared only as mini loaves of compressed nuts wrapped in a white shroud. Toasting it would have produced chipboard.

The omnipresent, but never-seen owner, allowed the operation of electronic equipment in the rooms – but not outside. If you were caught speaking on your mobile phone in a public space, you had to sit under the naughty palm. The atmosphere had to be kept meditative at all times. No showy Americans doing gazillion-dollar deals. Apart from some restaurant saxophone music that sounded as though it was coming through a pile of grey blankets, all was quiet. The other exception was the local pianist who filled the lounge with broken chords and impromptu twiddles for an hour-and-a-half each evening. He played a Yamaha very-baby grand and spent his time trying to catch the eye of anybody who would look at him for an exchange of nods and grins. He arrived each evening with a pile of music, which he seldom opened, because his broken chords and occasional trills sufficiently entertained the listeners. The top two treble notes of the keyboard were in need of repair. They sounded like an angry woodpecker. To stop people like me from playing the piano, there was a sign on its cover saying that it would play very badly for all but the nightly piano-man.

Chiva-Som only catered for about one hundred people. The guests often walked about trancelike, not looking right or left. They also dressed oddly. The hotel issued us with lemon-coloured, long-leg jersey pyjamas upon arrival, which we had to return or buy at departure. But some people, obviously not constrained by the etiquette of pyjamas being confined to the bedroom, wore them everywhere. They could appear at dinner in their pyjamas. At lunch one day, a man wore his pyjamas and added the hotel dressing gown to be really chic.

Another highlight of arrival was our health check. We had to confess all our flaws to the assessment officer who then passed them on to the vast health repair team, readying them to suggest treatments and exercises — some of which were included in the tariff, while others were extras. At health check time, we were issued with a substantial book laying out the treatments available. They were all aimed at transforming us into the people we could be and should be. It was an overwhelming list from which I realised that I'd arrived at the resort little more than a revolting receptacle of toxins and fast-breeding, nasty microorganisms.

The management gave us a free allowance of a thousand dollars to spend in the caverns of wellness. In addition, there was a free massage every day and a number of other activities, such as water aerobics and stretching, that we could share with other toxin-filled guests. One day, we did a class in metabolic breathing in which we had to assume a number of challenging poses and then try to inhale and exhale deeply. It was very difficult trying to breathe at all when I was perched on one hand and one leg while waving my big toe in a circle at the ceiling. I fell over a number of times.

Another day we took a class called H2O Body Complex in which a diminutive Thai girl took charge of Michelle and me in the swimming pool. We had a floatie noodle each, a strapped-on buoyancy band, a heart monitor and a pulse watch. Thus equipped, we attempted to exercise without drowning. Michelle did better than I, usually getting to the end of the pool way ahead of me. After an hour of that we were allowed to return to dry land — but what a shock. As we stepped up out of the water, we felt heavier and heavier — so much so that it was difficult to waddle along the path. We had become accustomed to the buoyancy, so that when it was taken away, gravity was intolerable. I would not have made a good returning astronaut.

I celebrated my birthday at Chiva-Som. Michelle had booked a table overlooking the sea. We tucked into a delicious four-course meal of very few calories while I toasted and lamented wasted years with a can of watery, non-alcoholic beer. There was more. Michelle had made secret arrangements with the kitchen. A birthday cake appeared with one candle, accompanied by a quavering duet from the waiter and waitress and general applause from the big table of growling Russians behind us. I did not rise to make a speech but instead attacked my cake of quivering jelly and embedded strawberries.

It was not fair to generalise, but our Russian colleagues en masse were an uncouth lot. They descended upon the establishment and made a mockery of courtesy, especially to the Thai staff who were gentle, naturally polite people, and trained to be even more so at the resort. The Russians broke the mobile phone rule, they smoked, they piled their plates, and they took tables that had been reserved by other people. They sat in clumps, snarling and harrumphing at one another and shouting for service to have plates brought or taken away.

In contrast to the Russians, we met a friendly Dutch couple who sat near us at dinner by the sea. They were taking a year off from work. During their conversation, they uttered the magic word: Herbalife. Had it come to Australia? Yes, it had, but low key. They left a couple of days later but I think they would have prospected us if they'd stayed longer. Michelle found them on the Dutch Herbalife website. We realised that we had been in the presence of Herbalife royalty. They were inner circle, President's Club members of the Herbalife grand family of international wellness, bright eyes and flat bellies. To their credit, they didn't get going on the abundance of benefits or set up a whiteboard. They really were the golden couple. He, very tall, deep-voiced and handsome and she, also tall, blonde with a beautiful face. They had paid the premium tariff and booked a villa overlooking the pond 'vit many vaterfoll'. But they had trouble sleeping because, 'Ve are kept avake by the froks croakink and croakink.'

Chiva-Som literally abutted the beach. Most nights we ate at a table within sight of gentle waves which were about as threatening as those in a bath tub. The water looked clean and inviting but we had to obey Chiva-Som's swimming semaphores. A notice at the front gate said that a red flag told us not swim — it was probably too rough. The green flag said it was safe to swim. The yellow flag meant to swim with caution. As it turned out, the green flag was never used but the yellow flag was virtually permanent. The reason: 'Sir, you go in the water, nice, but many jellyfisss. Always jellyfisss, so never safe to swim,' as was the case with so many idyllic beaches like those in northern Australia.

Chiva-Som specialised in treating the body with every fix imaginable. The assessors found bodily fails we didn't know we had. They even had visiting mind-altering people if you wanted to recalibrate your life path, but the body was the primary concern.

I booked in for many encounters with angelic, whispering therapists who gently massaged me with rare oils. I went for a treatment called detoxifying skin therapy. First a shower, then a layer of warm paint-stripper after which I was wrapped up like a fast-food sandwich, followed by another shower and then a slathering of green seaweed, more plastic wrapping plus towels and a final coat of a heated towel which was snap fastened snugly around my body. The heat was cranked up and I slow-cooked like a piece of Beef Wellington. It was really very hot and oppressive. To counteract the fear of emollition, they dipped a flannel in icy water and laid it over my face. Finally, they unwrapped me for a third shower to wash off the seaweed, which had become quite attached to its new host. I walked out of the treatment room alive and better for the experience or, at worst, relieved from the feeling of life as a sausage roll.

I'm never far away from textiles. I have to touch them, even if people are wearing them as clothing and then, blushing, I have to explain that I've come from a textile family. While shopping in Shanghai we came upon the silk shop, an absolute delight if you like the best silk fabrics on the planet. After declaring that I wasn't going to buy anything, I emerged with two metres of a classic, woven check that would transform me into George Clooney if I had it made into a jacket. I schlepped the fabric to Hua Hin and looked for a tailor whose low price would offset the high price I'd paid for the silk. The TripAdvisor recommendation was closed but we found another tailor down the street, unusually not Indian, who looked at my silk fabric and quoted a price to make it into a jacket. It was reasonable and I didn't haggle. Two days later, I went in for the first fitting. The tailor, it transpired, was not the tailor at all, but the measurer/interface man for the real tailor, whose wife arrived breathless at the shop, carrying the preliminary cut of my jacket's body. I tried it on as they fussed about with pins. Wasn't it usual for at least one trial sleeve to be attached? Much eye-play between the two and some quick-fire exchanges in Thai. Um, sir, there is not enough fabric to finish the jacket, the measurer said. But 2 m was plenty, I replied. I should know. I'm from the garment industry. In any case, you measured me and also measured the fabric. No problem, then. More urgent Thai conversation. The terrible truth was, I was now expected to accept a vest – in my prized Chinese silk. The George Clooney idea died. We will search in the factory sir, and call you. Later that day, he called with the news that the sleeves had been located under the cutting table. George Clooney came back to life. The second fitting included the sleeves and I looked forward to the job being finished with all the parts necessary to make a jacket. Michelle wanted me to get some trousers made but I feared I'd end up with a pair of shorts or maybe trousers with one leg.

Most people at the resort were exhausted by the daily exercises or the therapeutic corrections, meaning that night-time activities were limited. Television was dismal, specialising in movies that didn't make the box office for good reasons, or hysterical Wall Street reports on the micro-movements of economic indicators. Thus, when guest speakers offered wisdom in the library after dinner, we attended. The first was a vague Thai woman flogging an expensive course in life mapping. My map was already too near the edge of the page to bother risking a change from current happiness to future unhappiness. Michelle also had a satisfactory life map. The next speaker was a Zen master who'd come to talk about breathing. He began by asking how we could define life. That was a hard one. After our feeble answers, he defined it as a containment that breathes and is programmed to reproduce itself. He said that for life, a brain was not a necessity. A *jellyfisss* had no brain, he pointed out, and neither did a bacterium. He went on to demonstrate various kinds of breathing to assist in life's challenges. He'd written four books, but all in un-translated Japanese, unfortunately. He finished by saying that the best way to breathe was to laugh. We all had to stand up and start laughing – for no reason. An American woman saw the funny side of laughing not being funny and went out of control as she doubled up close to hysterics.

After a week, the world we had come from was fading, bringing into question the many views we all had of reality. If we'd lived at Chiva-Som for six months, we'd emerge as different people and maybe we wouldn't be able, or want, to return to our former lives. The limiting factor was, of course, money. Chiva-Som was far from cheap – a benefit in disguise.

I was fortunate in that I hadn't winked inappropriately at one of the guests at Chiva-Som. A rare, polite Russian (actually born in Kazakhstan, so I didn't mention Sacha Baron Cohen), Natascha, was a tall, statuesque, platinum blonde with mysterious, pale eyes and a most inviting smile. I labelled her a fitness fanatic as I saw her powering through swimming pool water, and running 4 km along the beach before going into a punishing aerobics class. Michelle spoke to her first when they met in the fragrant massage department and said she was friendly – which was not the case with the impenetrable, vacant expressions of some other guests. Then we came across her in the indoor pool where she'd been thrashing up and down with a personal trainer trying to keep up with her. We introduced ourselves. She said she was Natascha Ragosina, added, 'verld champion boxaar,' and punched the air twice just short of my nose. Was this a joke? We couldn't wait to get back to in-room Google and find out. It was true. Natascha had been world female boxing champion in three weight divisions simultaneously, one being the heavyweight where she gave away nearly half her bodyweight to a huge, grizzly British opponent and beat the tripe out of her. Many of her bouts were on YouTube. She was taller than most of her opponents and lightning fast – meaning that she was seldom hit. Her beautiful face showed no sign of damage. She'd had fifty professional bouts and won them all, knocking out many of her opponents. Before she retired (she was thirty-six and still stunning), she had wanted to fight the much-praised daughter of Mohammed Ali. The fight was arranged twice but Ms Ali backed out. Natascha got sick of all the waiting and all the talking, so she hung up her gloves, undoubtedly the greatest woman boxer to date. She'd also done catwalk modelling and currently had a sports segment on Moscow television – but she said the pay was hardly worth the trouble. 'Why do you keep training?' I asked. 'Because now I am hockey player,' she replied, laughing at my incredulous expression. 'I play professionally for Moscow in a team of men. I am the only woman. I want to play Olympic hockey.'

While the weather had been relatively calm, the jellyfisss ruled the waves but one morning we awoke to a right old gale and the sea had turned into petulant waves. The direction of the powerful wind blew away the jellyfisss but that didn't change the yellow flag because now we had to exercise caution in choppy conditions. I decided to go for a swim and went down to the beach. Sitting on the sea wall, I found one of our guests who had decided to light up a risky cigarette – since you could be sent to the naughty palm tree if caught smoking inside the resort. She made the mistake of smoking with her fag facing the wind, with the result that it feasted upon the oxygen and lasted about ten seconds. Being a non-smoker, I thought this was hilarious. She didn't, and looked sourly at me while she ignited the next one downwind and got some value out of it. I thought the government could make use of this unappreciated fact about smoking, by decreeing that all smoking outdoors must be done into an oncoming wind. If there was no wind, smoking should not be permitted.

The saga of the jacket and the tailor did not end where it should have. I went to pick up my George Clooney transformer only to find that the tailor had now let it out too much so that instead of fitting a stove pipe, the jacket would now fit me and a friend. Furthermore, the burgundy-coloured buttons agreed upon had turned into black buttons. The sleeves, however, did exist and were of excellent cut and length. But for the body, it was back to the factory. 'So sorry, sir, the factory not lucky for you. Come back day after tomorrow and all fix.' When I returned as agreed, the tailor was closed with a notice in the window saying, 'Back 1600. Sorry.' I did not believe this, but decided to settle in for a long wait by taking up a front position in the open bar opposite and ordering a beer I didn't want. The minute the beer arrived, so did the tailor. Now I was afraid that he might just be dropping in and would soon be gone. I might never see my jacket again. I gulped down my beer and rushed across the hot street. He was still there and greeted me by pulling the jacket from the rack with a flourish. The buttons had changed to pink, but that was okay, I'd get better ones in

Sydney. I slipped it on. It was perfect! All of a sudden there was a crowd of women outside the tailor's window. They were pressing their faces against the glass, pointing at me, and holding up autograph books. One pushed the door open a little and called out, 'George, I love you!' The tailor slipped the jacket off my shoulders and apologised that he had forgotten to sew some spare buttons on to the lining. Before I could say don't bother, he had dived out of his shop, grabbed his motorbike helmet, and he was gone, leaving me alone in the shop. What would happen if a gang of Russians came in demanding service? I'd have to pretend to be the tailor and start measuring them, inside legs and all. Thankfully, the tailor returned before I had to change my career. He put the jacket into a zipped bag. I paid the balance and caught a tuk-tuk back to the hotel where I discovered that the spare buttons he had given me were black so didn't match the pink ones on the jacket.

During the tailor saga, we moved from the purity of Chiva-Som to the mixed world of the InterContinental Hotel. We took an hour to pack, a three-minute taxi ride up the same road and unpacked it all again in a delightful room overlooking the swimming pool. Now, we were surrounded by people smoking, drinking alcohol, yelling, and spoiling kids. But this hotel turned out to be a grand halfway house between the health monastery and the lives we would return to at home. One of the eating options was to sit in a sunken little dining nook with water on three sides. Michelle had researched this restaurant as the best Thai food in Hua Hin. I looked at the menu, my eyes coming to rest on a dish offering Hua Hin crab meat, coconut cream spicy red curry and wild betel leaf. It was called Gaeng

Poo. I didn't order it, seeing no point in starting at the finishing line. It came as a shock to have two normal-sized courses each. One would have satisfied our now smaller stomachs.

Hotel Toaster Report

The hotel breakfast toaster at the Hua Hin InterContinental dragged down an otherwise excellent breakfast offering. The Hinder Tinder, a wide, single-grate model, moving at a snail's pace, delivered the under-toasted bread into a tray with a bent-up end to stop my much-anticipated slice from becoming airborne and landing on the floor. The problem was that I had to risk burning my wrist trying to retrieve it. I was reminded of a section in one of Derek Breadchamber's books which dealt exclusively with hotel toaster burns, how to treat them and some excellent advice on how to successfully sue the hotel.

All InterContinental Hotels were not born equal. The Hong Kong one was virtually built out into the harbour (a bit like the Sydney Opera House) with correspondingly water-dominated views. But by contrast, this was a bland building with low ceilings – even in the foyer. To create some illusion of height, the foyer desks and chairs stood on shortened legs. Bad knees were not taken into account, so that many elderly, over-nourished people could not get up from a chair without help from the staff who were trained in the dead lift. I supposed the good thing about that was, if you fell down drunk, you didn't have far to fall. But the cost of getting drunk would be beyond the means of most people. Money ruled at this InterContinental. The minibar was set like a bear-trap ready to devour wandering savings, while a light breakfast cost as much as a lavish dinner outside the hotel. Consequently, I was not able to report on the hotel toaster because I couldn't afford to enter the room where it was situated. But I imagined it would be high tech, combined with artistically hand-worked marble and brass, polished daily, and operated by four uniformed breakfast toaster technicians who would assist you to select bread from a massive array of international styles and then take instruction on the colour of the toast you preferred. You would then be asked to sit at your table and await the arrival of the runner bearing your piece of toast, still hot.

There was a sport played between guests, like us, who had paid money to join the InterContinental Hotel Ambassadors Club with the intention of cajoling the hotel into giving upgrades and privileges that exceeded the joining fee. The other team was the hotel, which added lightweight frippery to entry-level rooms with the intention of making a profit out of the joining fee. This was an engrossing team competition in which both sides were equipped with grizzle, stonewalling and nasty comparisons. Instead of a room upgrade, we got free WiFi, which had been free anyway in every other hotel we'd stayed at, a free movie to watch in bed, a harbour view to make the tiny room look bigger, late checkout, which we couldn't use, a small bottle of scent and some fresh fruit – delivered with all-consuming rote-enthusiasm by middle management. I couldn't say that we didn't like staying at the hotel. Everything worked, including a complex bedroom lighting system that took persistent study to master, and a toilet that flushed with a deep roar because, instead of a cistern, it was worked by some massive vacuum machine deep in the basement.

I was really taken with the harbour view from our room until I saw the same Chinese down-market cruise ship, the *Ji Mei*, go back and forth each day, accompanied by a tug. This ship was in need of paint and some panel work where the captain had run into something tougher than his ship. But was this a deception? Maybe we didn't have a harbour view room at all but a sub-entry-level room with a movie screen behind the picture window showing repeating harbour scenes from a video. I voiced my suspicions at the low-down reception desk but didn't get much of a hearing.

It would come as no surprise that we ate out on our first night. We found a restaurant on Nathan Road by following pictures and arrows up to the 27th floor of a building where we joined the clatter and hubbub of Chinese serving and eating. We ordered chicken with ginger sauce and, while we waited, Michelle was horrified by plates of Peking duck that waiters carried past with the bird's head as part of the offering. Apparently, it was there to prove to the diner that this was an authentic duck and not a flattened out chicken. 'I can see poor ducky's face,' Michelle moaned. 'Don't look,' I consoled her. 'It's normal here.' When our chicken arrived, it too came with a detached head that looked none too pleased at being separated from its body. Michelle couldn't look at it. Neither could I, actually. I began thinking that this chicken had started out with hopes and dreams for a long, meaningful life in the chook-yard and we had indirectly caused it to be unfulfilled. I called the waiter and asked for the head to be removed because it upset my wife. He complied, but with a look of incredulity on his face.

Michelle had done some research on the best dim sum lunch in Hong Kong. The vote went to Tim Ho Wan, which was the only restaurant of its type to have been awarded a Michelin star in the previous three years. We took a long, challenging taxi ride down Nathan Road until we found a group of people on the pavement outside an unpretentious doorway. In front of the door a woman was yelling into a microphone. After some enquiry, we found that this was not a political rally, but a woman announcing numbers from slips of paper which the intended diners held until they were called by her. This gained entry into the restaurant. Our number was eighty-six. First problem: The numbers were being announced in Cantonese. Solution: Find out who was holding number eighty-five so we'd know when we were next. I found number eighty-five, held by a nervous little woman who didn't know why I was looking over her shoulder. Second problem: If number eighty-five was waiting for a table of eight, then eighty-six, wanting only a table for two, might be taken in ahead of it. Solution: Continue to hold up eighty-six in front of the announcer's nose and point at the door. This seemed to work because we were propelled to a table for one-and-a-half in this tiny, very noisy restaurant. Third problem: I had come out bravely wearing a short-sleeved cotton polo shirt and was pretty cold when I sat down — only to find that I was under the air-conditioner outlet. I began to freeze. Michelle marked the menu card while I assumed the resigned face of Shackleton sitting in his Antarctic hut. We also discovered that our minute table was for four and that we were seated with two other people of unknown origin. The food had better be good, I said between vibrating teeth as I buttoned up my polo to the neck and hugged myself. When it arrived, I couldn't believe how good it was. This grotty little restaurant was world famous, with a cult following for a very good reason. The food was sensational and cost us less than AUD$20 for two.

Back in the street, Shackleton thawed out and we found we were in the wholesale garment district. The wholesalers operated distribution and retail simultaneously. The rule was, we could buy at wholesale price, but not try on until we'd paid, and returns were not accepted. This led to lots of speculation and holding up in front of the body before taking the purchase plunge. But the garments were so cheap that if we made a mistake, we could give them away immediately to the disadvantaged without crippling our budget.

On our second night out of three, we ate at our favourite restaurant, The Red Pepper in Causeway Bay. It specialised in Szechuan Chinese food, which relied chiefly on chillies to define it. Many people thought the food was inedible, but if you could tolerate fire in the mouth, and later further down, this was the best. We ordered three dishes, resulting in Michelle's partial loss of hearing and my partial blindness as we rode through a gastronomical bushfire. For me, cold beer, administered often, offered some extinguishing of the flames. That, in turn, left me intoxicated as I sat in the final smouldering ruins of empty plates.

CHAPTER 15

China – 2013

Michelle had wangled a spectacular deal at The Peninsula Beijing, a hotel where we took up residence in a two-level suite overlooking one row of buildings across the road before smog swallowed the world beyond. Our loft-style apartment had two separate washbasins, a shower, bath with TV set into the marble wall and two toilets.

The day we 'did The Wall' we were blessed by the only smog free day Beijing has had for at least a hundred years. After driving through snow-covered countryside, we began our ascent to the summit. Advice from locals: Very slippery, icy steps, so creeping-style walk advised. Special Beijing hospital for the broken bone because fall down on the ice. T-shirts with print selling for one dollar before bargaining. Guaranteed not dissolve in the washing machine on first wash. After that, no guarantee.

The Wall was spectacular and quite moving with its audacity and presence. It was worth the taxing walk. Our guide said that the Wall had been built to keep out the invading Mongols. Conversely, Michelle thought that China was trying to invade Mongolia and that the Wall had been built to keep out the invading Chinese. Whichever was correct, the Wall held two warring armies back while the soldiers on the top of the Wall poured boiling wonton soup over both sides to stop them. That hardly made sense to me. Who did the soldiers on top of the Wall belong to? Maybe the Brits, who traditionally didn't like anybody. Our guide became so confused by the question that he said it was time to catch the death-defying cable car back to the street vendors who all had the same stuff at the same price and drove us crazy. You could also pay to sit on a smelly, resentful camel for a picture.

We visited the Temple of Heaven. The park surrounding it was covered in snow. Unemployed people from cramped flats practiced dancing because it was a cheaper way to get warm than burning briquettes. The dancing was led by a similarly unemployed person who had done a course in ballet for seniors and beginners. Other people played cards, *mahjong*, foot badminton, or generally horsed about to keep from icing up.

Later, we crept along the ice-covered pavements and steps of the Forbidden City, peering into windows of temples. Our guide, Mark, told us that the palace had 9999 rooms, one less than heaven, which clocked up ten thousand rooms – although nobody had returned from a trip there to confirm the number.

The walk was gruelling, always with the fear of falling down on the ice and getting taken to the bone hospital in a pedal-powered three-wheeler, which posed a greater risk than the fall. We also circumnavigated Tiananmen Square by car to say that we'd been there, but it was too cold to get out and risk falling down again. In any case, I couldn't get former Prime Minister Bob Hawke's tearful story out of my head when he had described the massacre to the Australian Parliament in 1989.

The most impressive monument we saw in Beijing was the Lama Temple with its huge standing Buddha (by the time you got to Thailand, he was reclining owing to exhaustion from holding up so much gold), but here he stood, 30 m high, in a temple with rooms reserved for ghosts, and chanted to by brown-robed monks.

The Peninsula had an outstanding restaurant specialising in Beijing duck. Chef Donald of the Duck attended our table, dressed in white, plus a hat, which nearly doubled his height. He looked like a Mongol warrior as he flourished his knives and carved our duck with surgical precision. The dish used to be called Peking duck until Mao decided otherwise. I washed it down with Chinese rice wine that would intoxicate a horse. It easily accounted for me, and Michelle had to guide me back to the room as I performed an unrequested floorshow for the foyer guests.

Upstairs, in the double pad, I turned on the television. It certainly had a big, flat screen but everybody's head looked like a sat-on orange. It was showing a documentary of the history of the Peninsula Hotel in Hong Kong. After some jerky black-and-white footage of seaplanes taking a week to travel from England, we cut to colour, and an interview with Mr Khedouri, whose family had built the Peninsula Hotel. He spoke with style to the camera, since he had been educated as an English gentleman, accent and all, but when he stood next to the Duke of Kent, who had been invited to open the new tower, Mr Khedouri hardly made it past the Duke's naval. The Duke adopted the royal stoop, also perfected by Prince Philip when talking to short people, and proceeded to pull the cord which parted the curtains to reveal a commemorative plaque. In my drunken state, I imagined, instead of a plaque, a puppet show, where the Duke was short and Mr Khedouri was tall, and continually hit the Duke on the head with a cucumber sandwich. After I laughed myself hoarse at this idea, I struggled up the stairs to bed.

While I was bargaining for a beanie to reclaim my frozen ears, Michelle bought a Samsung computer tablet for a quarter of what it would cost in Australia. Too good to be true? Verily. The Samsung brand was not very clearly written on the back and there was no guarantee card. I suspected it was a Copysung. Nevertheless, it turned on and a little green animal scurried across the screen. She also bought a black telephone handset that plugged into her iPhone to stop cancer of the brain, and a diminutive speaker that claimed to do the job of a big, expensive pair.

One of the features of Beijing was its Hutongs – tiny streets that recalled old Beijing. They were so narrow that many of them couldn't fit a car, with the houses so small that the front door was almost the back door as well. There were no toilets or washing facilities in these houses, meaning that you must get out of bed in the night and walk down the street to the communal loo.

We took a train from Beijing to Shanghai. It was electric, but still managed to get along at 300 clicks. Michelle booked the express, which it was – but it only expressed itself between the twelve stations it stopped at. It therefore took over five hours, during which we observed, at great length, the countryside: quite remarkable in that it was either intensively cultivated or had stands of huge apartment buildings that formed cities – many of them still being built or, if finished, were empty because people couldn't afford to live in them.

Shanghai, a gracious, huge city, was bracingly cold when we arrived and then it became freezing. After a demonstration of multiple lane changing from the airport, the flimsy taxi deposited us at the Langham Hotel – the 'old' Langham for those in the know. This Langham was a 1930s art deco masterpiece with a huge bedroom and bathroom, small lifts, lots of dark red drapes, lead lights, and a restaurant where you'd expect to find Humphrey Bogart smoking a cigar between courses.

The Langham was a rewarding place to stay, its diminutive seven-storey height a reminder of old Shanghai in an otherwise sky-reaching city. The buildings of Shanghai were staggering in size and architectural diversity. After trudging through snow and dangerous fall-down ice, we went up the Oriental Pearl TV Tower, a very high spike with doughnuts around its legs, waist and neck. We took a lift to the neck doughnut where we could walk around and gaze at this remarkable city and its khaki-coloured river system. The outer rim of the doughnut was made of glass. It took courage to step onto it, looking down at a 200 m drop. Michelle did it easily, and stood looking nonchalantly down through the glass without a problem. My turn. If she hadn't been there, I would have chickened out, but to keep up with my self-designated fearless image, I had to do it. As I stepped onto the glass, my stomach and all below it wanted to migrate to my head and hide in my hair. I'm generally not too bad with heights, but this was past my limit. I'd been flying in a microlight in Thailand but it was not nearly as scary as the drop from the doughnut.

I allowed myself to be dragged grumbling into the Shanghai History Museum, but then loved it. The Chinese specialty was a miniature model of a street scene from the early 1900s, accompanied by dawn to dusk lighting, all achieved in two minutes, along with full-sized scenes of old Shanghai life with people grinding, weaving, pleading cases in court, going to crowded restaurants and generally trying to survive.

We ate at the Hyatt to celebrate Chinese New Year, ordering superb Shanghai duck – like Peking and Beijing duck by yet another name. I couldn't imagine the same dish served at home being called Sydney duck. People would think it was one of Donald's uncles.

Unlike our New Year, with the Sydney Harbour Bridge and sky lit up with fireworks , and everybody outdoors, Chinese New Year cleared the city as though there'd been an alien gas attack. The shops had closed, along with many other attractions, as most people had gone home to their families. Taxis were also scarce.

We had arranged to go to dinner the next night at another retained relic of old Shanghai – a 1930s theatre restaurant that put on some screeching Chinese opera highlights and served traditional dishes made from recipes found in Emperors' tombs. While Michelle was preparing to change in our hotel room, she began to feel sick and decided to lie down. From the horizontal, she said that she was now feeling worse and might throw up on the carpet, therefore would I please call housekeeping and ask them to send up a large plastic or metal bowl. This was very difficult to convey to housekeeping, especially when explaining what the bowl was for. I made vomiting noises to augment the explanation but this made matters worse because they thought I was sick too. The request did the rounds of several earnest people until one lady said she understood and would have it sent up immediately. Metal or plastic might be difficult but she would do her best. Shortly after, a knock on the door revealed a formally attired waiter with two dinner plates, two small soup bowls and two soup spoons. Seeing this, Michelle leaped off the bed, a towel over her mouth, and bolted for the cavernous, marble bathroom to drive the porcelain bus – on a long journey, it turned out. We both diagnosed her complaint as food poisoning.

We were covered by our never-before-used Amex health insurance and decide to give it a run by declaring a medical emergency. This entailed asking hotel reception to call Australia reverse charges – a huge struggle to begin. Who did I get patched through to? A lady in India who first had to know our credit card details, dates of birth, medical history, home contact, travel plans – and then went away to verify it all while Michelle continued driving the bus over potholes in the kneeling position. The Indian lady then called back to tell us the good news that we were covered, and that she would now call hotel reception and make enquiries about medical assistance. She called back to say that no doctor was available to come to the hotel and that we should load Michelle into a taxi (New Year's Eve, remember) and take her to the Shanghai United Family Hospital where some English was understood. There was a closer hospital but it was only Chinese speaking, and not recommended because they might take Michelle's tonsils out by mistake. We were implored to keep details of all bills we paid so we could make a claim later. 'This is very, very important, sir.' Never mind the patient. The paperwork must be comprehensive and correct otherwise your claim may be refused. Now, do you want to speak to a medical officer? No, my wife is throwing up, vomiting, hurling, chucking, heaving — take your pick — and I need to get her some physical assistance, not talk to an Indian medical officer. Very well sir, you must forthwith get her to the hospital. Hotel reception assures me that they can get a taxi, even at this difficult time. Is there anything else I can help you with?

Michelle parked the bus and returned to bed. I told her to get back out of bed so we could take a taxi to the hospital. Michelle refused, saying she'd rather stick with food poisoning in private. She then went to sleep, leaving me sitting in the art deco gloom for an hour wondering what to do. Since Michelle had shown no inclination to return to the bus (a nice art deco reproduction) I decided to go to bed too, while the city around us exploded tons of gelignite to scare off evil spirits. It certainly scared us, because next to The Langham was a small building forecourt which provided a launch pad for rockets and explosions that sounded as though they were in our bedroom. Happy New Year. Year of the Snake. Year of the Porcelain Bus. Year of the Shanghai United Family Hospital.

While Michelle lay in bed waiting for the war to be won by the good guys in her stomach, I donned my faithful, puffed-up jacket and went for a walk. This was the first day of the snake and nothing was open. There was not even the threat of being run over. The only place with an unlocked door was the massage therapist establishment – not parlour, because that denotes the other kind of massage that every man has heard about but never experienced. I felt that my body needed toning up, so I went in.

Once used to the interior gloom, I found a price list and slid my finger down to the one-hour oil massage, ideal for dry skin like mine. Out skipped number 36 and took me up to a neat room with very subdued lighting. I was asked to don a pair of uncomfortable blue paper underpants, which I later discovered were on backwards. Nevertheless, we began. Little 36 had hands of steel and the grip of a top-quality vice. She didn't speak English but managed to tell me I was fat and had many poorly functioning muscles. At one point, she excused herself and returned with a dangerously hot towel, which she laid on my back. Another trip away resulted in the arrival of a series of hot rocks, which she assembled down my backbone. Usually, groaning in a massage establishment signifies certain pleasures, but my groans designated pain. At the end of the hour, she said that there was much work left to do on my steamed dumpling of a body, so I gave the nod for another half hour. This time, she gave my stomach the hot towel treatment and then powered into some reflexology on my feet with her probing, heartless fingers. Her last act was to tie clear plastic bags around my ankles and put my socks on over them Why, I asked. She explained the reason at length in Mandarin. I wore the bags all night but had to abandon them the next morning when I showered without ever knowing what they were for.

I hobbled out, more than happy to pay for my escape to the hotel where I lay down next to Michelle to recover. By the following morning, I was able to cautiously move about, but

I was always reminded of places where little 36 had tried to tear me apart. Did I really feel better? Well, as the day wore on, yes, but I doubted that the pain/benefit analysis came out in my favour.

Michelle's recovery was greatly enhanced by the prospect of going shopping. We rugged up and made off down Nanjing Road to join a river of people all heading in the one direction. It was like joining a football crowd going to a grand final. But this crowd appeared to be walking for the sake of it. While some of them went into the shops, most simply walked and talked.

Michelle was vacuumed up into Forever 21, a Zara-like store for the teen sector. Forever 21 had attractive merchandise in a very austere, brightly lit building of seven floors. Michelle bought bling and tops for our two nieces. Outside, we found a hop-on-hop-off city tour bus. We hopped on and then had to hop upstairs onto the open deck to find a seat. That wasn't too bad until the bus started moving and then the wind chill factor threatened snap freezing. In order to stay alive, we hopped off at the museum, thinking that a bit of warming culture would be good — until we found a queue several kilometres long of people with the same idea. A fellow in a smart uniform marched up with a sign saying it would be at least an hour before we'd get in. We then decided to swap that culture for another by walking along the famous Bund, where grand old buildings were left as a testament to Shanghai's glorious — and not so glorious — past. Michelle was a collector of hotels. She loved inspecting rooms, sizing up foyers, nosing into accommodation rates and assessing dining. Thus missioned, we took in the Peninsula, Peace and Waldorf Astoria hotels. At the Waldorf, we paid three times as much for tea and coffee as we had for an earlier, huge lunch but the view of the world from the gallery was worth it.

Hotel Toaster Report

Like the hotel, the Langham's machine seemed to have been preserved from art deco times. I laid three pieces of bread on the moving belt where they crept into the glowing interior of the toaster, then disappeared. I called the waitress who called the other waitress who called the toast captain. This chatty trio all but dismantled the toaster and eventually discovered that it was throwing the half-toasted bread off the hidden end of the belt and waiting, with a grin on its knobbed face, to see what we thought about that. Now watched by six officials, I loaded in another three pieces of bread and, after an interminable time, it produced my three pieces barely warmed. It was clearly sulking.

We finally made it to the museum, largely because some official left a sign outside that said it was closed and that reduced the queue. It was well and truly open, with spectacular showings of jade, old clobber, pottery, furniture, currency and art.

We had tickets to take the fast train to the airport. This train could get up to 400 kph but apparently only loped along at 300 because of magnetic arthritis. We'd be going from the chill of China to the steamy heat of Thailand and I looked forward to the change. Waiting at the airport, I discussed China's one-baby policy with an English businessman who had been trading in China most of his working life. Along the way, he had learned to speak competent Mandarin and had a good understanding of Chinese culture. He said that the one baby was over-cherished by the mother, father and grandparents. In infancy, the baby thought it sat at the pinnacle of the universe. As a young child, it behaved like a brat in public and nobody dared discipline it, nor did it learn to share or interact with siblings. At school, the parents both protected it and intensively assisted in its learning. Any natural talents were exploited. Then suddenly, it was in competition with other one-off kids. As the pressure to succeed built, it produced rebellious, difficult teenagers. What sort of adults would these people make, and how would they shape the future of China? My businessman could see a huge mass-personality shift coming.

Boys were highly favoured over girls. In one small village, I was told, there were 300 single men and no women. Becoming gay or having sex change operations must have been tempting. Then there was the story about four enterprising single men who pooled their resources to appear on a high-visibility billboard showing them posing in trendy clothes, stating their assets and their aspirations. Single women were invited to apply and enquire about marriage. Apparently, they harvested a reasonable selection. 'The Farmer Wants a Wife' equivalent in China was 'The Man Wants Anything that is Approximately Female'.

We took our first trip in an A380 with Emirates, business class, and loved our muffled, silky trip between Hong Kong and Bangkok – where we moved through startling steam into the InterContinental Hotel. We had ahead of us one day and two nights of exhaustive walking and shopping for stuff we didn't know we so desperately needed.

CHAPTER 16

Update – 2022

Stories of travel are always frozen at the time they take place. They are consigned to the past the moment they are written because, after that, change is inevitable. Weather, war, politics and popular pastimes pile in to outdate the traveller's experience. These accounts begin in 2013 and finish in 2020. They are therefore not necessarily about where to go, how to get there or what you might find today.

Covid-19 sent travel into an intermission, but it will crank up again once a sufficient level of vaccination has been achieved by travellers and the countries who receive them. At the time of writing, cruise ships were already heavily booked on the anticipation that vaccines would soon see them all back on the seven seas. Airlines were stirring too, retrieving parked aeroplanes from desert storage and taking bookings to an ever-increasing number of destinations.

I admit to sometimes making airlines look worse than they

really are. Michelle and I like Singapore Airlines above the rest, although we had good experiences with Cathay, Vietnamese, and Silk Air. We didn't love Delta or American, finding them more like budget bus travel. Then there was our run-in with Emirates, during which neither side was happy with the outcome. Although we may never travel Emirates again, based on our first flight, I still rank it as a top airline. As they say, shit happens.

The two health resorts, The Orchard in Malaysia and Chiva-Som in Thailand, have changed since we were there. The Orchard is now well organised while retaining its outstanding facilities. Sadly, Dr Muscles is no longer on the personal training staff. His stories were the stuff of legend or fantasy – depending upon which way you wanted to take them.

Since we were there, Chiva-Som rebuilt its bedrooms and public spaces to match its world class health and diet programs. But its daily rates can still only be afforded by the well-heeled. Having said that, we did an off-season deal that was financially manageable, so it's worth keeping in touch for specials. Anybody who could stay for two weeks at Chiva-Som would come away transformed. Four weeks and you may never want to leave.

One of my recurring subjects has been hotel toasters. I can't remember when it began, but I do remember sitting at a hotel breakfast when a toaster shot its output behind the cupboard on which it stood. At that moment, I felt a heavenly call that I should make reporting on these machines a regular segment of my travel writing. Of course, I needed a mentor, and that's when I imagined into life Derek Breadchamber, hotel toaster critic for *The New York Times*. Over my many years of travel and comment, Derek has become a real person to me. He's an historian, a writer of books on hotel toasters, an important contributor to hotel toaster publications and a keynote speaker at hotel toaster conventions. I wouldn't be surprised if, one day, in a distant city, a tall man in rather old-fashioned academic attire comes up to me in the street, holds out his hand and says, 'I'm Derek Breadchamber.'

Some of the places we visited have since undergone radical change. I suppose that goes for every place to a degree, but it especially applies to Hong Kong. I loved it most when I first went there in the 1960s as a journalist. Hong Kong Island was a patchwork of low-rise buildings and greenery, leading emphatically into the harbour, where the world's busiest ferry service took people to and from the mainland. For decades, Hong Kong was where many people had their indicative experience of China and the Chinese. Today, Hong Kong has lost its personality as China has imposed national laws and regulations upon it. It is not for me to judge whether this has been justified, but I felt as though an old friend had died.

Many places are changing for the worse, but not with the speed and brutality of Hong Kong. Places like Angkor Wat in Cambodia, the Greek Islands and Venice in Italy spring to mind as being in danger of death by a thousand cuts as they deal with the trampling and touching by tourists. Poorer countries are often the ones with the most to offer and are the quickest to lose it. Money in exchange for the obliteration of their antiquities is often too tempting to refuse. I'm not an activist about this, but I do see value in constraint and the development of technology where virtual tours are indistinguishable from the real thing.

I've taken the piss out of many of the hotels we've stayed

in without praising their good sides. For that, I apologise, but there is much more fun in failure than in success. Michelle and I have an affinity for the InterContinental Hotels group, but more expensive hotels have sometimes been disappointing while we have found delight in virtually unknown boltholes. The vast amount of conventional travel reporting is spent looking for positive experiences, but I celebrate the stuff-ups. Consequently, I'll never get a job as a copywriter for travel advertising. But I might get a laugh from those who like the unexpected, the absurd and the quirky.

Travel, of course, costs money. Like rich people and poor people, one level doesn't experience what the other does. We've found the greatest rewards have come from purposely mixing the two. If we booked a five-star hotel and hired guides and drivers, we balanced that by staying in dives and taking public transport or walking. The guiding light is to have vivid experiences and make memories. You can get those from either end of the travel spectrum.

In writing this book, I have many people to thank. There is my long-time friend, Ray Stewart, who provided guidance and his considerable editing skills, my actor cousin, Mark Mitchell, who went out of his way to encourage my travelogues, and the many friends who expressed their pleasure at the emails I sent while on the road. Writers are more sensitive to reactions and responses than readers imagine. And a special thanks to Alice Hubbers, an English lady who would not let me rest until I had welded my travelogues into a book.

One of the greatest rewards of travel is sharing it with somebody. For me, that somebody is Michelle, my wife and incomparable travelling companion. Michelle battles travel gremlins, joins hotel clubs and elongates our travel budget. She knows where to go in a city she's never visited before. She carries emergency provisions for every possible disaster on her back. Her suitcase contains a compact pharmacy which she happily dispenses to anybody in need. She reads brochures, chats to people in lifts and loves conquering subway train systems. I could never contemplate travelling without her.

www.ingramcontent.com/pod-product-compliance
Lightning Source LLC
Chambersburg PA
CBHW020134130526
44590CB00039B/166